A Concise Guide to the Nuts and Bolts of Estates and Future Interests

A Concise Guide to the Nuts and Bolts of Estates and Future Interests

Second Edition

Andrew Beckerman-Rodau

PROFESSOR OF LAW
SUFFOLK UNIVERSITY LAW SCHOOL
BOSTON, MASSACHUSETTS

Edited by Molly Rodau

CAROLINA ACADEMIC PRESS
Durham, North Carolina

Library of Congress Cataloging-in-Publication Data

Beckerman-Rodau, Andrew.
  A concise guide to the nuts and bolts of estates and future interests / Andrew
Beckerman-Rodau. -- 2nd ed.
    p. cm.
  Includes index.
  ISBN 978-1-59460-710-3 (alk. paper)
  1. Estates (Law)--United States. 2. Future interests--United States. 3. Real
property--United States. I. Title.

  KF575.B43 2009
  346.7304'3--dc22

                                                              2009011596

CAROLINA ACADEMIC PRESS
700 Kent Street
Durham, North Carolina 27701
Telephone (919) 489-7486
Fax (919) 493-5668
www.cap-press.com

Printed in the United States of America

Contents

Preface

Estates, future interests and the Rule Against Perpetuities are topics which have confused students for generations. This book is designed to demystify this area of law. The goal is to provide the reader with a basic understanding of this subject matter and to enable sufficient mastery of the material to correctly answer questions on both law school and bar examinations.

This book is not intended to be a comprehensive treatment of these subjects, nor is it intended to provide an historical overview of this area of the law. The history can explain why and how this body of law developed, but it does not facilitate a basic understanding of how to apply this law today. For an excellent overview of the historical aspect of this subject, see MOYNIHAN'S INTRODUCTION TO THE LAW OF REAL PROPERTY (Fourth Ed.) by Cornelius J. Moynihan and Sheldon F. Kurtz.

This book focuses on the modern common law application of this law. However, many states have statutorily modified aspects of the common law, so this book should not be relied on as an accurate source of modern law in reference to a particular jurisdiction.

One of the more difficult aspects of this area of law is learning the definitions of the numerous unique terms that have developed over the centuries. To ease this task, important terms are highlighted and clearly defined. Typically, examples follow a definition to illustrate and reinforce what a term means. Additionally, numerous explanatory examples are used throughout the book to provide a clear understanding of the material.

I have used certain conventions throughout the book:

- O refers to the original land owner. Unless otherwise stated, O owns a fee simple absolute in the land. (You will know what a fee simple absolute is when you finish studying this book!)
- Blackacre is the name of the land involved in all the transactions in this book.
- Reference to A, B, C, C1, or C2, etc. refers to a living person.

The final chapter includes sample exam questions to test your understanding of the material. Answers with detailed explanations are provided.

I would like to thank Professor Stephen C. Veltri, Ohio Northern University Pettit College of Law, Ada, Ohio, for his numerous helpful comments and suggestions, which are incorporated into this second edition. I would like to thank Molly Rodau for her expert editing and Marie Frito for her tireless proofreading. Finally, I would like to thank Ruth who provides inspiration and support for all my endeavors.

If you have any comments, suggestions or questions feel free to contact me.

Professor Andrew Beckerman-Rodau
Suffolk University Law School
120 Tremont St.
Boston, MA 02108
E-mail: arodau@suffolk.edu
www.lawprofessor.org

A Concise Guide to the Nuts and Bolts of Estates and Future Interests

Chapter One

An Introduction to Basic Property Concepts

The law of estates and future interests deals with creating and transferring different interests in land. Some basic background information about property will allow an enhanced understanding of this area of law.

The basic idea of private property is the foundation of our economic system. Through the means of work, individuals earn money which is used to purchase both necessities such as food and shelter as well as luxuries. All of the various things available for purchase in our society are property. The law has developed a classification system for different types of property.

Types of Property

Land is referred to as **real property** or **realty**. Most other things are classified as **personal property** or **personalty**. In the modern world many things, such as a building or a fence, are attached to land. Many of these items are initially classified as personalty; however, once permanently affixed to land these items become part of the land for purposes of the law and are called **fixtures**.

The majority of everyday personal property, such as automobiles, clothing or books, is tangible and can be physically held, possessed or transferred. This type of property is called **tangible personal property**. Increasingly in the United States the most important types of property for many business enterprises are ideas and information which cannot be physically held or possessed. This property is categorized as **intangible personal property**. Much intangible property represents the creative endeavors of individuals. Such property is often designated as intellectual property and may be protected by a variety of intellectual property laws, including patent, copyright, trademark and trade secrets law.

Division of Property

As a practical matter, it is often necessary to divide property. For example, the owner of a multistory building may want to transfer different parts of the building to different business enterprises. Likewise, the owner of a one-thousand acre parcel of land may want to divide it into one acre parcels to allow a real estate developer to build one house per one acre of land. While it is often necessary to divide realty, the division of intangible personal property is equally important. For example, the owner of intellectual property rights in a movie may want to sell different distribution rights to different buyers in different markets. This division could enable the owner to sell one enterprise the right to show the movie in movie theatres, another business the right to sell copies of the movie on DVD and a third enterprise the right to make the movie available on pay-per-view television.

From an economic standpoint the division of property is often necessary to maximize its value. It may also provide a property owner the ability to exert some degree of control over property despite the sale or transfer of some portion of it to a third party. Historically, the legal rules for dividing interests in property have developed differently for personal property and for real property. The law has allowed the marketplace to freely develop many new and varied approaches for the division of personal property. Many of these approaches have enabled the development of numerous new financial products. In contrast, many of the rules regarding the division of real property are ancient rules inherited from England. Such rules, in general, have undergone significant changes, but many persist as valid rules of law today. Many of the original underlying reasons for these rules, to a large extent, are no longer relevant today. Nevertheless, the rules themselves remain important inasmuch as they provide a framework for the division of real property that is still applicable in varying degrees today. Unlike personal property, which an owner can divide up in almost any manner, the division of real property is governed by relatively rigid rules. An understanding of these rules is necessary to fully comprehend how real property can be divided. Perhaps even more importantly, these rules are common subject matter on law school and bar exams.

Summary of Main Points

A. Types of property
   1. Real property (also called realty or land)
   2. Personal property (also called personalty)
      a. Tangible personal property (also referred to as goods)
      b. Intangible personal property (also referred to as intellectual property)
B. Division of property
   1. Division of real property must conform to rigid rules
   2. Division of personal property can either conform to rigid rules developed for real property, or an owner can develop new methods solely for the purpose of dividing personal property

Chapter Two

Transferring Property: Basic Vocabulary

A variety of situations exist that allow ownership of real property to be transferred. For example, property may be sold by an owner or given away as a gift. Furthermore, it may be transferred upon the death of an owner either by a will or, in the absence of a will, via intestate succession law. Specific terminology has developed to act as a shorthand designation for each of these transfers.

Transfer is the generic term describing the act of a property owner giving ownership of her property to another person. The original owner is referred to as the *transferor* and the new owner or recipient is referred to as the *transferee.* The specific terms used to identify specific types of transfers are discussed below.

Voluntary Transfers

Types of Voluntary Transfers

conveyance/grant

A *conveyance* (or *grant*) typically refers to the voluntary transfer of ownership of real property to another person. This can be accomplished by a sale, a gift or via a will upon the death of a property owner (a will is typically a written document that must comply with certain formalities to be legally valid; the owner of property can utilize a will to distribute ownership rights to chosen recipients).

An *inter vivos conveyance* refers to a conveyance by sale or gift while a transferor is alive. *alive*

A *testamentary conveyance* (also called a *devise* when it involves land or a *bequest* when it involves personal property) refers to a conveyance made by a will. *will* A will allows a person to decide in advance who gets ownership of property upon death. A valid will has no legal effect until the person whose will it is dies. Prior to death, a party can freely change a will at any time. A will only transfers ownership of property actually owned at the time of an owner's death. A person who dies with a valid will is referred to as having died *testate.* *died w/ valid will*

7

Parties Involved in a Voluntary Transfer

A person making a voluntary conveyance is called a *grantor*. A grantor who sells land may also be called a *seller*, and a grantor who gives land away via a gift may be called a *donor*. A person who gives land away at death via a will may be called a *testator* or a *decedent.*⊘ death

The recipient of a voluntary conveyance is called a *grantee.* A grantee who buys land from a grantor may also be called a *buyer* or a *purchaser.* A grantee of a gift may be called a *donee.* A grantee of real property that is transferred via a will may be called a *devisee or a beneficiary.*

Explanatory Examples

(1) **O sells Blackacre to A for $10,000.** This is an inter vivos conveyance. O is the grantor (or seller) and A is the grantee (or buyer) of Blackacre.

(2) **O gives Blackacre to B as a wedding gift.** This is an inter vivos conveyance. O is the grantor (or donor) and B is the grantee (or donee) of Blackacre.

(3) **O dies with a will which leaves Blackacre to X.** This is a testamentary conveyance or a devise. O, the decedent, is the testator. X is the devisee (or beneficiary) of the will and the new owner of Blackacre.

Involuntary Transfers

Types of Involuntary Transfers (or Transfers via Operation of Law)

Intestate succession law (also called an *intestacy statute*, a *statute of descent and distribution,* or the *law of descent and distribution*) provides default provisions that determine who receives ownership of a person's property at the owner's death in the absence of a will (or if an existing will is held to be invalid). If a person dies with a valid will, ownership of property is transferred in accordance with that will. When a person dies without a valid will, intestate succession law controls property distribution. A person who dies without a will or with an invalid will is referred to as having died *intestate.* The transfer of property ownership via intestate succession law is called *inheritance* (or *descent*).

Partial intestacy is possible when a will transfers ownership of some but not all of the property a person owns at death. In such situations the will controls all the property it specifically refers to. Property not covered by the will is transferred via intestate succession law. It is common for a will to contain a *residuary clause* which applies to any property not specifically mentioned. The use of a residuary clause typically avoids partial intestacy.

Dower and *curtesy* refer to common law property rights a surviving widow or widower, respectively, receive in a deceased spouse's property. These common law rights generally could not be defeated or destroyed by will or by inter vivos conveyance. Most states have abolished dower and curtesy rights today.

If a spouse dies intestate today the surviving spouse is generally entitled to all or a share of the deceased spouse's property via intestate succession laws.

A *forced share* or *elective share* statute typically applies when a spouse dies testate. Such statutes allow a surviving spouse to either elect to accept the decedent's will or to take a statutorily set percentage of the decedent's property regardless of the share provided by the will. Such statutes effectively prevent a deceased spouse from conveying all of his or her property to a party other than the surviving spouse. Generally, these statutes do not provide any rights to children.

Parties Involved in an Involuntary Transfer

Heirs (also called *next-of-kin, heirs at law, rightful heirs* or *legal heirs*) refer to the persons alive at someone's death who receive ownership of the decedent's property via intestate succession law. Heirs do not exist prior to a decedent's death because it cannot be known in advance who will be alive at the time of death. Originally, heirs only referred to blood relatives. Most modern intestate succession statutes however, include surviving spouses and adopted children as heirs even though they are not blood relatives.

Intestate succession laws vary by state. They typically transfer property to the surviving spouse and children; in the absence of children, to grandchildren; in the absence of both children and grandchildren, to great-grandchildren; etc. Children, grandchildren, great-grandchildren, etc. are *lineal descendents* (also called *issue*).

If there is no surviving spouse or lineal descendents, intestate succession laws usually provide for the property to go to the decedent's *parents*; if no parents, to grandparents; etc. (also called ancestors).

In the absence of a surviving spouse, lineal descendents and ancestors, other *blood relatives* such as brothers, sisters, nephews, nieces, uncles, aunts and cousins take the decedent's property. These relatives are referred to as *collaterals.*

If a decedent dies intestate without any heirs the decedent's land is transferred to the state where it is located. This is called *escheat.*

Explanatory Examples

(1) **O, a single mother, dies owning Blackacre but she does not have a will. Her parents predeceased her but she is survived by a child, C.** O died intestate. C is O's lineal descendant or issue and her heir. C is the owner of Blackacre.

(2) **O dies owning Blackacre but he does not have a will. He is survived by his wife, W, and two children, C1 and C2.** O is intestate. At common law, W, as a surviving spouse, would have dower rights in Blackacre. However, most states have abolished dower rights. Therefore, under most modern intestate succession laws W (or, in some states W along with C1 and C2) would inherit an interest in Blackacre. The size of the interest inherited varies in different states.

(3) **H dies with a valid will leaving all of his property to X. H is survived by a spouse, W, and two children, C1 and C2.** W, pursuant to a forced share or elective share statute, can elect to obtain a statutorily set percentage of H's property in lieu of the will which left nothing to W. This forced share statute applies without regard to the intent of the testator. The children, C1 and C2, however, have no right to any of H's property because they were not provided for in his will.

(4) **O dies owning Blackacre but without a will. Blackacre is located in Ohio. O's spouse, children and all blood relatives predecease her.** O is intestate but she does not have any heirs. Blackacre escheats to the state of Ohio who becomes the new owner.

Review Questions

(1) What is the difference between an inter vivos conveyance and a testamentary conveyance?

(2) When is a will effective?

(3) When does an intestate succession statute apply?

(4) Henry gives Ellen ownership, via a valid deed, of Blackacre. How would you describe the transfer from Henry to Ellen?

(5) Henry dies with a valid will giving Ellen ownership of Whiteacre. How would you describe the transfer of Whiteacre from Henry to Ellen?

(6) Henry never married. He has two brothers, Bob and Bill. Bob dies before Henry. At Henry's death, his only surviving relative is Bill. Henry owned Blackacre at his death. Henry never drafted a will. Who owns Blackacre at Henry's death?

(7) Alice makes a valid will leaving Blackacre and Whiteacre to Bob. Subsequently, Alice makes a gift of Blackacre to Carole. Who owns Blackacre and Whiteacre when Alice dies eight years later?

(8) Alice makes a will leaving Blackacre to her cousin, Sam. At Alice's death, Sam is alive. Alice's husband, Harold, is also alive at her death. Who owns Blackacre when Alice dies if her will is held to be invalid?

(9) Jane owns Blackacre at her death. She dies with a valid will leaving all of her property to her spouse Steve. The jurisdiction has enacted a forced share statute entitling a surviving spouse to 50% of a deceased spouse's property. Does Steve own Blackacre at Jane's death?

(10) Jane owns Blackacre at her death. She dies with an invalid will leaving all of her property to her spouse Steve. The jurisdiction has enacted a forced share statute entitling a surviving spouse to 50% of a deceased spouse's property. The jurisdiction also has an intestate succession statute giving a surviving spouse 100% of the deceased spouse's property. Does Steve own Blackacre at Jane's death?

Review Questions: Answers

(1) An inter vivos conveyance is a transfer of property made by a person while alive. A testamentary conveyance is a transfer made at a person's death.

(2) A will is only effective at a person's death. A person is free to change or alter his or her will at anytime while alive.

(3) Typically, a person can decide who gets her property at her death by writing a valid will. If a person dies without a valid will an intestate succession statute determines who gets the person's property at death.

(4) Inter vivos conveyance.

(5) Testamentary conveyance.

(6) Bill owns Blackacre. Henry died intestate so intestate succession law determines who gets his property at his death. Under intestate succession law, only heirs—relatives alive at a person's death—get his property.

(7) Carole owns Blackacre. Bob owns Whiteacre. Alice's will has no legal effect until Alice's death. Alice is free to transfer property mentioned in the will prior to her death. If she does that, the transferred property is no longer conveyed by her will. When Alice made the inter vivos transfer of Blackacre to Carole, the property belonged to Carole so it could no longer be subsequently transferred via Alice's will. Alice continued to own Whiteacre until her death so that property was transferred to Bob via the will.

(8) Harold owns Blackacre. The will is invalid so it cannot transfer any property interests. Intestate succession law controls who gets Blackacre at Alice's death. Typically, intestate succession statutes give the decedent's real property to the surviving spouse.

(9) Steve owns all of Blackacre. Jane died testate because she left a valid will. Under the forced share statute Steve can elect to rely on either the will or the forced share statute. The will gives Steve ownership of all of Blackacre. The forced share statute only gives Steve ownership of 50% of Blackacre. Steve would opt to take under the will so he would own all of Blackacre.

(10) Steve owns all of Blackacre. Jane's will is invalid so it cannot transfer any interest in Blackacre to Steve. The forced share statute is not applicable since Jane died intestate. Therefore, the intestate succession statute controls.

Summary of Main Points

A. Voluntary property transfers
1. Conveyance via sale, gift or will
    a. Inter vivos conveyance refers to a conveyance made while the transferor is alive
    b. Testamentary conveyance refers to a conveyance via a will at the transferor's death
B. Involuntary property transfers
1. Dower and curtesy
    a. Property right surviving spouse had in property of deceased spouse
    b. Most states have abolished dower and curtesy and now provide the following:
        i. If deceased spouse died intestate the surviving spouse takes deceased spouse's property via intestate succession; or
        ii. If deceased spouse died testate, the surviving spouse, via forced share or elective share statutes, can elect to take the deceased spouse's property via the decedent's will or a fixed statutory percentage of the decedent's property
2. Intestate succession
    a. Statutory law that determines who gets decedent's property if decedent dies without a valid will
    b. Typically, the following rules apply under intestate succession:
        i. Property first goes to surviving spouse and lineal descendants
        ii. If no surviving spouse or lineal descendants then to ancestors (parents)
        iii. If no surviving spouse, lineal descendants or ancestors then to collateral blood relatives (brothers, sisters, uncles, aunts, cousins)
        iv. If no relatives at death then property goes to state (called escheat)

Chapter Three

Types of Real Property Interests: Introductory Background

Ownership of real property provides an owner certain rights. These rights, often referred to as a bundle of rights, consist of the right to exclusive possession of property, the right to use property and the right to transfer all or part of property to a third party. Such ownership rights are sometimes called possessory rights.

A property owner can jointly own property with another party. Such ownership is called concurrent ownership. The two common types of concurrent ownership are joint tenancy with a right of survivorship and tenancy in common. A third type of concurrent ownership, tenancy by entirety, is similar to a joint tenancy with a right of survivorship but can only exist between a husband and wife. Some states have abolished tenancy by entirety.

A property owner has the ability to retain ownership while allowing someone the right to use his or her property. These rights are typically called easements, profits, covenants, licenses or servitudes and are not considered possessory rights. They can be referred to as non-possessory rights or use rights because they merely provide a right to the limited use of property while the property owner continues to have possession of the property. Such use rights are not exclusive. The owner of a use right is allowed to use property concurrently with a property owner. For example, assume Sally owns Blackacre. Sally grants an easement to her neighbor, Oscar, which allows him to cross her land on an established trail. Oscar has a non-exclusive right to use the trail. Sally continues to have a right to use the trail as the owner of Blackacre.

> The law of estates and future interests deals with three aspects of real property ownership:
> (1) It determines when you have the right to possession of your property interest;
> (2) It determines how long your property interest lasts; and
> (3) It determines whether your property rights can be lost prematurely

The law of estates and future interests has developed specific words that act as a short-hand for defining property interests. The remainder of the chapter will discuss several terms and accompanying definitions which provide the basic vocabulary for this area of law.

> "Estate" is the generic legal term for a possessory interest in real property. Different types of estates exist. Each different type of estate is defined by how long it lasts and/or how it terminates

Explanatory Examples

(1) **S graduates from law school. As a gift for graduating, S's aunt conveys her summer house in Maine to S without any conditions or limitations.** S's aunt has conveyed a property interest in the house to S which gives S the right to immediate possession of the house. The property interest in the house is an estate.

(2) **B is a first year law student. As an incentive to complete law school, B's aunt conveys to B her summer house in Maine. However, the conveyance states that B cannot have the house until he completes law school.** B's aunt conveyed a property interest in the house to B. Although B does not have a right to immediate possession of the house he does have a right to future possession of the house once he completes law school. The property interest in the house is an estate.

> A "present estate" is an interest in real property that grants an immediate right of possession of property

Explanatory Examples

(1) S graduates from law school. As a gift for graduating, S's aunt conveys her summer house in Maine to S without any conditions or limitations. This is a present estate because S has the right to occupy or possess the house immediately.

(2) **O writes a valid will in 1990 and subsequently dies in 1992. The will devises Blackacre to A.** In 1990, O is still the owner of Blackacre because a will has no legal effect until the testator dies. At O's death in 1992, A has a present

estate in Blackacre because upon O's death the will became effective and therefore it transferred Blackacre to A who now has the right to immediate present possession of Blackacre.

> A "future interest" is an interest (estate) in real property that is presently owned but which only grants a future right to possession of property

Explanatory Examples

(1) S is a first year law student. As an incentive to complete law school, S's aunt conveys to S her summer house in Maine. However, the conveyance states that S cannot have the house until she completes law school. This is a future interest because S does not have a right to possession of the house until the future when she graduates from law school. S does, however, have an immediate ownership interest (estate) in the house even though her right to possession of the house is postponed to the future.

(2) O leases Blackacre to A for five years. During the fourth year of the lease, O leases Blackacre to B for five years commencing upon the end of A's lease. B has a future interest in Blackacre because the right to possession does not arise until A's lease ends. O has a future interest in Blackacre because a future right to possession of Blackacre arises when B's lease ends.

Review Questions

(1) What is an estate?

(2) What is a present estate?

(3) What is a future interest?

(4) O conveys her summer house in Maine to A for A's lifetime. The conveyance provides that the house shall go to B upon A's death. At the time of the conveyance both A and B are alive and in good health. At the time of O's conveyance does A and/or B have a present estate or a future interest in the house?

(5) O leases Blackacre to A for ten years. During the third year of the lease does A have a present estate or a future interest in Blackacre? During the third year of the lease does O have a present estate or a future interest in Blackacre?

Review Questions: Answers

(1) The generic term for a possessory ownership interest in real property.

(2) An estate which gives an estate owner the present right to possession of the real property.

(3) Ownership of an estate where the right to possession of the estate is postponed to a future time.

(4) A has a present estate in the house because she has the right to immediately possess it. B has an ownership interest in the house, created at the time of O's original conveyance. B's interest is a future interest because he cannot use or possess the house until the future (after A dies).

(5) A has a present estate because she has the immediate right to possession of Blackacre for the next ten years. O continues to own an interest in Blackacre throughout the ten year lease term. O's interest is a future interest because his right to possession of Blackacre must wait until A's ten year lease ends.

Summary of Main Points

A. Purpose of estates & future interests
   1. To tell you when you have a right to present possession of property
   2. To tell you how long your right to present possession lasts
   3. To tell you if or when and under what circumstances your right to present possession will terminate
B. Definitions of important terms
   1. Estate refers to a possessory real property interest
   2. Present estate refers to a real property interest that grants a present or immediate right of possession
   3. Future interest refers to an interest in real property that grants a future right to possession

Characteristics of Present and Future Interests

Type of Interest	Characteristics
Present estate	(1) Ownership of an interest in real property (2) The right to immediate possession of property (sometimes called a present possessory interest in real property)
Future interest	(1) Ownership of an interest in real property (2) The right to possession of real property is postponed until the future

Chapter Four

Types of Estates

The concept of an *estate* was introduced in Chapter Three. This chapter will explain the different types of estates that exist.

> "Fee simple absolute" estates (also called fee simple estates) are estates that have the potential to last indefinitely:
> (1) This is the largest estate someone can own
> (2) Today, fee simple absolute estates are one of the most common types of estates created

Explanatory Example

O **conveys a fee simple absolute estate in Blackacre to A.** After the conveyance O no longer owns any interest in Blackacre because she conveyed her entire interest to A. A is now the sole owner of Blackacre.

> "Fee tail" estates are a series of life estates that pass from one lineal descendant to another:
> (1) The estate continues until the line of lineal descendants ends
> (2) Most states no longer allow the creation of fee tail estates

Fee tail estates can be limited to specific lineal descendants in terms of gender. Such estates would be called *fee tail male* or *fee tail female* estates. Fee tail estates can also be limited to the lineal descendents of a specific spouse. Such an estate would be called a *fee tail special*.

Historically, a fee tail was used to keep property within a family. Today, the vast majority of states have abolished all fee tail estates. The few states (Delaware, Maine, Massachusetts and Rhode Island) that still recognize fee tails allow, by statute, a person with a present estate in fee tail to convert the fee tail into a fee simple absolute estate during their lifetime (this is called *disentailing* the fee tail estate).

If a person attempts to create a fee tail estate in a state that does not permit fee tail estates, the estate, by operation of law, is automatically converted typically into a fee simple absolute estate.

Explanatory Examples

(1) **O conveys a fee tail estate in Blackacre to A.** This conveyance creates a present fee tail estate in Blackacre which means A is entitled to immediate possession of Blackacre. Upon A's death, Blackacre automatically passes to A's lineal descendants; and, upon the death of those lineal descendants, to the next generation of lineal descendants. This continues until no lineal descendants exist. O's conveyance creates a property right in A and property rights in future lineal descendants of A even though such descendants may not yet exist.

(2) **O conveys a fee tail estate in Blackacre to her daughter Z. Z subsequently dies without ever having any children.** This conveyance gives Z a present estate in Blackacre. However, the estate ends upon Z's death because there are no lineal descendents of Z; and, it is impossible for Z to have any lineal descendants in the future.

(3) **O conveys a fee tail female estate in Blackacre to Y. Y has four sons during her lifetime but no daughters.** This conveyance gives Y a present fee tail estate in Blackacre. However, the fee tail estate ends upon Y's death because there are no female lineal descendents of Y; and, it is impossible for Y to have any female lineal descendents in the future.

(4) **O conveys a fee tail estate in Blackacre to S. S conveys a fee simple absolute estate in Blackacre to X.** In a state that does not allow the creation of fee tail estates the original conveyance from O to S conveys a fee simple absolute estate to S. If the original conveyance was in a state that allows fee tail estates the conveyance would give S a fee tail estate in Blackacre. S disentailed the fee tail estate when she conveyed a fee simple absolute estate to X. Therefore, in either state X has a fee simple absolute estate in Blackacre.

> "Life estates" are estates that last for the lifetime of one or more natural persons:
>
> > (1) A natural person refers to an actual human in contrast to a legal person which can include a legal entity such as a corporation
> > (2) An "ordinary life estate" lasts for the lifetime of the estate owner *(ends @ their death)*
> > (3) A "life estate pur autre vie" lasts for the lifetime of a third party
> > (4) Life estates are commonly used today as an estate planning tool

↳ natural persons ✓ corporations

Explanatory Examples

(1) **O conveys a life estate in Blackacre to A.** This conveyance creates a present estate in A in Blackacre which means A is entitled to immediate possession of Blackacre. A's estate is an ordinary life estate that ends at A's death.

(2) **O conveys a life estate in Blackacre to A. A then conveys Blackacre to B. A then dies before B.** A's conveyance of the life estate in Blackacre to B cannot change the duration of the estate. It does not become an estate based on B's life because that would alter the original estate conveyed by O. The life estate continues to be measured by A's life after it is conveyed to B. The estate owned by B is a life estate pur autre vie because it is a life estate based on the life of a third party (A). When A dies B's life estate pur autre vie ends. *ex.*

(3) **O conveys Blackacre to A for the lives of A, B and C.** This conveyance creates a present estate in Blackacre in A which means A is entitled to immediate possession of Blackacre. A's estate is a life estate based on the lives of A, B and C. More specifically, it is a life estate pur autre vie because it is based on his life as well as the lives of third parties (B and C). The life estate ends only when A, B and C are all dead. *ex. 2*

(4) **O conveys Blackacre to A for the lives of A, B and C; B subsequently dies; then A dies with a will leaving all of her property to X.** A's life estate does not end at A's death because it is a life estate pur autre vie based on the lives of A, B and C. C is still alive so the estate does not end upon either A's death or B's death. A died with a will so A's life estate pur autre vie passes by her will to X. X owns a life estate pur autre vie based on C's life. Upon C's death the life estate ends.

(5) **O conveys Blackacre to Big Corporation for the life of X.** O's conveyance to Big Corporation is measured by X's life so Big Corporation owns a life estate pur autre vie.

> "Leasehold estates" (also called "non-freehold" estates or "leases") comprise the common landlord-tenant relationship (also called "lessor-lessee" relationship):
>
> (1) Unlike fee simple absolute estates which have the potential to last indefinitely, leaseholds are similar to life estates in that leaseholds typically end at some time in the future
>
> (3) Four types of leasehold estates exist:
>> (a) "Estate for years" (also called a "term of years")
>> (b) "Periodic tenancy" (also called an "estate from period to period")
>> (c) "Tenancy at will" (also called an "estate at will")
>> (d) "Tenancy at sufferance" (also called a "holdover tenancy" or an "estate at sufferance")

The four types of leasehold estates are described in detail below:

(A) *Estate for years* (also called a *term of years*) leaseholds have a specific ending date agreed upon at the time the estate is created. For example, if an apartment is leased on January 1, 2000 for two years, the estate ends on December 31, 2002. If a leasehold estate does not have a fixed date of termination at the time of creation it is not an estate for years. At common law, the duration of an estate for years lease can be any fixed time period; it could be for one day or for nine-hundred years.

An estate for years leasehold cannot be unilaterally terminated by either the lessor or the lessee prior to the ending date specified in a lease.

Residential estate for years leaseholds most commonly last for one or two years. Commercial estate for years leaseholds often last for substantially longer periods of time.

Explanatory Examples

(1) **O leases Blackacre to A for a term beginning on January 1, 2002 and ending on June 15, 2004.** At the time of creation it was determined that the lease-

hold estate would end on June 15, 2004. O created an estate for years leasehold. This leasehold gives A the right to present possession of Blackacre during the term of the lease.

(2) **O leases Blackacre to B for one year beginning on January 1, 2008.** By agreeing to a one year lease starting on January 1, 2008 both the lessor and lessee know the lease ends on December 31, 2008 which makes it an estate for years lease.

(B) *Periodic tenancy* (also called an *estate from period to period*) leaseholds do not have a specific end date. Instead they continue to exist until either the lessor or the lessee terminates the estate by providing proper notice to the other party. A periodic tenancy has a specific recurring or successive time period. For example, a year to year periodic tenancy initially lasts for one year upon its creation; it then continues to exist for successive one year periods until it is terminated by one party providing proper notice of termination to the other party.

At common law, six months notice is required to terminate a year to year periodic tenancy. Shorter periodic tenancies require notice equal to at least the period of the tenancy. For example, a month to month tenancy requires a notice to terminate at least one month prior to the termination date.

The most commonly created periodic tenancies are month to month and year to year periodic tenancies.

Explanatory Examples

(1) **O leases Blackacre to A. The lease is a month to month periodic tenancy.** The lease continues for successive monthly periods until the lessor or the lessee give proper notice to the other party that he or she is terminating the lease. Unlike an estate for years leasehold, it is unknown at the time a periodic lease is created when it will end. At common law, proper notice is one month prior to the start of the next monthly lease period.

(2) **O leases Blackacre to A. The lease is a month to month periodic tenancy which begins on January 1. On February 15th, O decides to cancel the lease as soon as possible.** The next period for the periodic tenancy begins on March 1st. February 15th is less than one month before March 1st. O cannot terminate the lease as of March 1st. On March 1st the lease automatically continues for another month. The earliest O could cancel the lease would be April 1st.

(C) *Tenancy at will* (also called an *estate at will*) leaseholds, like periodic tenancies, have an indefinite duration. However, unlike a periodic tenancy, under the common law a tenancy at will can be terminated at any time for any reason by either the lessor or the lessee without any notice.

effective immediately

Explanatory Examples

(1) **O leases Blackacre to A. The lease is a tenancy at will. After eight months O decides to terminate the lease.** O can tell A to leave the leased property immediately because, at common law, there is no notice requirement for termination of a tenancy at will.

(2) **O leases Blackacre, via a tenancy at will, to B. B decides to terminate the lease after only three days.** B is free to terminate the lease immediately due to the absence of any notice requirement, at common law, for terminating this type of lease.

(D) *Tenancy at sufferance* (also called a *holdover tenancy* or an *estate at sufferance*) leaseholds are created when a person continues in possession of property after a leasehold estate ends. The distinction between a trespasser and a tenant at sufferance focuses on whether the person ever had rightful possession of the property. For example, a lessee who possesses property pursuant to a one year lease becomes a tenant at sufferance if she remains in possession of the property after the one year lease ends. In contrast, a trespasser is someone who enters the property without ever having the lawful right to enter the property.

A tenancy at sufferance will often arise following a long-term commercial lease. When a business lessor decides to move to a new location at the end of a long-term lease numerous things can interfere with the move occurring on time. A delay in moving can create a tenancy at sufferance. A lessor and a lessee can contractually agree in advance how any holdover tenancy will be dealt with by the parties. Absent an agreement, the common law requires the lessor to elect one of the following: (1) treat the holdover tenant as a trespasser and sue for damages, or (2) renew the prior lease (in many states the prior lease can only be renewed for up to one year if the prior lease was for a term greater than one year). Some states have statutes providing for double rents or other remedies for holding over.

Explanatory Examples

(1) **O leases Blackacre to A. The lease is a ten year estate for years leasehold. At the end of the ten year period A is still in possession of the property because the moving company failed to show up on time.** Once the ten year lease period ends A becomes a tenant at sufferance if she remains on the property beyond the ten year period.

(2) **O leases Blackacre to A. The lease is a tenancy at will. After ninety days, O notifies A that the lease is terminated effective immediately.** If A continues in possession of Blackacre, his status changes from a tenant at will, prior to the notice, to a tenant at sufferance after the notice.

Leasehold estates, historically, were typically viewed as personal property. Additionally, leasehold estates are referred to as *non-freehold estates*. Fee simple, fee tail and life estates are referred to as *freehold estates*. Such distinctions have historical origins but are of little importance today.

A substantial body of law (both common and statutory) has developed with regard to modern leasehold estates. Residential leasehold estates in particular are the subject of much statutory modification. Much of the common law regarding leaseholds has been eliminated or modified by modern law. This has occurred to such an extent that leaseholds have become a separate and distinct area of law that is typically studied as a separate self-contained topic. The creation of the typical leasehold estate involves a contractual agreement between the lessor and the lessee which includes a conveyance of the leasehold estate. This has caused many courts to view a landlord-tenant relationship as a contractual agreement such that they apply contract law principles in lieu of some property law rules. The detailed study of leasehold estates goes beyond the scope of this book.

Review Questions

(1) What is a fee simple absolute estate?

(2) What is the difference between a life estate and a life estate pur autre vie?

(3) What is the difference between an estate for years and a periodic tenancy?

(4) What is the difference between a periodic tenancy and a tenancy at will?

(5) What common law freehold estate is no longer recognized in most states?

(6) O conveys a life estate in Blackacre to A; at A's death her will conveys all of her property to Z. Does Z own an interest in Blackacre upon A's death?

(7) O conveys a life estate in Blackacre, based on the life of S, to B. At B's death her will conveys all of her property to Z. If S is alive does Z own an interest in Blackacre upon B's death?

(8) O conveys a fee simple absolute in Blackacre to A. A subsequently dies with a will leaving all of his property to X. Who owns Blackacre upon A's death?

(9) O conveys a fee tail in Blackacre to M. What interest does M own in Blackacre in the majority of jurisdictions? In Massachusetts?

(10) O conveys a fee tail in Blackacre to the lineal descendants of his spouse, S. O subsequently divorces S and marries Z. Do the lineal descendants of S and Z have any interest in Blackacre?

(11) O leases Blackacre to A for an unspecified term and without any agreement for A to make rental payments. A lives on Blackacre but he never makes any rental payments to O. O informs A he must vacate the property immediately. Has O given A proper notice of termination of the lease?

(12) O leases Blackacre to A for one year starting on January 1, 2008. Can A decide to end the lease early on June 15, 2008?

(13) O leases Blackacre to A for one year starting on January 1, 2008. A takes possession of Blackacre on January 1, 2008. On January 2, 2009, A is still in possession of Blackacre. What interest does A have in Blackacre on January 2, 2008? On January 2, 2009?

Review Questions: Answers

(1) The largest ownership interest in real property which can potentially last forever.

(2) A life estate lasts for the lifetime of the life estate owner provided the life estate owner is a natural person. A life estate pur autre vie lasts for the lifetime of a natural person other than the life estate owner.

(3) An estate for years leasehold interest ends on a specific calendar date which is agreed to by the parties at the start of the lease. A periodic tenancy is a leasehold interest that continues for successive time periods (i.e. thirty days) until either the lessor or the lessee terminates the leasehold by giving proper notice. Typically, notice must equal one successive time period.

(4) A periodic tenancy can only be ended by one party providing proper notice to the other party. A tenancy at will can be ended immediately by either the lessor or lessee without any specific notice period being required.

(5) Fee tail.

(6) No. A's life estate is measured by A's lifetime. At A's death the life estate has ended. Therefore, Z cannot inherit an interest in Blackacre via A's will.

(7) Yes. B's life estate is based on the life of another person—S. Therefore, B has a life estate pur autre vie. At B's death S is still alive so the life estate pur autre vie does not end at B's death. Z inherits, via B's will, the estate pur autre vie. Z has a life estate in Blackacre that lasts until S dies.

(8) X owns a fee simple absolute in Blackacre upon A's death. X acquired the estate via A's will.

(9) M owns a fee simple absolute in the majority of jurisdictions. In Massachusetts M owns a life estate. The majority of states do not permit fee tail estates to be created. Typically, an attempt to create a fee tail estate in these jurisdictions creates a fee simple absolute estate. In a state such as Massachusetts which allows the creation of fee tail estates, the owner of a fee tail estate has a life estate which passes to his or her successive lineal descendants at death.

(10) Lineal descendants of S have an interest in Blackacre. The lineal descendants of Z do not have any interest in Blackacre. O created a fee tail special which is limited to the lineal descendants of S.

(11) Yes. The parties created a tenancy at will which does not require any notice period to terminate the lease.

(12) No. The parties created an estate for years lease which cannot be unilaterally ended by A prior to the end of the lease term. The one year lease ends on December 31, 2008.

(13) A has an estate for years leasehold in Blackacre on January 2, 2008. A is a tenant at sufferance on January 2, 2009. A lease with a fixed calendar end-

ing date that is agreed to in advance is an estate for years leasehold. A tenant who remains in possession of leased property after the lease ends is a holdover tenant or tenant at sufferance.

Summary of Main Points

A. Types of freehold estates
  1. A fee simple absolute estate is the largest real property interest that can be created
     a. It is the most common estate created today
  2. A fee tail estate creates a series of consecutive ordinary life estates in a natural person and subsequent lineal heirs until the line of lineal descendants ends
     a. A fee tail estate can be limited to specific lineal descendants:
        i. A fee tail male is limited to male lineal descendants
        ii. A fee tail female is limited to female lineal descendants
        iii. A fee tail special is limited to lineal descendents of a specific spouse
     b. Fee tail estates can no longer be created in most jurisdictions
     c. In the few jurisdictions that allow a fee tail estate to be created, any present estate holder of a fee tail may convert the estate into a fee simple absolute (called disentailing)
  3. Life estates
     a. An ordinary life estate lasts for the life of the transferee of the estate
     b. A life estate pur autre vie is a life estate measured by the life of a third party rather than the life of the transferee of the estate
        i. Only the lifetime of a natural person (human) can be used for the term of an ordinary life estate and a life estate pur autre vie
B. Types of non-freehold estates (commonly called leasehold estates)
  1. An estate for years leasehold lasts for a fixed time period that is set at the time the leasehold is created
     a. It cannot be terminated by lessor or lessee prior to expiration of the fixed time period
  2. A periodic tenancy lasts for successive periods that continue until lessor or lessee terminate the leasehold by providing proper notice to the other party
     a. The successive period can be for any time period—one day; one month; one year; etc.
     b. Proper notice for termination must equal at least one successive period but no more than six months
  3. Tenancy at will lasts until either the lessor or lesse terminate it
     a. Either party can terminate the lease at any time without any notice

4. Tenancy at sufferance arises when a lessee continues in possession of leased property after the lease has terminated and the lessee no longer has a right to be on the leased property
   a. A lessor can elect to treat a tenant at sufferance as a trespasser or renew the prior for lease up to one year

Types of Estates

Estate	Characteristics
Fee simple absolute	Freehold estate Largest real property interest which can potentially last forever
Fee tail	Freehold estate Successive lineal descendants of transferor own property for their respective lifetimes (essentially a series of successive life estates which lasts as long as successive lineal descendants exist)
Life estate	Freehold estate A property interest whose duration is measured by the lifetime of the life estate owner or some other designated person(s) Only a natural person(s) (human) can be used as the measuring lifetime If the measuring lifetime is someone other than the life estate owner the life estate is called a life estate pur autre vie
Estate for years	Non-freehold leasehold estate Lease is for a fixed length of time which is set at the beginning of the leasehold and lease automatically terminates at end of that fixed time period
Periodic tenancy	Non-freehold leasehold estate Lease is for a set period of time (such as 30 days or one year) and it automatically continues for each new successive period until terminated by either lessor or lessee with proper notice
Tenancy at will	Non-freehold leasehold estate No fixed term Lasts until either lessor or lessee terminates
Tenancy at sufferance	Non-freehold leasehold estate which describes a lessee who has remains in possession of the estate after the lease has ended

Chapter Five

Estates Subject to Conditions

All of the estates discussed in Chapter Four can be created subject to one or more conditions which provide for the estate to end upon violation of the condition or conditions. This chapter will discuss the different types of conditions that an estate can be subject to.

A *defeasible estate* (also called a *qualified estate*) is an estate subject to a condition that provides for early or premature termination of the estate if the condition is violated. All estates can be made defeasible. It is important to distinguish between the normal or natural end of an estate and the premature termination due to violation of a condition. Only estates subject to conditions that have the potential to prematurely terminate the estate are defeasible estates.

> A "defeasible life estate" is an ordinary life estate that:
> (1) May last until its natural end upon the death of the life estate holder; or
> (2) Can terminate prematurely during the lifetime of the estate holder if a condition is violated
> Likewise, a "defeasible life estate pur autre vie" can end upon the death of the measuring lifetime or prior to death of the measuring lifetime due to violation of a condition

Explanatory Examples

(1) **O conveys Blackacre to A for life subject to the condition that if A sells alcohol on Blackacre A's estate will immediately end.** A has a present life estate that will end naturally at his death. However, the estate is subject to a condition—if A sells alcohol on Blackacre his life estate will immediately terminate. This condition will not end A's life estate if A never sells alcohol on Blackacre. If A does sell alcohol on Blackacre, however, his life estate will be prematurely terminated during his lifetime. This condition makes A's estate a defeasible life estate. A's life estate will either end prematurely upon violation of the condi-

tion or it will last until its natural end upon A's death if the condition is never violated.

(2) **O conveys Blackacre to A for the life of B but subject to immediate termination if Blackacre is ever used for gambling.** A has a present life estate pur autre vie because the life estate is based on B's life. The life estate is also subject to premature termination during B's lifetime if Blackacre is used for gambling. A has a defeasible life estate pur autre vie because the estate will either end prematurely upon violation of the condition or it will last until its natural end upon B's death if the condition is never violated.

> A "fee simple defeasible" estate is a fee simple estate that can either:
>   (1) Last indefinitely if the condition is never violated; or
>   (2) Can terminate if the condition is violated

Explanatory Examples

(1) **O conveys a fee simple estate in Blackacre to B subject to the condition that the estate will immediately terminate if Blackacre is ever used for commercial purposes.** B has an estate in Blackacre that could last forever if Blackacre is never used for commercial purposes. However, the estate will prematurely terminate if the condition (no commercial use) is violated. B has a fee simple defeasible estate because it may last forever if the condition is never violated or it may be prematurely terminated if the condition is violated.

(2) **O devises a fee simple estate in Blackacre (which is a farm) to W so long as Blackacre continues to be used for farming.** W's estate in Blackacre will last forever unless Blackacre stops being used as a farm. W has a fee simple defeasible estate because the estate may last forever or it may be prematurely terminated due to violation of the condition (it stops being used as a farm).

> A "defeasible leasehold" is a leasehold estate that may prematurely end prior to the time it would normally end due to violation of a specified condition

Explanatory Examples

(1) **O leases Blackacre to A for ten years subject to the condition that the lease will immediately end if Blackacre is used for residential purposes at any time during the term of the lease.** A has an estate for years leasehold which

will normally end after ten years. The lease has the potential to be prematurely terminated prior to the end of the ten year term if A breaches the condition by living on the property. A has a defeasible ten year estate for years leasehold.

(2) **O leases X a monthly periodic tenancy in Blackacre subject to the condition that the tenancy will immediately terminate if X keeps a pet on the property.** X has a monthly periodic tenancy. Such a tenancy will last until one party provides proper notice to end the lease. Proper notice for a monthly periodic tenancy is at least one month. If X keeps a pet on Blackacre the lease will terminate immediately. Therefore, X has a defeasible monthly periodic tenancy because it can terminate normally if proper notice is provided or it can terminate prematurely if the condition is violated.

> **Three types of conditions that can make an estate defeasible (or qualified):**
> (1) **Determinable condition**
> (2) **Condition subsequent**
> (3) **Executory limitation**

Each type of condition is explained in detail below:

(A) A *determinable condition* causes an estate to automatically end or terminate when a condition is violated and the original transferor becomes the present estate owner upon violation of the condition. Defeasible estates subject to a determinable condition are called *determinable* estates.

[handwritten: auto-matic]

(B) A *condition subsequent* allows an original transferor the right to retake present possession of an estate when a condition is violated. Defeasible estates subject to a condition subsequent are called estates *subject to a condition subsequent* (also called *interests subject to divestment*).

[handwritten: not automatic]

The key distinction between a determinable estate and an estate subject to a condition subsequent relates to what happens when a condition is broken. Determinable estates *automatically* end and revert back to the original transferor. Once the condition is broken the breaching party is essentially a trespasser. Estates subject to a condition subsequent do not automatically end. Breach of the condition in this case, merely gives the original transferor the *right to retake* possession of the property. The breaching possessor continues to have an estate in the property until the original transferor takes action to retake possession of the property.

[handwritten: distinction]

(C) An *executory limitation* is a condition that provides that upon breach of a condition an estate goes to someone other than an original transferor. Ordinarily, the estate automatically transfers to a third party upon breach of a condition (analogous to a determinable estate). Alternatively, the grant can expressly provide that the third party only has a right to retake possession (analogous to an estate subject to a condition subsequent). This type of defeasible estate is typically called an estate *subject to an executory limitation* (also called *subject to an executory interest*). This is in contrast to the fist two conditions, which cause an estate to revert to the transferor as opposed to a third party.

Explanatory Examples

(1) O conveys a fee simple estate in Blackacre to A. However, the conveyance provides that Blackacre automatically reverts to O if alcohol is ever sold on Blackacre. O conveyed an estate to A that may go on forever if alcohol is never sold on Blackacre. The estate will automatically be cutoff or prematurely terminated and revert back to O if alcohol is sold on Blackacre. O has conveyed a fee simple determinable estate to A.

(2) O conveys a fee simple estate in Blackacre to A. However, the conveyance provides that O has the right to retake Blackacre if alcohol is ever sold on Blackacre. O conveyed to A an estate that may go on forever if alcohol is never sold on Blackacre. If alcohol is sold on Blackacre, O has the right to retake possession of Blackacre. Unlike the previous example, Blackacre does not automatically revert to O if and when the condition is violated. O must take action to retake possession of Blackacre. O has conveyed a fee simple subject to a condition subsequent estate to A.

(3) O conveys a fee simple estate in Blackacre to A. However, the conveyance provides that Blackacre automatically goes to B if A, during her lifetime, engages in the sale of alcohol on Blackacre. O conveyed an estate to A that may go on forever if A never sells alcohol on Blackacre. The estate will be cutoff or prematurely terminated and the estate will automatically go to B if A sells alcohol on Blackacre. O has conveyed a fee simple subject to an executory limitation estate to A. It is not a fee simple determinable estate because upon breach of the condition the present estate automatically goes to B. If it automatically reverted back to O it would be a fee simple determinable. Note that the way the grant is written, present possession of the estate automatically goes to B if A violates the condition. This makes the grant essentially the same as a fee simple determinable except that a third party automatically gets the right to present possession upon violation of the condition rather than the original grantor.

(4) O conveys a fee simple estate in Blackacre to A. However, the conveyance provides that B shall have the right to take possession of Blackacre if A, during her lifetime, engages in the sale of alcohol on Blackacre. O conveyed an es-

tate to A that may go on forever if A never sells alcohol on Blackacre. If A sells alcohol on Blackacre B will have the right to take possession of Blackacre. O has conveyed a fee simple subject to an executory limitation estate to A. It is not a fee simple subject to a condition subsequent because upon breach of the condition the right to take possession of Blackacre goes to B. If O had the right to take possession of Blackacre it would be a fee simple subject to a condition subsequent. The way the grant is written the right to take possession of the estate goes to B if A violates the condition. This makes the grant essentially the same as a fee simple subject to a condition subsequent except that a third party, B, gets the right to take possession of Blackacre rather than the original grantor.

(5) **O conveys Blackacre to A for life; but if A becomes an attorney Blackacre shall automatically revert to O.** A has a defeasible life estate because her estate can be terminated prematurely prior to its natural end if A becomes an attorney. If A does not become an attorney her life estate will last until its natural termination at her death. Because the estate will automatically revert to O if the condition is broken, A has a determinable life estate.

(6) **O leases Blackare to A for five years. The lease provides that O shall have the right to immediately reenter and retake possession of Blackacre if A allows the property to become run-down.** A has a five year estate for years leasehold interest. It is a defeasible leasehold because it can terminate prematurely if A violates the condition. O only has the right to reenter and retake Blackarce upon violation of the condition so A has an estate for years leasehold subject to a condition subsequent.

Review Questions

(1) What is a defeasible estate?

(2) What are the three types of defeasible conditions?

(3) What is the difference between a determinable condition and a condition subsequent?

(4) How is an executory limitation different than both a determinable condition and a condition subsequent?

(5) A fee simple determinable estate, a fee simple subject to a condition subsequent estate, a fee simple subject to an executory limitation estate, a determinable life estate and a determinable estate for years lease can *all* be described by which of the following?

    (a) Freehold estates

    (b) Non-freehold estates

    (c) Defeasible estates

    (d) Determinable estates

(6) Which of the following is correct?

    (a) All determinable estates are defeasible estates

    (b) All defeasible estates are determinable estates

    (c) All defeasible estates include a condition and if the condition is violated the estate always reverts to the original grantor

    (d) All defeasible estates include a condition and if the condition is violated the estate always reverts to a third party

(7) Identify what type of defeasible estate O creates in each of the following:

    (a) O conveys a life estate in Blackacre to X provided X never becomes an attorney; and if X does become an attorney Blackacre shall automatically go to O

    (b) O devises a life estate in Blackacre to X provided X never becomes an attorney; and if X does become an attorney Blackacre shall automatically go to Z

    (c) O conveys a 15 year estate for years leasehold in Blackacre to L but O shall have the right to reenter and retake possession of Blackacre if L fails to properly maintain Blackacre

    (d) O conveys a fee simple estate in Blackacre to X provided X never becomes a veterinarian; and if X does become a veterinarian Blackacre shall automatically go to O

(8) O conveys a fee simple estate in Blackacre to A but the conveyance provides that the estate shall automatically revert to O if A sells alcohol on Blackacre; and that the estate shall automatically go to B if A engages in gambling

on Blackacre. Assuming A has not sold alcohol on Blackacre nor engaged in gambling on Blackacre, what interest in Blackacre does A own?

Review Questions: Answers

(1) An estate that is created subject to a condition that can prematurely terminate the estate if the condition happens or is violated.

(2) Determinable condition; condition subsequent; executory limitation.

(3) If a determinable condition is violated the right of possession and ownership of the estate automatically goes to the original transferor who created the defeasible estate. If a condition subsequent is violated the original transferor who created the defeasible estate only has the right to retake possession and ownership of the defeasible estate.

(4) Violation of a determinable condition or a condition subsequent gives the original transferor who created the defeasible estate automatic ownership and possession of the defeasible estate (determinable condition) or the right to retake ownership and possession of the defeasible estate (condition subsequent). Violation of an executory limitation causes a third party, named in the original transfer, to get possession and ownership of the defeasible estate.

(5) (c) All of the estates are qualified or subject to conditions. The generic category of defeasible estates describes estates subject to conditions. (a) is incorrect because a lease is a non-freehold estate. Likewise, (b) is incorrect because a fee simple and a life estate are freehold estates. (d) is incorrect because a determinable estate is only one type of defeasible estate. Other types of defeasible estates are estates subject to a condition subsequent and estates subject to an executory limitation.

(6) (a) Defeasible estate is the generic category for estates subject to conditions which can lead to premature termination of an estate. (b) is incorrect because determinable estates are a specific type of defeasible estate. Therefore, all determinable estates are defeasible estates but all defeasible estates are not determinable estates. (c) and (d) are incorrect because violation of the condition causes some defeasible estates to revert back to the grantor and some to revert to a third party.

(7) The conveyance in (a) creates a determinable life estate because upon violation of the condition the estate automatically goes back to the grantor, O. The devise in (b) creates a life estate subject to an executory limitation because upon violation of the condition the estate automatically goes to a third party, Z. The conveyance in (c) creates a 15 year estate for years leasehold subject to a condition subsequent because upon violation of the condition the original grantor has the right to retake possession of Blackacre instead of the estate automatically reverting back to O. The conveyance in (d) creates a determinable fee simple estate because upon violation of the condition the estate automatically goes back to the grantor.

(8) O has given A a defeasible estate with two conditions. Each condition can independently prematurely terminate the estate. If A sells alcohol on Blackacre the estate automatically reverts to the original grantor. This condition makes A's estate a determinable fee simple. If A engages in gambling on Blackacre the estate automatically goes to a third party. This condition makes A's estate a fee simple subject to an executory limitation. A has a determinable fee simple estate that is also subject to an executory limitation.

Summary of Main Points

A. Estates can be created subject to a condition
   1. A defeasible estate (also called a qualified estate) is an estate subject to a condition where violation of the condition prematurely terminates the estate prior to when it would normally end absent the condition
      a. A life estate normally ends at the death of the measuring life for the life estate (typically the life of the life estate owner, or the life of a third party if it is a life estate pur autre vie)
         i. A defeasible life estate is subject to a condition that, if violated, would end the life estate before the death of the measuring life
      b. A five year estate for years leasehold normally ends at the end of the five year lease term
         i. A defeasible five year estate for years leasehold is subject to a condition that, if violated, would terminate the estate prior to the end of the five year lease term
      c. A fee simple estate will potentially last forever
         i. A fee simple defeasible estate is subject to a condition that, if violated, would terminate the estate
   2. All estates can be made defeasible
B. Types of defeasible conditions
   1. Determinable condition (such as a fee simple determinable estate, a determinable life estate and a determinable leasehold)
      a. If a determinable condition is violated the estate automatically and immediately goes back to the original transferor
   2. Condition subsequent (such as a fee simple subject to a condition subsequent, a life estate subject to a condition subsequent, and a leasehold subject to a condition subsequent)
      a. If a condition subsequent is violated the original transferor automatically has the right to retake possession of the estate
      b. The transferor does not gain the right to possession of the estate until she takes action to retake possession of the estate
   3. Subject to an executory limitation (such as a fee simple subject to an executory limitation, a life estate subject to an executory limitation, and a leasehold subject to an executory limitation)
      a. If a condition creating an executory limitation is violated the estate will automatically and immediately go to a third party named in the transfer who can be anyone other than the transferor

      i.   This type of condition is the same as a determinable condition except that the estate goes to a third party rather than to the original grantor

b. It is possible to draft the condition so that it specifies that violation of the condition results in a third party only having the right to take possession of the estate

      i.   This type of condition is the same as a condition subsequent except that a third party has the right to take possession of the estate rather than the original grantor

Types of Conditions that Make an Estate Defeasible

Type of Condition	Characteristics
Determinable	*When condition violated:* (1) Ownership of present estate automatically terminates; and (2) Original transferor automatically becomes owner of the present estate
Condition subsequent	*When condition violated:* (1) Original transferor automatically has the right to retake possession of the present estate (2) If original transferor does not retake possession, the transferee's rights are unaffected and the transferee remains the owner of the present estate subject to the transferor retaking possession in the future (3) If the original transferor takes action which amounts to retaking possession of the present estate, the transferee's ownership of the present estate terminates and the original transferor becomes the owner of the present estate
Executory limitation	*When condition violated:* (1) Ownership of present estate automatically terminates and a third party named in original transfer automatically becomes owner of present estate OR (2) Third party named in transfer automatically has a right to take possession of present estate if the transfer provides for this

Chapter Six

Types of Future Interests

The basic concept of a future interest was introduced in Chapter Three. This chapter will explain the different types of future interests that exist. Future interests can be divided into two general categories: **Reversionary** and **Nonreversionary**.

> "Reversionary" future interests are future interests retained by an original transferor when the transferor transfers an estate that is smaller than the estate owned by the transferor. Three types of reversionary interests exist:
> (1) **Possibility of reverter**
> (2) **Right of entry**
> (3) **Reversion**

The three types of reversionary future interests are explained in detail below:

(1) A **possibility of reverter** is a future interest that is retained by a transferor when an estate subject to a determinable condition is created. The possibility of reverter may become a present possessory estate in the future upon violation of a condition contained in the original transfer, or it may never become a present possessory estate because the condition is never violated. Whether the transferee will breach the condition is unknown at the time of the transfer. The present estate has the potential to last indefinitely if the condition is never breached. The possibility of reverter provides that a present estate automatically terminates upon violation of the condition. Upon such termination, the original transferor automatically becomes the owner of the present estate.

A transfer does not have to expressly mention the creation of a possibility of reverter. A possibility of reverter is automatically created by operation of law whenever a determinable estate is created.

Explanatory Example

O conveys Blackacre to A. However, the conveyance provides: (a) A loses all rights in Blackacre if he ever uses it for commercial purposes; and (b) if A loses all rights in Blackacre O automatically becomes the owner of the present estate in Blackacre. O has a possibility of reverter in Blackacre because breach of the condition automatically eliminates A's rights in Blackacre in favor of O.

(2) A right of entry (also called a **right of re-entry, right of entry for condition broken** or **power of termination**) is a future interest that is retained by a transferor when an estate subject to a condition subsequent is created. A right of entry is very similar to a possibility of reverter. The key difference between a possibility of reverter and a right of entry lies in what happens upon breach of the condition.

If an original transferor has a possibility of reverter a transferee's breach of the condition automatically terminates her present estate and makes her a trespasser. The original transferor then automatically becomes the owner of the present estate. In contrast, if an original transferor has a right of entry, the breach of the condition by the transferee does not automatically terminate her present estate. In this case, upon breach of the condition, the original transferor has the right to terminate the transferee's present estate and to retake possession. The transferee's present estate (and right to possession) continues to exist until the original transferor takes action. Breach of the condition will have no effect upon the transferee's present estate if the original transferor fails to take appropriate action subsequent to the transferee's breach. A transferor could physically enter the property and retake possession or could bring a law suit seeking to have the transferee removed from the property. Either action will terminate the ownership interest of the transferee and give the original transferor the right to present possession of the property.

A grant or conveyance does not have to expressly mention the creation of a right of entry. A right of entry is automatically created by operation of law whenever an estate subject to a condition subsequent is created.

Explanatory Example

O conveys Blackacre to A. However, the conveyance provides: (a) O shall have the right to retake Blackacre if A uses it for commercial purposes; and (b) A only loses his rights in favor of O if O takes steps to retake possession of Blackacre. O has a right of entry in Blackacre because A only loses his rights in Blackacre if O takes action to retake Blackacre. Even if A uses Blackacre for commercial purposes he continues to own Blackacre and he continues to have the right to present possession of Blackacre. A only loses his rights to Blackacre if and when O retakes possession of Blackacre.

(3) A reversion is any future interest retained by a transferor which is not a possibility of reverter or a right of entry. A reversion can be identified as a future interest that is retained by a transferor that will only become a present estate at the natural end of the prior present estate. For example, life estates naturally end when the life estate holder dies. An estate for years leasehold naturally ends when the fixed time period specified in the leasehold ends. Therefore, a future interest retained by a transferor that follows the natural end of a life estate or the natural end of an estate for years leasehold is a reversion.

A grant or conveyance does not have to expressly mention the creation of a reversion. A reversion is automatically created by operation of law whenever a defeasible estate, other than a determinable estate or an estate subject to a condition subsequent, is created.

Who Retains the Reversionary Interest if the Original Transfer Is via a Will?

If a will creates a defeasible estate, any retained reversionary interest is viewed as property owned by the decedent at death. The will determines who gets the reversionary interest just like any other property owned by the decedent at death. If the will does not make any provision for who gets the reversionary interest, it will go to the decedent's heirs via intestacy.

Explanatory Examples

(1) **O conveys Blackacre to A for life.** The life estate naturally ends at the death of A. At A's death, O owns Blackacre. O's right to Blackacre does not arise due to termination of A's estate caused by breach of a condition. Instead, O gains a present estate in Blackacre at the normal end of A's interest which is at A's death. O's future interest is neither a possibility of reverter nor a right of entry, so by default it must be a reversion. It does not matter in this example that the original conveyance fails to mention creation of a reversion in O. O, who had a fee simple absolute in Blackacre, only conveyed a life estate to A. He made no other conveyance so O still owns the rest of the interest in Blackacre since a life estate is less than a fee simple absolute estate. O's right to present possession is merely postponed until A's life estate ends.

(2) **O leases Blackacre to A for ten years.** O has a reversion because he is entitled to present possession of Blackacre only after the normal end of the estate for years leasehold. He does not gain the right to present possession of Blackacre by terminating A's estate prematurely due to breach of a condition placed on the estate. O's interest is not a possibility of reverter or a right of entry. Therefore, by default it must be a reversion.

(3) **O conveys a fee tail in Blackacre to his only child, C.** The fee tail may continue forever. It is also possible that at some point in the future O's lineal descendants will die out. If this happens, the fee tail will end because no lineal descendant will exist to take possession of the property. O has a reversion in Blackacre which will only become a present possessory interest if the fee tail terminates because the line of descendants ends.

> "Nonreversionary" future interests are future interests
> created and transferred by an original transferor to a
> third party instead of being retained by the transferor.
> Two types of nonreversionary future interests exist:
> (1) Remainder
> (2) Executory interest

The two types of nonreversionary future interests are explained in detail below:

(1) A **remainder** is a future interest created in a person other than the original transferor which can only become a present estate, if ever, immediately at the natural end of the prior present estate.

Explanatory Examples

(1) **O conveys Blackacre to A for life, and then to B upon A's death.** B's future interest will become a present estate immediately at the natural end of A's present life estate which is at A's death. B has a remainder.

(2) **O leases Blackacre to T for fifteen years pursuant to an estate for years lease. The lease also provides that upon the end of the fifteen year lease term Blackacre shall go to P.** P only gets present possession at the natural end of the prior possessory estate (the leasehold). P's interest is a remainder.

(3) **O devises Blackacre to A for life, then to B for life, then to C in fee simple absolute.** A has a present life estate in Blackacre. Both B and C have future interests in Blackacre because their respective rights to present possession of Blackacre are delayed until the future. B has a remainder because B will get present possession of Blackacre immediately at the natural end of the prior estate (A's

life estate) at A's death. C has a remainder because C will get present possession of Blackacre immediately at the natural end of the prior estate (B's life estate) at B's death.

(2) An executory interest is a future interest created in a person other than the original transferor which can only become a present estate, if ever, if the prior estate is prematurely terminated or cutoff.

How Do You Distinguish between a Remainder and an Executory Interest?

The distinction between a remainder and an executory interest is based on when the future interest becomes (or may become) a present estate. If this can only occur immediately at the natural end of the prior possessory estate, it is a remainder. If this can only occur by prematurely terminating the prior possessory estate before it naturally ends, it is an executory interest. If a gap exists between the end of the prior possessory estate and the time the future interest can become a present estate, the future interest is an executory interest.

Explanatory Examples

(1) **O conveys Blackacre to A forever, but if A uses Blackacre for commercial purposes then to B for life.** A's present estate can potentially last forever if she never uses Blackacre for commercial purposes. Such an estate has no natural end. B's future interest can only become a present estate if A's interest is prematurely terminated or cutoff because A violates the condition by using Blackacre for commercial purposes. B has an executory interest.

(2) **O conveys Blackacre to A for life, then one year after A's death to B.** A has a present life estate in Blackacre. B has a future interest which cannot become a present possessory estate immediately at the natural end of A's estate (at A's death). The conveyance states that B's interest only becomes a present estate one year after A's death. Therefore, a one year gap exists between the end of the prior possessory estate (A's life estate) and the time when B's interest can become a present estate. Due to this gap B's interest is an executory interest. If B's interest could become a present possessory estate immediately after A's death, B's interest would be a remainder.

(3) **O conveys a life estate in Blackacre to W; and in the same conveyance O simultaneously conveys a fee simple absolute interest in Blackacre to M which can only become a present estate if W marries.** W has a present life es-

tate in Blackacre. M has a future interest in Blackacre. M's interest is an executory interest because it can only change from a future interest to a present estate if W marries. If W marries his life estate is prematurely terminated or cutoff prior to its natural end which would be upon W's death. M will not get present possession of Blackacre upon W's death. M gets a right to present possession only if W marries. If W dies without having married M does not have a right to Blackacre because the condition has not been breached.

Review Questions

(1) What are the three types of reversionary interests and the two types of nonreversionary interests?

(2) What is the key difference between a reversionary interest and a nonreversionary interest?

(3) What is the key difference between a possibility of reverter and a right of entry?

(4) What is the key difference between a remainder and an executory interest?

(5) O conveys a fee simple absolute interest in Blackacre to A. Which of the following is correct?

  (a) O has a possibility of reverter

  (b) O has a right of entry

  (c) O has a remainder

  (d) O has no interest

(6) O, the fee simple absolute owner of Blackacre, conveys a life estate in Blackacre to A. Which of the following is correct?

  (a) O has a possibility of reverter

  (b) O has a right of entry

  (c) O has a reversion

  (d) O has an executory interest

(7) O leases Blackacre to T for fifteen years pursuant to an estate for years lease. The lease provides that upon the end of the 15 year lease term Blackacre shall go to P; but if T fails to pay rent for two consecutive months, Blackacre shall go to Z. Describe the interests granted to P and Z by O.

(8) O conveys a life estate in Blackacre to A, then a life estate in Blackacre to B, then ten days after B's death Blackacre shall go to C for life. Describe the interests in Blackacre created by O's conveyance.

(9) O leases Blackacre to A for ten years. The lease provides: (a) A loses all rights in Blackacre if he ever uses it for commercial purposes; and (b) if A loses all rights in Blackacre O automatically becomes entitled to the present estate in Blackacre. Describe any interests retained by O after the original conveyance.

Review Questions: Answers

(1) Reversionary interests are possibility of reverter, right of entry and reversion. Nonreversionary interests are remainder and executory interest.

(2) Reversionary interests are future interests retained by the original transferor. Nonreversionary interests are future interests transferred to someone other than the original transferor.

(3) If the original transferor has a possibility of reverter she automatically gets possession of the defeasible estate upon breach of the condition. If the original transferor has a right of entry she does not automatically get possession of the defeasible estate upon breach of the condition; she only has the right to take possession of the defeasible estate.

(4) Both are future interests created in someone other than the original transferor. A remainder only becomes a present possessory interest, if at all, immediately at the natural end of the prior possessory estate. An executory interest only becomes a present possessory estate, if at all, either because: (a) the prior possessory estate is prematurely terminated; or (b) there is a gap in time between the end of the prior possessory estate and the future interest becoming a present possessory interest.

(5) (d). (a) and (b) are incorrect because O conveyed her entire interest to A so O did not retain any interest in Blackacre. (c) is incorrect because a remainder is a future interest in someone other than the original grantor.

(6) (c). O conveyed only a life estate to A so O retained part of her interest in Blackacre because the life estate is a smaller interest than the fee simple absolute interest O owned. Both (a) and (b) are incorrect because O's interest will not become a possessory interest by prematurely terminating A's life estate. O must have a reversion which is the only remaining type of reversionary interest. (d) is incorrect because an executory interest is a future interest in someone other than the original grantor.

(7) P and Z have future interests in Blackacre. P only gets present possession, if at all, immediately at the natural end of the prior possessory estate (the leasehold). Therefore, P's interest is a remainder. Z only gets present possession of Blackacre, if at all, if the leasehold estate is prematurely terminated or cutoff by T's breach of the condition (failure to pay rent for two consecutive months) during the lease term. Z has an executory interest in Blackacre.

(8) A has a present life estate. B has a remainder in Blackacre because B's interest is a future interest that will only become a present possessory estate at the natural end of A's life estate. C has a future interest. C's interest does not become a present possessory estate by prematurely terminating B's prior possessory estate. It only becomes a present possessory estate ten days after B's

death. Due to this ten day gap C has an executory interest rather than a remainder. O retains an interest in Blackacre (a reversion) that will become a possessory interest after all three life estates end.

(9) O has retained two future interests: (a) a reversion which becomes effective at the end of the ten year lease which is the natural end of A's estate; and (b) a possibility of reverter because breach of the condition prematurely and automatically eliminates A's rights in Blackacre in favor of O.

Summary of Main Points

A. Reversionary future interests
   1. Future interests retained by the original transferor
      a. Created when original transferor transfers a smaller estate then the transferor owns
      b. Created by operation of law so they do not have to be expressly mentioned in the grant, will or other document creating/transferring the property interest
   2. Types of reversionary future interests:
      a. Possibility of reverter
         i. Created automatically whenever a determinable estate is created
         ii. The possibility of reverter automatically becomes a present possessory estate if the condition in the determinable estate is violated
      b. Right of entry
         i. Created automatically whenever a defeasible estate subject to a condition subsequent is created
         ii. The right of entry does not automatically become a present possessory estate if the condition in the defeasible estate is violated
         iii. The owner of the right of entry must take steps to retake possession of the estate
      c. Reversion
         i. Created automatically whenever the future interest retained by the original transferor is not a possibility of reverter or a right of entry
B. Nonreversionary future interests
   1. Future interests created by the original transferor in a third party (someone other than the original transferor)
   2. These interests are only created if they are expressly mentioned in the grant, will or other document creating/transferring the property interest
   3. Types of nonreversionary future interests
      a. Remainder
         i. Future interest in a third party that can only become a present possessory estate, if at all, immediately at the natural end of the prior possessory estate
      b. Executory interest

i. Future interest in a third party that can only become a present possessory estate, if at all, by prematurely terminating or cutting off a prior possessory estate; or,

ii. Future interest in a third party that can only become a present possessory estate, if at all, after a time gap following the end of the prior possessory estate

Reversionary Future Interests
(Interests Retained by Original Transferor)

Type of Interest	Examples
Possibility of Reverter - Automatically created by operation of law when determinable interest is created - May or may not become present possessory estate - If defeasible condition is broken original transferor automatically becomes present possessory estate owner	(1) O conveys Blackacre to A so long as Blackacre is only used for non-commercial purposes (2) O conveys Blackacre to A for life, however the estate shall automatically terminate if alcohol is sold on Blackacre, and upon such termination it shall automatically revest in the grantor or her heirs (3) O gives A a ten year leasehold interest in Blackacre, so long as A shall not sell alcohol on Blackacre, and if alcohol is sold on Blackacre it shall automatically and immediately revert to the lessor
Right of Entry - Automatically created by operation of law when estate subject to a condition subsequent is created - May or may not become present possessory estate - If defeasible condition is broken original transferor automatically has power to retake possession of estate; unlike possibility of reverter, a right of entry requires action for it to become a present possessory estate	(1) O conveys Blackacre to A, but if Blackacre ceases to be used for residential purposes O shall have the right to retake possession of Blackacre (2) O conveys Blackacre to A for life, however the grantor shall have a right to reenter and retake possession of Blackare if alcohol is sold on Blackacre (3) O gives A a ten year leasehold interest in Blackacre, but if A sells alcohol on Blackacre the lessor shall have the right to reenter and retake possession of Blackacre
Reversion - Automatically created by operation of law - May or may not become a present possessory interest - Any future interest retained by original transferor which is not possibility of reverter or right of entry is a reversion	(1) O devises Blackacre to A for life, then to B for life (2) O conveys a ten year leasehold interest in Blackacre to A (3) O conveys Blackacre to A for life, then to B provided that B does not predecease A

Nonreversionary Future Interests
(Third Party Future Interests)

Type of Interest	Examples
Remainder - Can only follow an estate that is not a fee simple absolute estate - Can only become a present possessory estate, if at all, immediately at natural end of prior possessory estate - Cannot become a present possessory estate by prematurely terminating prior estate	(1) O conveys Blackacre to A for life, then to B (2) O conveys a 20 year leasehold interest in Blackacre to A, then to B (3) O devises Blackacre to A for life, then to B if B survives A (4) O conveys Blackacre to A for life, then to B if B reaches 25 years old
Executory Interest - Can only become a present possessory estate, if at all, by prematurely terminating prior estate - Third party future interest that follows defeasible estate	(1) O conveys Blackacre to A, but if Blackacre ceases to be used for residential purposes to B for life (2) O conveys Blackacre to A for life, but Blackacre shall go to B if A gets married (3) O leases Blackacre to A for 10 years, but if A sells alcohol on Blackacre the leasehold shall automatically transfer to B
Key Distinction between Remainder and Executory Interest - Focus on when future interest is capable of becoming a present possessory estate - If it can only become a present possessory estate when prior possessory estate naturally ends, it is a remainder - If it can only become a present estate by prematurely terminating prior estate, it is an executory interest	(1) O devises Blackacre to A for life, then to B for life (B has a remainder because it will only become a present possessory estate at natural end of prior estate – A's death) (2) O conveys Blackacre to A for life, then to B provided that B does not predecease A (B has a remainder because it will only become a present possessory estate at natural end of prior estate which is when A dies. B may lose estate if he predeceases A but his estate can only become a present possessory estate, if at all, at death of A) (3) O conveys Blackacre to A for life, but if A marries then to B for lifetime of A (B has an executory interest because his interest will only become a present possessory estate, if at all, if A gets married. It will not become a present possessory estate at the natural end of A's estate which is at A's death)

Chapter Seven

Types of Remainders

Remainders were introduced in Chapter Six. This chapter will explain the different types of remainders that exist.

Remainders can initially be divided into two main categories: **vested remainders** and **contingent remainders**.

> A remainder is a "vested remainder" if *both* of the following are true:
>
> (1) At the time the remainder is created a specific person is identified as the owner of the remainder and that person is actually living at that time (this is typically referred to as the "known and ascertained" requirement); and
>
> (2) At the time the remainder is created no condition exists which must be satisfied before the remainder can become a present possessory estate at the natural end of the prior possessory estate (such a condition is called a "condition precedent")

vested

(not subsequent)

> Any remainder that is not a vested remainder is a "contingent remainder"

contingent

Explanatory Examples

(1) **O conveys Blackacre to A for life, remainder to B.** A has a present life estate. B is an existing person at the time O made the conveyance. When the prior present possessory estate naturally ends (at A's death) B's future interest in Blackacre will automatically become a present possessory estate without having to satisfy any condition. B has a vested remainder in Blackacre at the time of the conveyance by O. A's death signifies the natural end of her present possessory estate. Waiting for A to die is not considered a condition precedent which must be satisfied before B is entitled to present possession of Blackacre.

(2) **O conveys Blackacre to A for life, remainder to A's first child. At the time of the conveyance A does not have any children.** A has a present life estate followed by a remainder in A's first child. At the time of the conveyance A does not have any children. O has created a remainder for a person that does not yet exist. The owner of the remainder is not known or ascertained at the time the conveyance is created so it cannot be a vested remainder. By default it is a contingent remainder.

(3) **O conveys Blackacre to A for life, remainder to A's first child. At the time of the conveyance A has one child, C.** O created a present life estate in A followed by a remainder in C. At the time of the conveyance, A's first child, C, exists so she is known and ascertained. A condition precedent does not exist. C has a vested remainder. As noted in example (1), the fact that C must wait until A dies before C obtains a present estate is not a condition precedent.

(4) **O conveys Blackacre to A for life, and if A's first child is alive at A's death, remainder to A's first child. At the time of the conveyance A has one child, C.** O created a present life estate in A followed by a remainder in C. At the time of the conveyance A has a child, C, so her first child is known and ascertained. A condition precedent exists which must be satisfied (C must be alive at A's death) before C's interest can become a present possessory estate. C has a contingent remainder because a condition precedent exists.

(5) **O conveys Blackacre to A for life, and if B has reached twenty-one years of age, remainder to B. B is nineteen years old when O makes the conveyance.** O created a present life estate in A followed by a remainder in B. B exists at the time of O's conveyance so he is known and ascertained. B must satisfy a condition precedent (reaching twenty-one) before his future interest can become a present possessory estate. B's interest must be a contingent remainder.

(6) **O conveys Blackacre to A for life, and if B has reached twenty-one years of age, remainder to B. B is twenty-two years old when O makes the conveyance.** This example is the same as the previous one except that B is twenty-two at the time O makes the original conveyance. B does not have to satisfy any condition precedent since he satisfied the condition before O made the conveyance. B's interest is a vested remainder because at the time of O's original conveyance B is known and ascertained and does not have to satisfy any condition precedent.

(7) **O conveys a fee simple defeasible estate in Blackacre to A subject to the condition that a remainder exists in B if A, during her lifetime, ever sells liquor on Blackacre.** Despite what the conveyance says, B cannot have a remainder. A remainder must be capable of becoming a present possessory estate, if ever, immediately at the natural end of the prior present estate. B's future interest can only become a present possessory estate if the prior present possessory es-

tate is prematurely terminated due to A violating the condition by selling alcohol on Blackacre. B has an executory interest in Blackacre.

(8) **O leases Blackacre to A for thirty years. Does O have a remainder in Blackacre at the end of the lease term?** No, because a remainder is a future interest in a party other than the transferor. O, the original transferor, has a future interest at the end of A's present estate. Future interests in the original transferor must be a possibility of reverter, a right of entry or a reversion. The original transferor did not create a determinable estate or an estate subject to a condition subsequent. O's future interest cannot be a possibility of reverter or a right of entry because those interests are associated with a determinable estate or an estate subject to a condition subsequent, respectively. By default, O must have a reversion.

(9) **O leases Blackacre to A for ten years. The lease also provides that failure to maintain the premises in a habitable state shall result in the termination of the lease with the remainder of any lease term going to B. It also provides that at the end of the ten year lease term C shall have a life estate.** O created a present possessory estate in A. O also gave B and C future interests in Blackacre. B's interest can only become a present estate if A's leasehold is prematurely terminated due to A's breach of the condition by failing to maintain the premises in a habitable state. B's interest is an executory interest. C's future interest will become a present estate at the natural end of A's lease at the end of the ten year lease term. C has a remainder. Since C exists at the time of O's original conveyance she is known and ascertained. Additionally, no condition precedent exists which must be satisfied. C has a vested remainder.

Only one type of contingent remainder exists but three types of vested remainders exist. If it is determined that a vested remainder exists it must be further classified as either an indefeasibly vested remainder, a vested remainder subject to complete defeasance or a vested remainder subject to open. Each type of vested remainder is discussed below.

> An "indefeasibly vested remainder" (also called an "absolutely vested remainder") is a vested remainder that satisfies *both* of the following at the time of the original conveyance:
>
> (1) It can be said with absolute certainty that the future interest will become a present possessory estate in the future; and
>
> (2) Once it becomes a present possessory estate it cannot expire (naturally end) or be prematurely terminated by violation of a condition

Pursuant to the above definition, an indefeasibly vested remainder is not subject to any conditions or limitations, nor can the future interest naturally end before or after it becomes a present possessory interest. Only a vested remainder in a fee simple absolute estate can be an indefeasibly vested remainder.

Explanatory Examples

(1) **O conveys Blackacre to A for life, remainder to B in fee simple absolute.** B's remainder will absolutely become a present possessory fee simple absolute estate at the natural end of A's life estate. Nothing will prevent it from becoming a present possessory interest in the future. B's right to possession is merely delayed until the future (at A's death). Notice that B's future interest is not subject to any condition precedent or any condition subsequent. Once B's interest becomes a present possessory fee simple absolute estate it cannot be prematurely terminated and it cannot naturally end. Once an indefeasibly vested remainder is created the subsequent death of the owner of the remainder does not terminate the interest. The interest is a property interest that will simply pass via will or intestate succession upon the death of the owner of the interest. If B died during A's lifetime leaving a will giving all of her property to S, upon B's death S would acquire the future interest in Blackacre via B's will. If B died during A's lifetime without a will B's heirs would inherit B's future interest.

(2) **O wills Blackacre to A for life, then to B for life, then to C in fee simple absolute.** O's will creates a present life estate in A, followed by two successive future interests. Both B's and C's future interests will become present possessory estates at the natural end of the respective prior estates. Neither future interest is subject to a condition precedent. B and C both have vested remainders in Blackacre. More precisely, B has a vested remainder in a life estate in Blackacre and C has a vested remainder in a fee simple absolute estate in Blackacre. It is possible that B could predecease A, and therefore B's future interest would never become a present possessory estate because it would naturally end at B's death. Consequently, B does not have an indefeasibly vested remainder. In contrast, it can be stated with absolute certainty that C's future interest will become a present possessory estate in the future after both A and B die. Nothing can prematurely terminate C's interest either before or after it becomes a present possessory estate. Nor can C's interest naturally end before or after it

becomes a present possessory estate. C has an indefeasibly vested remainder in Blackacre in fee simple absolute.

> A "vested remainder subject to complete defeasance" (also called a "vested remainder subject to a condition subsequent", or a "vested remainder subject to complete divestment") is a vested remainder that meets *any* of the following criteria at the time of the original transfer:
>
> (1) It could naturally end prior to the future interest becoming a present possessory estate;
>
> (2) It could naturally end after it becomes a present possessory estate;
>
> (3) It could prematurely terminate prior to the future interest becoming a present possessory estate (If the remainder is subject to a condition precedent it is a contingent remainder); or
>
> (4) It could prematurely terminate after it becomes a present possessory estate due to breach of a condition subsequent (If the remainder is subject to a condition precedent it is a contingent remainder)

In light of the above definition, a vested remainder in a defeasible estate, a vested remainder in a life estate or a vested remainder in a leasehold estate will be a vested remainder subject to complete defeasance.

Explanatory Examples

(1) **O conveys Blackacre to A for life, remainder to B, but if B dies during A's lifetime Blackacre shall immediately go to C in fee simple absolute.** O's original conveyance creates a present defeasible life estate in A, a remainder in B and an executory interest in C. B has a vested remainder because B is known and ascertained and no condition precedent must be satisfied. A condition subsequent (B dies while A is alive) could prematurely terminate B's interest before it becomes a present possessory estate. B has a vested remainder subject to complete defeasance.

(2) **O conveys Blackacre to A for life, remainder to B if B is alive at A's death, but if B dies during A's lifetime then Blackacre shall immediately go to C in fee simple absolute.** The wording of this conveyance is only slightly different

than the wording of example (1). This difference changes the interests created by the conveyance. In this example, B is known and ascertained but B is subject to a condition precedent (B must be alive at A's death) so B has a contingent remainder in Blackacre. In example (1) O conveyed a vested remainder to B which could be subsequently prematurely terminated or divested if B died during A's lifetime. In contrast, here O conveys a contingent remainder to B that requires B to satisfy a condition precedent (be alive at A's death) before it can be become a vested remainder. In example (1) the condition acts to prematurely terminate or divest a remainder that is already vested. In this example the condition acts as a prerequisite to the remainder vesting. (Distinguishing between a condition precedent and condition subsequent is not always easy. This issue will be discussed in detail in Chapter Eleven).

(3) **O conveys Blackacre to A for life, then to B in fee simple, but if B sells alcohol on Blackacre then to C in fee simple absolute.** O's conveyance creates a present life estate in A, a remainder in B and an executory interest in C. B is known and ascertained and no condition precedent exists. B's interest will become a present possessory interest at the natural end of the prior present possessory estate (at A's death). B has a vested remainder. B's remainder is subject to a condition subsequent (selling alcohol on Blackacre) which means B's fee simple estate can be prematurely terminated or cutoff if the condition is violated after he obtains present possession of Blackacre. B's interest can be fully described as a vested remainder subject to complete defeasance in Blackacre in a fee simple subject to an executory limitation. C has a shifting excecutory interest in fee simple absolute because C's interest will only become a present possessory estate if B's interest is prematurely terminated or cutoff due to B's violation of the condition subsequent.

(4) **O conveys Blackacre to A for life, then to B in fee simple, but if A sells alcohol on Blackacre then Blackacre shall go immediately to C in fee simple absolute.** O's conveyance creates a present defeasible life estate in A, a vested remainder in B and an executory interest in C. C has a shifting excecutory interest in fee simple absolute because C's interest will only become a present possessory estate if B's interest is prematurely terminated or cutoff due to A's violation of the condition subsequent (selling alcohol on Blackacre). B has a vested remainder subject to complete defeasance because B's vested remainder can be prematurely terminated before B gets a present possessory interest in Blackacre if A violates the condition subsequent by selling alcohol on Blackacre. B's interest can only be divested or prematurely terminated while A has present possession of Blackacre. Upon A's death, A can no longer violate the condition so B would end up with a fee simple absolute since B's interest cannot be divested if A dies without violating the condition. B's future interest can be fully described as a vested remainder subject to complete defeasance in Blackacre in a fee simple absolute.

(5) **O conveys Blackacre to A for life, then to B for life, and then to C in fee simple absolute.** O's conveyance creates a present life estate in Blackacre in A and vested remainders in B and C. Both B and C have remainders because they have a right to present possession of Blackacre immediately upon the natural end of the respective prior estate. B and C are known and ascertained and no condition precedent or subsequent exists with regard to either B or C taking possession at the end of the respective prior estate. However, B could predecease A which would prevent B from ever having a present possessory estate in Blackacre. Note that B would not lose the right to present possession due to violation of a condition. It would simply be due to his life estate naturally ending upon his death. B cannot have an indefeasibly vested remainder because it cannot be said with absolute certainty that he will definitely get a present estate in Blackacre. B has a vested remainder subject to complete defeasance in Blackacre in a life estate. C will definitely get a present possessory estate in Blackacre at some future date and that estate cannot be prematurely terminated nor can it naturally end. C has an indefeasibly vested remainder in Blackacre in fee simple absolute.

> A "vested remainder subject to open" (also called a "vested remainder subject to partial defeasance" or a "vested remainder subject to partial divestment") is a vested remainder transferred to a group of people. This type of vested remainder only exists if *all* of the following conditions are satisfied at the time of the original conveyance:
>
> (1) At least one member of the group must currently exist (be known and ascertained);
> (2) The group is capable of increasing in size (the "subject to open" language refers to this requirement); and
> (3) There is no condition precedent which must be satisfied before the remainder can become a present possessory estate at the natural end of the prior possessory estate (if the remainder is subject to a condition precedent it is a contingent remainder)

An understanding of class gifts is necessary to fully comprehend vested remainders subject to open. The following provides an explanation of class gifts.

A transfer made to a group is a class gift if:

(1) The number of individuals in the group can change (increase or decrease) subsequent to the original transfer; and

(2) The percentage ownership interest of individual group members in the transferred property can increase or decrease due to members entering or leaving the group.

A transfer to a group of persons who have indefeasibly vested interests is not a class gift. Such individuals do not drop out of the group if they die. Death merely transfers a deceased person's interest via will or intestate succession to the person's will beneficiaries or heirs, respectively.

A group receiving a class gift is typically referred to as a class.

Children and grandchildren are groups that commonly receive class gifts. A gift to a group of people that is fixed at the time of the original conveyance is not a class gift. For example, a gift "to my grandchildren, Sam and Alvin," is not a class gift because the group of transferees is specifically defined. Additional persons cannot enter the class. If the gift states "to my grandchildren" it would be a class gift since at the time of the conveyance it is unknown if additional grandchildren might be born in the future and thereby enter the class. The gift "to my grandchildren" is a class gift.

General Rules — Class Gifts

(1) Typically, a future interest transferred to a group that only identifies the group members by a group label (e.g. my children; my grandchildren; the students in my property class; my first cousins) is a class gift.

(2) Typically, a future interest transferred to a group is not a class gift if the group members are identified by name (e.g. my children A and B; my grandchildren C and D; my first cousins E and F).

A class gift can be a contingent remainder if no members of the class exist at the time the original transfer created the class gift. If a condition precedent exists at the time the class gift is created and no class member has satisfied the condition it is also a contingent remainder in a class. A class gift can be an executory interest as well. In all cases, a class gift exists if the size of the class can change subsequent to its creation.

The same rules that determine if a contingent future interest is a contingent remainder or an executory interest apply to determine if a class gift is a contingent remainder or an executory interest.

Explanatory Examples

(1) **O transfers Blackacre to A for life, then to A's children, B1, B2 and B3.** O's transfer creates a present life estate in A followed by a vested remainder in the named children, B1, B2 and B3, as a group. This is not a class gift. The size of the group cannot change. Each named child gets 1/3 of an interest in Blackacre. If B1 predeceases A, B2 and B3 still only get a 1/3 interest. B1's 1/3 interest passes via her will or via intestacy absent a will. The future interest in B1, B2 and B3 is an indefeasibly vested remainder in Blackacre with each child entitled to a 1/3 fractional share of Blackacre.

(2) **O transfers Blackacre to A for life, then to A's children, B1, B2 and B3, but if B1, B2 or B3 attend law school during A's lifetime the interest of the child attending law school shall be forfeited.** O's transfer creates a present life estate in A followed by a vested remainder in the named children, B1, B2 and B3. Each child initially is entitled to 1/3 of an interest in Blackacre but a condition subsequent (attending law school during A's lifetime) can terminate the interest of B1, B2 or B3. If a child's interest is terminated the interest of the remaining children will increase. If B1 attends law school during A's lifetime B1 is divested of his interest in Blackacre. B2 and B3 are now each entitled to a fractional 1/2 interest in Blackacre. O's conveyance created a vested remainder subject to complete defeasance in B1, B2 and B3 that is a class gift.

(3) **O transfers Blackacre to A for life, then to A's children, B1, B2 and B3, but if B1, B2 or B3 attend law school during A's lifetime the interest of the child attending law school shall automatically go to C.** This transfer is very similar to example (2), except that B1, B2 and B3 do not forfeit their future interest if they go to law school. Instead their interest is automatically transferred to a third party, C, if they attend law school. The interest of B1, B2 and B3 cannot increase or decrease in size. They are only entitled to a 1/3 fractional interest. O's conveyance created a vested remainder subject to complete defeasance in B1, B2 and B3 but it is not a class gift.

A vested remainder in a class gift is specially designated as a vested remainder subject to open if the number of persons in the class can increase. The wording "subject to open" refers to the possibility that the membership of the class can increase. This is in contrast to the definition of a class gift which includes a class that can increase in size or decrease in size. Therefore, only some future class gifts will be vested remainders subject to open.

class gift ↑ ·or ↓
svbj. to open ↑

Explanatory Examples

(1) **O conveys Blackacre to A for life, then to A's children. Assume A has one child, B, at the time of the conveyance.** The interest created in A's children is a class gift. The interest in the children can only become a present possessory estate at the natural end of the prior life estate. This makes the children's interest a remainder. Only one member of the class, B, exists at the time of the original conveyance but the class could subsequently increase in size since A could have more children. Additionally, no condition precedent exists which must be fulfilled before A's children have a right to present possession at the natural end of the prior life estate. Therefore, A's children have a vested remainder subject to open. It is vested because at the time of the original conveyance B exists and there is no condition precedent which B must satisfy. It is "subject to open" because at the time of the original conveyance by O there is a possibility more children could enter the class in the future since A is alive at the time of the conveyance.

(2) **O conveys Blackacre to A for life, then to A's children. Assume A has no children at the time of the conveyance.** This is the same conveyance as in example (1). However, no children of A exist at the time of the original conveyance. Like example (1), O creates a class gift in A's children which will become a present possessory interest at the natural end of A's life estate. Therefore, the children of A have a remainder. A vested remainder subject to open requires at least one member of the class to be known and ascertained at the time of the conveyance. In this example, no children exist at the time of the original conveyance so no class member is known and ascertained at the time of the conveyance. Therefore, A's children have a contingent remainder.

(3) **O conveys Blackacre to A for life, then to A's children. Assume A has no children at the time of the conveyance. However, she had a child, B, who died two weeks before the conveyance, and she has a child, C, who was born two years after the conveyance.** The interest created in A's children by O's original conveyance is a class gift. A vested remainder subject to open requires at least one member of the class to be known and ascertained at the time of the original conveyance. In this example, no children existed at the time of the conveyance. B died prior to the conveyance and C was born after the conveyance. Therefore, O's conveyance created a contingent remainder in A's children. It should be noted, however, that the contingent remainder in A's children changes to a vested remainder subject to open once C is born.

(4) **O conveys Blackacre to A for life, then to A's children, but if any of A's children shall attend law school during A's life such child shall be automatically divested of any interest in Blackacre. A has no children at the time of O's**

conveyance. The interest created in A's children is a class gift because it is unknown at the time of the original conveyance who the class members will be and how big the class will be. No children exist at the time of the original conveyance. Therefore, the interest in A's children cannot be a vested remainder. By default it is a contingent remainder.

(5) **O conveys Blackacre to A for life, then to A's children, but if any of A's children shall attend law school during A's life such child shall be automatically divested of any interest in Blackacre. A has one child, X, at the time of O's conveyance.** This conveyance is the same as example (4) except that one child, X, is alive at the time of the original conveyance. In light of the existence of X, the children of A have a vested remainder subject to open. Note that the divesting condition (attending law school) is a condition subsequent rather than a condition precedent so it does not make the children's interest a contingent remainder.

(6) **O conveys Blackacre to A for life, then to B's children. At the time of O's conveyance, B is deceased and three of B's children, B1, B2 and B3, are alive.** This conveyance is not a class gift. No additional children can enter the class since B died prior to the conveyance by O. The interest created by O in B's children is an indefeasibly vested remainder because the children exist at the time of the conveyance and no condition precedent exists that must be satisfied in order for them to take their interests at the natural end of A's life estate. Additionally, no condition subsequent exists which can divest B1, B2 and B3 of their future interests. Therefore, even if B1, B2 or B3 predecease A their future interests will not be destroyed because they are indefeasibly vested. If they do predecease A their interest will simply pass to their will beneficiaries or, in the absence of a will, to their heirs via intestate succession.

(7) **O conveys Blackacre to A for life, then to B's children. At the time of O's conveyance, B is alive and three of B's children, B1, B2 and B3, are alive.** This conveyance is the same as the grant in example (6) except that B is alive in this example. As a result, the conveyance to B's children is a class gift because additional children could enter the class after O's original conveyance since B could potentially have more children. The class gift is a remainder because it can only become a present possessory interest at the natural end of A's life estate which occurs at A's death. Additionally, three children of B (B1, B2 and B3) exist at the time of O's original conveyance and no condition precedent exists. Therefore, the remainder in B's children is a vested remainder subject to open.

(8) **O conveys Blackacre to A for life, then to B's children subject to the condition precedent that a child of B must be alive at A's death. At the time of O's conveyance, B has one child, X.** During A's lifetime B could have more children or some of B's children could predecease A. Therefore, the future

interest in B's children is a class gift since the size of the class will be un-known until A dies. However, since the interest of every class member is subject to a condition precedent (at least one child of B must outlive A) the children of B have a contingent remainder rather than a vested remainder subject to open.

Some special rules, discussed below, exist for vested remainders subject to open.

> The "closed class rule" states that once it is impossible for the number of persons in a class to increase it is no longer subject to open. The class is then referred to as a "closed class." Such class closure occurs when class membership can no longer increase due to subsequent occurrences following the original transfer that created the class gift

Explanatory Examples

(1) **O conveys Blackacre to A for life, then to B's children. At the time of the conveyance B is alive and has one child, C.** B's children have a vested remainder subject to open because at the time of the conveyance by O, B has one child, C, who is not subject to any condition precedent. However, other children could enter the class if B has additional children during A's lifetime.

(2) **Assume in the preceding example, that during A's lifetime B has another child, D, and then B dies during A's lifetime.** B obviously cannot have any more children after she dies so the class closes at B's death because her death makes it impossible for any additional members to enter the class. Additionally, the interests of the existing children are indefeasibly vested since they are not subject to any conditions subsequent. Therefore, if either C or D predecease A their interests pass via will or intestacy. Nevertheless, C and D must wait until A dies before they are entitled to present possession of Blackacre.

The 'rule of convenience' states that once any member of a class is entitled to present possession of property the class closes even if it is possible for subsequent class members to enter the class

(1) This is a default rule so it will not apply if the original transferor clearly stated an intent for the class to remain open until all possible persons could become class members

(2) This rule may have the effect of cutting off future potential class members because once a class closes no one else can become a class member

(3) Typically, if a class has not closed prior to the natural end of the prior possessory estate it will be closed when the prior possessory estate ends under the rule

Explanatory Examples

(1) **O devises Blackacre to A for life, then to B's children. Assume B is alive at A's death, and B has one child, X, alive at A's death.** Subsequent to A's death B could have additional children. However, at the natural end of A's estate (upon her death) X is available to take Blackacre. Therefore, under the rule of convenience the class of B's children is closed upon A's death and X takes Blackacre. In this example, the rule of convenience cuts off any subsequently born children of B who would be class members absent the rule of convenience.

(2) **O devises Blackacre to A for life, then to B's children. Assume B is alive at A's death but she does not have any children.** The rule of convenience would not be applied to close the class of B's children because no class member (child of B) exists to take Blackacre at the end of the prior possessory estate.

Review Questions

(1) What is the difference between a vested remainder and a contingent remainder?

(2) Is a remainder interest that is subject to a condition subsequent a contingent remainder?

(3) How many types of contingent remainders exist?

(4) How many types of vested remainders exist?

(5) What is a class gift?

(6) Are all class gifts vested remainders subject to open?

(7) What is the closed class rule?

(8) What is the rule of convenience?

(9) O conveys Blackacre to A for life but subject to the condition that A's life estate shall automatically terminate if A uses Blackacre for commercial purposes, and if it terminates due to violation of the condition Blackacre goes to B in fee simple absolute. Does B have a remainder?

(10) O conveys Blackacre to A for life, then to B in fee simple absolute. What interest does B have?

(11) O conveys Blackacre to A for life, then to B in fee simple, but if B attends law school Blackacre shall go to C in fee simple absolute. Does this conveyance create any remainders?

(12) O wills Blackacre to A for life, then to A's children in fee simple absolute. If A has no children at O's death does the will create a vested remainder subject to open?

(13) O wills Blackacre to A for life, then to A's children in fee simple absolute. If A has one child, X, alive at O's death does the will create a vested remainder subject to open?

(14) O wills Blackacre to A for life, then to B's children in fee simple absolute. B has one child, X, alive at O's death and another child, Z, born after A dies. Does Z have any interest in Blackacre?

Review Questions: Answers

(1) A vested remainder exists if the remainder person actually exists at the time of the original conveyance and no condition precedent must be satisfied before the remainder interest can become a present possessory estate in the future. If a remainder is not a vested remainder it is a contingent remainder by default.

(2) No. A remainder subject to a condition precedent is a contingent remainder but a remainder subject to a condition subsequent is a vested remainder.

(3) One.

(4) Three. Indefeasibly vested remainder, vested remainder subject to complete defeasance, vested remainder subject to open.

(5) A transfer made to a group or class of individuals where the people included in the class can change (increase or decrease) subsequent to the original transfer.

(6) No. A class gift is a vested remainder subject to open only if it meets the following: (a) satisfies the requirements to be a remainder; (b) it is possible for the number of members in the class to increase; and (c) at least one class member must both exist and not be subject to a condition precedent at the time of the original transfer.

(7) The class in a vested remainder subject to open closes once it is impossible for the number of persons in the class to increase due to occurrences subsequent to the original transfer. The class would then be referred to as a "closed class."

(8) It is a default rule which automatically closes the class in a vested remainder subject to open once any member of the class is entitled to present possession of the property. Once the class closes no additional people can be added to the class. This default rule can only be avoided if the original transferor clearly states her intent for the class to remain open until all possible persons could become class members.

(9) No. B does not have a remainder because B will only get a right to present possession of Blackacre if A prematurely terminates her life estate by violating the condition. If A never violates the condition B will never gain a right to present possession of Blackacre. B has a shifting executory interest in Blackacre in fee simple absolute.

(10) An indefeasibly vested remainder in Blackacre in fee simple absolute. B only gets a right to present possession of Blackacre at the natural end of the prior possessory estate (at A's death). B is known and ascertained and his interest is not subject to any condition precedent or condition subsequent so he has a vested remainder. Nothing will prevent B's remainder from eventually

becoming a present possessory estate. Additionally, once B's estate becomes a present possessory estate it cannot be prematurely terminated. Therefore, B has an indefeasibly vested remainder in Blackacre in fee simple absolute.

(11) B has a vested remainder subject to complete defeasance in Blackacre. B has a right to present possession of Blackacre immediately at the natural end of A's life estate. Therefore, B has a remainder. The remainder is vested because B is known and ascertained and does not have to satisfy a condition precedent. A condition subsequent exists (B attends law school) that can terminate or divest B's future interest. B can attend law school during A's lifetime, so B's vested remainder can be divested prior to it becoming a present possessory estate. B's interest can also be prematurely terminated after it becomes a present possessory estate if he first attends law school after A dies. Therefore, B has a vested remainder subject to complete defeasance in Blackacre in a fee simple subject to an executory limitation. C's interest only becomes a present possessory interest if B prematurely terminates his interest by violating the condition (attending law school). C does not obtain the right to present possession of Blackacre at the natural end of the prior estate. Therefore, C has a shifting executory interest in Blackacre in fee simple absolute.

(12) No. O created a class gift in A's children. The children will get present possession of Blackacre at the natural end of the prior estate (at A's death) so the children have a remainder. However, since no children exist at O's death the remainder is a contingent remainder.

(13) Yes. The existence of one class member, X, who is not subject to a condition precedent makes the remainder a vested remainder. The vested remainder is subject to open because A can have more children who would become class members.

(14) No. O's will gives B's children a vested remainder subject to open because X is alive at O's death and not subject to any condition precedent. At A's death the class closes due to the rule of convenience because X has a right of present possession of Blackacre at A's death. Once the class closes no additional people can enter the class. Z was born after A's death so he cannot become a member of the class.

Summary of Main Points

A. Types of remainders
    1. Vested remainder
        a. A remainder is a vested remainder if:
            i.   The owner of the remainder exists; and
            ii. No condition precedent exists
    2. Contingent remainder
        a. By default, if a remainder is not a vested remainder it is a contingent remainder
B. Types of vested remainders
    1. Indefeasibly vested remainder
        a. Both of the following must be true for a remainder to be an indefeasibly vested remainder:
            i.   Remainder will definitely become a present possessory estate in the future; and
            ii. Once it becomes a present possessory estate it cannot expire (naturally end) or be prematurely terminated by violation of a condition
        b. Therefore, only a vested remainder in a fee simple absolute estate can be an indefeasibly vested remainder
        c. Death of remainder owner does not destroy remainder
    2. Vested remainder subject to complete defeasance
        a. If any one of the following are true the remainder is a vested remainder subject to complete defeasance:
            i.   Remainder can be divested by violation of a condition before it becomes a present possessory estate;
            ii. Interest can be prematurely terminated or cutoff after it becomes a present possessory estate; or
            iii. Interest may be prevented from becoming a present possessory estate in the future because the estate naturally terminates before it can become a present possessory estate
        b. Therefore, a vested remainder in a defeasible estate, a life estate or a leasehold estate will be a vested remainder subject to complete defeasance
    3. Vested remainder subject to open
        a. Applies only to class gifts when the number of persons in the class can increase

      i.   A class gift is a gift to a group of persons in which the number of persons in the group can change (decrease or increase) subsequent to the original conveyance

b.   At least one class member must have a vested interest at the time of the original conveyance (class member must both exist and not be subject to a condition precedent at the time of the original conveyance)

c.   It must be possible for the class to increase in size after the original conveyance

d.   Special rules apply to a vested remainder subject to open:

      i.   Closed class rule—once it is impossible for the number of members of a class to increase the class closes (for example, under this rule a class gift to the children of A closes when A dies)

      ii. Rule of convenience—once any class member is entitled to present possession of the estate the class closes (for example, under this rule when the prior present possessory estate naturally ends the class typically closes). This is a default rule which applies unless the original conveyance clearly states the class should remain open until all possible class members can be included in the class

Types of Remainders

Type of Remainder	Examples
Vested Remainder If both of the following are true the remainder is a vested remainder: -The remainder is given to a person who exists at the time of the original conveyance - There is no condition precedent that must be satisfied before the remainder can vest (existence of a condition subsequent does not make a remainder a contingent remainder)	(1) O conveys Blackacre to A for life, then to B (B has a vested remainder) (2) O wills Blackacre to A, then to B (B has a vested remainder) (3) O conveys a twenty year leasehold interest in Blackacre to A, then to A's first child. At the time of the conveyance A has one child, C (C has a vested remainder) (4) O conveys Blackacre to A for life, then to B, but if B does not go to law school then to C (the condition in this conveyance is a condition subsequent which can divest B's interest; it is not a condition precedent which must be satisfied before B's interest can vest so B has a vested remainder; C has a shifting executory interest)
Contingent Remainder - If a remainder is not a vested remainder it is a contingent remainder by default	(1) O conveys Blackacre to A for life, and if B graduates from law school to B. B is still in high school at the time of the conveyance. (B has a contingent remainder because he is subject to a condition precedent) (2) O conveys a twenty year leasehold interest in Blackacre to A, then to A's first child. A does not have any children at the time of the conveyance (A's first child has a contingent remainder because he or she does not exist yet) (3) O conveys Blackacre to A for life, then to B if B reaches twenty-five. B is twenty at the time of the conveyance. (B has a contingent remainder because he is subject to a condition precedent)

Types of Vested Remainders

Type of Vested Remainder	Examples
Indefeasibly Vested Remainder - Remainder will definitely become a present possessory estate in the future; *and* - Once it becomes a present possessory estate it cannot expire (naturally end) or be prematurely terminated by violation of a condition	(1) O conveys Blackacre to A for life, then to B in fee simple absolute (B has an indefeasibly vested remainder) (2) O conveys a twenty year leasehold interest in Blackacre to A, then to B in fee simple absolute (B has an indefeasibly vested remainder)
Vested Remainder Subject to Complete Defeasance - If vested remainder can expire (naturally end) prior to the future interest becoming a present possessory estate; - If vested remainder can terminate prior to the future interest becoming a present possessory estate due to breach of a condition subsequent (if the remainder is subject to a condition precedent it is a contingent remainder); *or* - If vested remainder can terminate after it becomes a present possessory estate due to breach of a condition subsequent (if the remainder is subject to a condition precedent it is a contingent remainder)	(1) O conveys Blackacre to A for life, then to B, but if B becomes an attorney to C (B has a vested remainder subject to complete defeasance) (2) O devises Blackacre to A for life, then to B, but if B predeceases A, then to C (B has a vested remainder subject to complete defeasance) (3) O grants Blackacre to A for life, then to B for life, then to C in fee simple absolute (B has a vested remainder subject to complete defeasance; C has an indefeasibly vested remainder)
Vested Remainder Subject to Open - A remainder to a class of persons where at least one person both exists and is not subject to any condition precedent at the time of the original conveyance; *and* - Others may enter the class subsequent to the original conveyance	(1) O conveys Blackacre to A for life, then to A's children. A has one child, C, alive at the time of the conveyance (A's children have a vested remainder subject to open because A could have more children) (2) O devises Blackacre to A for life, then to B's children. B has five children alive at the time of the conveyance (B's children have a vested remainder subject to open because B can have more children)

Chapter Eight

Types of Executory Interests

In Chapter Six the distinction between a remainder and an executory interest was discussed, and in Chapter Seven the different types of remainders were examined. In this chapter we will examine the two types of executory interests that exist.

First, it is important to recognize that executory interests are contingent future interests. In this regard they are very similar to contingent remainders which are also contingent future interests. Designation of an interest as a contingent future interest is a recognition of the fact that the interest may or may not ever become a present possessory estate in the future. Additionally, like a contingent remainder, an executory interest in a class of persons can be created without regard to whether the members of the class currently exist.

Only two types of executory interests exist—a *shifting executory interest* and a *springing executory interest*.

> A "shifting executory interest" refers to an executory interest where the holder of the executory interest will only obtain a present possessory estate, if at all, from another transferee (rather than from the original transferor)

> A "springing executory interest" refers to an executory interest where the holder of the executory interest will only obtain a present possessory estate, if at all, from the original transferor (or her heirs or will beneficiaries, if the original transfer is via intestate succession or via testamentary transfer, respectively)

The distinction between shifting and springing executory interests is best understood by studying the following examples.

Explanatory Examples

(1) **O conveys a defeasible life estate in Blackacre to B subject to the condition that Blackacre will go to C if B ever sells alcohol on Blackacre.** B has a present life estate that is subject to a condition (never sell alcohol). If the condition is never violated B's life estate will naturally end at B's death and C will never obtain a present possessory estate in Blackacre. However, if B violates the condition, B's life estate will be prematurely terminated and will go to C. C has an executory interest because she will only obtain a present possessory estate in Blackacre if B violates the condition. The next question is whether C's executory interest is a shifting or a springing executory interest. If the condition is violated, the right to the present estate in Blackacre will go from one grantee or transferee (B), to C. Therefore, C has a shifting executory interest.

(2) **O conveys Blackacre to A but if A dies without any surviving children to B.** A has a present fee simple estate that is subject to divestment or defeasance at A's death if she has no child alive at her death. Her estate is therefore a fee simple defeasible estate, or more specifically a fee simple subject to an executory limitation. A's estate might last forever or it may terminate at her death. If A dies with surviving children, B's interest will never become a present possessory estate because the condition will never be violated. However, if A violates the condition by leaving no surviving children at her death, her interest in Blackacre will be immediately cutoff or terminated in favor of B. Since B, under such circumstances, would be obtaining a present possessory estate in Blackacre from a grantee or transferee (A), B's interest is a shifting executory interest.

(3) **O conveys Blackacre to A for life and remainder to B, but if B dies without any children surviving her then B's interest will be divested in favor of her heirs.** A has a present life estate. B has a vested remainder in fee simple because B exists and no condition precedent must be satisfied before B's interest will vest. However, B is subject to a condition subsequent so her future interest is a vested remainder in fee simple subject to complete defeasance because her interest can be divested at her death if she does not leave any surviving children. If her interest is cut off or terminated at her death due to a lack of surviving children, a present estate in Blackacre will go to B's heirs. Note that a person does not have heirs prior to death. Heirs can only be determined at death because by definition heirs are your surviving relatives at your death. This illustrates the ability to create an executory interest in a class of individuals who are not known or ascertained at the time the original grantor creates the interest. This executory interest in B's heirs is a shifting executory interest because any transfer of a present possessory estate to B's heirs will come from B.

springing ex.

(4) O devises Blackacre to A so long as A marries B. A is unmarried at O's death. A does not get a present possessory estate upon O's death because A has not met the marriage condition at O's death. The condition appears to be a condition precedent since it must be met before A obtains a present possessory estate in Blackacre. This would suggest that A has a contingent remainder. However, a remainder must be capable of becoming a present possessory estate at the natural end of the prior possessory estate. A's interest can only become a present possessory estate if A satisfies the condition and thereby cuts off or terminates the prior possessory estate. At O's death, A only has a future interest since the condition has not yet been satisfied. Therefore, at O's death O's heirs or will beneficiaries inherit O's present possessory estate subject to its being terminated if A marries B. This means the heirs or will beneficiaries inherit a present possessory estate subject to an executory interest. If A marries B, the right to present possession of Blackacre transfers from O's heirs or will beneficiaries to A. Therefore, it is a springing executory interest.

(5) O transfers Blackacre to A for life and then ninety days after A's death to B. O's transfer creates a present life estate in A. B has a future interest that can only become a present possessory interest ninety days after A dies. B's interest is not a remainder because it cannot become a possessory interest at the natural end of the prior possessory estate (A's life estate). Therefore, O must have a reversion in Blackcacre upon A's death. Upon the end of the ninety day period the right to present possession of Blackacre transfers from O to B which means B's interest is a springing executory interest. Remember that a future interest in a third party must be either a remainder or an executory interest. In this example, since B's future interest cannot be a remainder, it must by default be an executory interest.

(6) O devises Blackacre to A upon the condition that A must have O cremated and must then spread his ashes on the surface of Lake Erie. O's will conveys all other property to X in fee simple absolute. A cannot get a present possessory estate in Blackacre until she meets the two conditions (cremation and spreading ashes on Lake Erie). It will take some time, after O's death, to fulfill the conditions. Therefore, A cannot take present possession of Blackacre immediately upon the natural end of the prior possessory estate. Consequently, A has a future interest but it cannot be a remainder. By default it must be an executory interest. Therefore, O retains a present possessory interest in Blackacre at his death. However, it is subject to a springing executory interest in A because A is entitled to present possession of Blackacre once A satisfies the two conditions. Of course, since the transfer is via a will the interest retained by O is transferred, by the will, to X because the will conveys all property, other than Blackacre, to X. As a result, X has a right to present possession of Blackacre in fee simple subject to a springing executory interest in A. The executory interest is a springing interest because it transfers present possession, upon satisfaction of the conditions, from O's will beneficiary (X) to a grantee (A).

Review Questions

(1) Is an executory interest a third party contingent future interest?

(2) How many types of executory interests exist?

(3) What is the key distinction between a shifting and a springing executory interest?

(4) O transfers Blackacre to A in fee simple but if A shall ever use Blackacre for commercial purposes it shall immediately go to B in fee simple absolute. What interest in Blackacre does B own?

(5) O devises Blackacre to A for life once A graduates from college, and all other property to B. A is a college freshman at O's death. What interest in Blackacre does A own?

Review Questions: Answers

(1) Yes. Third party future interests are either remainders or executory interests. An executory interest is a contingent future interest because it can only become a present possessory estate if the prior estate is prematurely terminated or cut off.

(2) Two. A shifting executory interest and a springing executory interest.

(3) The key distinction relates to who had present possession of the estate prior to the executory interest becoming a present possessory estate. If the original transferor had present possession it is a springing executory interest. If a transferee other than the original transferor had present possession it is a shifting executory interest.

(4) A has a present possessory estate in Blackacre which is subject to a condition (A's use of Blackacre for commercial purposes) that can terminate A's interest if it is violated. B only gets present possession of Blackacre if A violates the condition. If A violates the condition the present estate in Blackacre is transferred from A (a transferee) to B. Therefore, B has a shifting executory interest in Blackacre.

(5) A cannot get present possession of Blackacre at O's death because A has not satisfied the condition precedent (graduating from college) as of O's death. O retains present possession of Blackacre at his death. Present possession of Blackacre will only be subsequently transferred from O to A when A graduates. This transfer goes from O (original transferor) to A so it is a springing executory interest. The interest retained by O is a reversion subject to an executory interest which passes at O's death to B via will.

Summary of Main Points

A. Types of executory interests
   1. Shifting executory interest
      a. An executory interest whose immediate past possessor was a grantee or transferee of the original grantor
   2. Springing executory interest
      a. An executory interest whose immediate past possessor was the original grantor or transferor (or her heirs or will beneficiaries if a testamentary transfer is involved)
B. Key distinction between shifting and springing executory interests
   1. Who had a right to present possession of the estate immediately before the owner of the executory interest would have a right to present possession

Types of Executory Interests

Type of Interest	Examples
Shifting Executory Interest - Transferee named in conveyance had present possession of estate before executory interest can become a present possessory estate - Therefore, present possession of estate goes from one transferee named in the conveyance to the owner of the executory interest	(1) O conveys Blackacre to A for life, but if A ever uses Blackacre for commercial purposes it shall go to B (B has a shifting executory interest) (2) O conveys Blackacre to A, but if A marries, Blackacre shall immediately go to B (B has a shifting executory interest)
Springing Executory Interest - Original transferor had present possession of estate before executory interest can become a present possessory estate - Therefore, present possession of estate goes from the original transferor (or transferor's heirs or will beneficiaries if a testamentary transfer is involved) to the owner of the executory interest	(1) O conveys Blackacre to A for life, then to B ninety days after A's death (B has a springing executory interest) (2) O devises Blackacre to A so long as A marries B (if A is not married to B at O's death A has a springing executory interest)

Chapter Nine

Transferring Estates and Future Interests

The concept of transferring estates and future interests is often confusing. Understanding certain basic rules can simplify one's understanding of this area of law. This chapter will examine five general rules governing the transfer of different types of estates and future interests.

> **First general rule: Under the modern trend most estates and future interests are freely transferable**

Despite this general rule, some jurisdictions, as noted below, impose limitations on transferability of certain types of property interests.

A fee simple absolute estate is freely transferable.

Explanatory Examples   *fee simple absolute*

(1) **O conveys his fee simple absolute interest in Blackacre to A.** A now owns the entire estate in Blackacre. Subsequent to the conveyance, O has no interest in Blackacre because O's entire interest in Blackacre was transferred to A.

(2) **O devises a fee simple absolute estate in Blackacre to A, then a remainder to B. What interest does B own?** B does not own anything. When O devised a fee simple absolute in Blackacre to A she gave her entire interest in Blackacre to A. O retained no interest in Blackacre which could be transferred to anyone else.

A fee simple defeasible estate is freely transferable.

Explanatory Example   *fee simple determinable*

O conveys a fee simple determinable estate in Blackacre to A. The conveyance provides that alcohol shall not be served on Blackacre. A subsequently devises her estate to B. B owns a fee simple determinable estate subject to the same condition A was subject to. B cannot sell alcohol on Blackacre. Additionally, O continues to own a possibility of reverter in Blackacre because O never conveyed her entire estate to A.

A fee tail estate can be transferred inter vivos. However, a fee tail is essentially a succession of life estates in the lineal descendants of the creator of the fee tail. Therefore, a lineal descendant cannot make a testamentary transfer of an estate because it naturally ends at the decedent's death. Likewise, a transfer cannot occur via intestate succession.

Explanatory Examples *fee tail*

(1) **O conveys a fee tail in Blackacre to A. A subsequently makes an inter vivos transfer of her estate to her cousin, X.** The largest estate that A can transfer to X is a life estate based on A's life because the fee tail owned by A automatically passes to A's lineal descendants upon A's death. Therefore, X owns a life estate pur autre vie. When A dies Blackacre transfers automatically to A's lineal descendants. If A has no lineal descendants Blackacre goes back to O because as the original grantor, O retained a reversion.

(2) **O devises a fee tail estate in Blackacre to A. Several years later A dies with a will leaving all of her property to her friend, B. At A's death A has one child, C.** A has a fee tail in Blackacre so at her death Blackacre automatically goes to her lineal descendant, C. At A's death C has a present possessory life estate in Blackacre. A's will does not transfer any interest in Blackacre to B because A's interest in Blackacre naturally ended at A's death leaving A no interest to pass via a testamentary transfer.

A life estate is freely transferable. Of course, an ordinary life estate cannot be transferred by will or intestate succession because the estate naturally ends upon the death of the life estate owner. However, a life estate pur autre vie may be transferable via will or intestate succession.

Explanatory Examples *life estate estate*

(1) **O conveys a life estate in Blackacre to A. A subsequently makes an inter vivos transfer of her life estate to B.** O conveyed an ordinary life estate to A. When A transfers her life estate to B it is still measured by A's life. B has a life estate pur autre vie measured by A's life. When A dies B's estate naturally ends. O only conveyed a life estate to A so she retained an interest in Blackacre in the form of a reversion. At A's death O owns Blackacre.

(2) **O conveys a life estate in Blackacre to A. A subsequently devises his interest in Blackacre to B via a will.** When A dies the life estate naturally ends so A has no interest in Blackacre to transfer via will. O retained a reversion in Blackacre because he only conveyed a life estate. O owns Blackacre at A's death.

(3) **O conveys a life estate in Blackacre, based on X's life, to A. A subsequently predeceases X and dies leaving a will which conveys all of her property to B.** Upon A's death her will transfers her life estate to B because O conveyed to A a life estate pur autre vie (the estate is measured by X's life). A's life estate still exists at her death because X is still alive. B will have a life estate pur autre vie in Blackacre until X dies. O retained a reversion when he made the original conveyance so O will own Blackacre in the future when X dies.

(4) **O conveys a life estate in Blackacre, based on X's life, to A. A subsequently makes an inter vivos gift of her estate to B.** O's conveyance gives A a life estate pur autre vie. Likewise, A's gift transfers a life estate pur autre vie in Blackacre to B (measured by X's life). O retained a reversion when he made the original conveyance so O will own Blackacre in the future when X dies.

A leasehold (also called a lease) is generally freely transferable. The transfer by a lessee of the entire leasehold estate (or the entire remaining interest in the estate) is typically called an *assignment of the lease*. A transfer by a lessee of only a portion of the leasehold which ends prior to the end of the lease term is called a *sublet* or a *sublease*. A lease may contain restrictions which prohibit or limit transferability. Today, most lease agreements are contractual agreements that include a property conveyance.

Explanatory Examples

(1) **O leases Blackacre to A for twenty-five years. Ten years into the lease term A conveys the remaining fifteen year lease term to B.** The original conveyance to A creates a present possessory twenty-five year estate for years leasehold interest in Blackacre. B becomes the present owner of a possessory interest in the leasehold estate when A transfers (assigns) the remaining fifteen years of the lease term to B.

(2) **O leases Blackacre to A for one year. The lease includes a contractual agreement that limits Blackacre to residential use and prohibits any assignment or sublease of the leasehold.** A cannot assign or sublet his estate for years leasehold interest in Blackacre to anyone because he has contractually agreed not to do so.

(3) **O leases a one year estate for years determinable leasehold in Blackacre to A, subject to the condition that Blackacre shall not be used for commer-**

cial purposes. After three months, A transfers the remainder of the leasehold interest (an assignment) to B, who engages in commercial use of Blackacre. O has transferred to A a one year determinable estate for years leasehold. A possibility of reverter, which is implied in law, is retained by O. A is free to transfer the remaining lease term to B but B remains subject to the original condition placed on the leasehold. Since B violated the condition by engaging in commercial use of Blackacre, B automatically loses any rights to Blackacre. O's possibility of reverter automatically becomes a present possessory interest upon B's violation of the condition.

A reversion is generally freely transferable.

Explanatory Examples *Reversion*

(1) **O leases Blackacre to A for fifteen years. O subsequently conveys her entire remaining interest in Blackacre to X.** O never conveyed her entire interest in Blackacre to A. A only obtained an estate for years leasehold so O retained a reversion in Blackacre. O's conveyance to X transferred O's reversion to X. During the remaining lease term X has a future interest in Blackacre (a reversion). At the end of A's lease term X owns a present possessory estate in Blackacre.

(2) **O leases Blackacre to A for fifteen years. Two years later, O dies leaving a will which gives all of her property to X.** O never conveyed her entire interest in Blackacre to A. A only obtained a leasehold so O retains a reversion in Blackacre. O dies before the natural end of A's leasehold estate. O's will then transfers all of her property to X. Since O has a reversion in Blackacre her will transfers that reversion to X. At the end of A's lease X owns a present possessory estate in Blackacre.

(3) **O conveys a life estate in Blackacre to A. O subsequently conveys her entire remaining interest in Blackacre to X.** O never conveyed her entire interest in Blackacre to A. A only obtained a present life estate so O retains a reversion in Blackacre. O's conveyance to X transfers her reversion in Blackacre to X. Upon A's death X's reversion will become a present possessory interest in Blackacre.

A possibility of reverter is generally freely transferable. However, some states restrict certain types of transfers.

Explanatory Examples *possibility of reverter*

(1) **O conveys a fee simple determinable estate in Blackacre to A. Subsequently, O dies intestate leaving Z as her only heir.** O never conveyed her en-

tire interest in Blackacre to A. A only obtained a fee simple determinable so O automatically retains a possibility of reverter in Blackacre. At O's death her only heir, Z, inherits the property via intestate succession. O's property includes her possibility of reverter so at O's death Z has a possibility of reverter in Blackacre.

(2) **O leases Blackacre to A. The lease states that it shall have a term of ten years but if A uses Blackacre for commercial purposes it shall automatically revert to O who retains a possibility of reverter in Blackacre. One year after leasing Blackacre to A, O makes an inter vivos gift of all of his real property interests to Y. Ten days later A engages in commercial use of Blackacre.** O transferred a determinable ten year estate for years lease in Blackacre to A. O retained a reversion in Blackacre which will become a present possessory estate at the end of the lease term. O also retained a possibility of reverter which will only become a present possessory estate if A utilizes Blackacre for commercial purposes prior to the end of the lease term. O's gift to Y transfers both the reversion and the possibility of reverter to Y. Because A violated the condition (used Blackacre for commercial purposes), Y, as the owner of the possibility of reverter, immediately becomes the owner of a present possessory estate in Blackacre. If A had never violated the condition Y would have become the owner of a present possessory estate in Blackacre at the end of the lease term.

A right of entry is transferable via will or intestate succession. Some states permit inter vivos transfers. Other states prohibit inter vivos transfers except via the granting of a release of the condition to the holder of the present possessory estate, or if the transfer is incident to or accompanied by a reversion.

Explanatory Examples

(1) **O conveys a fee simple subject to a condition subsequent in Blackacre to A. Subsequently, O dies intestate with H as her only heir. A has not violated the condition.** O conveyed a present defeasible fee simple estate in Blackacre to A. O retained a right of entry which can only become a present possessory estate in Blackacre if A violates the condition. When O dies she still owns the right of entry so it is transferred to H via intestate succession. If A subsequently violates the condition H will be entitled, pursuant to the right of entry, to retake possession of Blackacre from A.

(2) **O conveys a fee simple subject to a condition subsequent in Blackacre to A. Subsequently, O transfers his right of entry to B as a gift. One week later O dies intestate leaving H as his sole heir.** O conveyed a present defeasible fee simple estate in Blackacre to A. O retained a right of entry which can only become a present possessory estate in Blackacre if A violates the condition. Dur-

ing O's lifetime he made a gift of the right of entry to B. Some states do not allow an inter vivos transfer of a right of entry. If the inter vivos transfer is not permitted, O still owns the right of entry at his death. Therefore, H would inherit the right of entry at O's death via intestate succession. If the state permits inter vivos transfers of a right of entry, B will own the right of entry.

(3) **O conveys a fee simple subject to a condition subsequent in Blackacre to A. Subsequently, O agrees to release A from the condition subsequent.** This is a permissible inter vivos transfer in all states since O has essentially conveyed her right of entry via release to A who currently is the holder of the present possessory estate. A now owns all of the interests in Blackacre. These interests merge together to create a fee simple absolute in Blackacre in A. (See Chapter Fourteen for a discussion of the merger doctrine).

(4) **O leases Blackacre to A for ten years subject to a condition subsequent. One week later, O conveys all her property interests in Blackacre to X.** O leased a defeasible estate for years leasehold interest to A. O retained a right of entry which gives her the right to retake possession of Blackacre before the end of the lease term if A, the lessee, violates the condition. O also retained a reversion which will automatically become a present possessory estate at the natural end of the lease term if A does not violate the condition. O can make an inter vivos transfer of both interests to a third party in all jurisdictions because the right of entry is accompanied by a reversion. X is entitled to present possession of Blackacre at the end of the ten year lease. Additionally, X is entitled to retake possession of Blackacre prior to the end of the lease term if the lessee, A, violates the condition imposed on the lease.

Vested remainders of all types are freely transferable.

Explanatory Examples

(1) **O conveys Blackacre to A for life, then a remainder to B. Subsequently, during A's lifetime B makes a gift of her remainder to C.** O's original conveyance creates a present life estate in Blackacre followed by a vested remainder in B. B is free to retain or transfer the remainder. In this example, B transfers it to C as a gift. Therefore, upon A's death C will have a present possessory estate in Blackacre.

(2) **O conveys Blackacre to A for life, then a remainder to B, but if B gets divorced during A's lifetime O shall have the right to reenter and retake possession of Blackacre. During A's lifetime B makes a gift of his remainder in Blackacre to C.** O's original conveyance creates a present life estate in A followed by a vested remainder in Blackacre in B. B's vested remainder is subject

to a divesting condition subsequent so it is a vested remainder subject to complete defeasance. As a result of B's gift C owns a future interest (vested remainder subject to complete defeasance) during A's lifetime. C's interest will become a present possessory estate in Blackacre upon A's death. However, the interest can be divested or lost if B gets divorced during A's lifetime and if O exercises her right to retake Blackacre.

(3) **O conveys Blackacre to A for life, then to A's children. A has one child, B, at the time of the conveyance. During A's lifetime B makes an inter vivos transfer of his interest in Blackacre to X.** O's conveyance creates a present life estate in A followed by a class gift in A's children. Since one child, B, is alive at the time of the conveyance and not subject to any condition precedent, O created a vested remainder subject to open in A's children. B's conveyance of this vested remainder to X essentially puts X into B's shoes so X has a vested remainder subject to open in Blackacre. X's interest may or may not be shared with other children depending upon whether A has any more children prior to her death.

A contingent remainder is generally freely transferable although a few states restrict inter vivos transfers. If a contingent remainder is given to someone who is not known and ascertained (does not exist) it may not be transferable because no one exists to make the transfer.

Explanatory Examples

(1) **O conveys Blackacre to A for life, and if B graduates from law school during A's lifetime a remainder to B. At the time of O's conveyance B is a first year law student. During his second year of law school B sells his remainder to X.** O's conveyance creates a present life estate in Blackacre in A followed by a remainder in B. B's interest is a remainder because it will only become a present possessory estate at the natural end of the prior present estate. B's remainder is a contingent remainder because B must satisfy a condition precedent (graduate from law school) prior to obtaining a present possessory estate in Blackacre. B sold his contingent remainder to X. Whether B graduates from law school during A's lifetime determines if X's interest will become vested and capable of becoming a present possessory estate in the future. Some states do not allow the inter vivos transfer of a contingent remainder to X.

(2) **O conveys Blackacre to A for life, remainder to the first child of A. A's first child, C, is born one year after the original conveyance.** O's conveyance creates a present life estate in Blackacre in A followed by a remainder in A's first child. At the time of O's original conveyance A has no children. O created a contingent remainder in a person who did not exist at the time of the

original conveyance. Since A's first child does not exist at the time of O's original conveyance no one exists to transfer the contingent remainder. Subsequently, when C is born, her existence converts the contingent remainder into a vested remainder which she is free to transfer.

An executory interest is freely transferable in most jurisdictions today. If an executory interest is given to someone who is not known and ascertained (does not exist) it may not be transferable because no one exists to make the transfer.

Explanatory Examples

(1) **O conveys a fee simple defeasible estate in Blackacre to A, subject to the condition that if A subdivides Blackacre it shall automatically go to B for life. B conveys his interest in Blackacre to X.** O's conveyance creates a present fee simple subject to an executory limitation estate in Blackacre in A and a shifting executory interest in B. B has an executory interest because the future interest will only become a present possessory estate by prematurely cutting off A's estate due to violation of the condition prohibiting subdivision of Blackacre. After B's conveyance X will automatically become the owner of a present life estate pur autre vie in Blackacre if A violates the condition during B's lifetime. X's interest will cease to exist upon B's death since the estate is a life estate pur autre vie measured by B's life.

(2) **O conveys a life estate in Blackacre to A, with a remainder to B, but if A sells alcohol on Blackacre during her lifetime, Blackacre shall automatically go to C in fee simple absolute. During A's lifetime C sells his entire interest in Blackacre to X. Two days later A dies. A never sells alcohol on Blackacre. Who owns Blackacre at A's death?** O's original conveyance creates a defeasible life estate in A, a vested remainder subject to complete defeasance in B and a shifting executory interest in C. X essentially steps into C's shoes when C sells his executory interest in Blackacre to X. If A violates the condition X will have a present fee simple absolute estate in Blackacre. However, A did not violate the condition so upon A's death B becomes the owner of a present possessory estate in Blackacre. X's executory interest is effectively destroyed when A dies without violating the condition because the condition can only be violated during A's lifetime. B owns a present possessory estate in Blackacre at A's death.

(3) **O conveys a life estate in Blackacre to A, with a remainder to B, but if A sells alcohol on Blackacre during her lifetime, Blackacre shall automatically go to C in fee simple absolute. During A's lifetime C sells his entire interest in Blackacre to X. Two days later A sells alcohol on Blackacre. The next day A dies. Who owns Blackacre at A's death?** This is the same as the previous ex-

ample except here A violates the condition. A's life estate in Blackacre is immediately terminated when A violates the condition. B's vested remainder was divested when A violated the condition. At A's death X has a present possessory fee simple absolute estate in Blackacre.

(4) **O conveys Blackacre to A for life but if A sells alcohol on Blackacre it shall go to A's first child in fee simple absolute. A's first child, C, is born one year after O's original conveyance.** O's conveyance creates a life estate subject to an executory limitation in A. A's first child has a shifting executory interest in Blackacre in fee simple absolute. At the time of O's original conveyance A has no children so no one exists at that time that could transfer the executory interest. When C is born she is free to transfer her executory interest.

> **Second general rule: A property owner can transfer less than she owns**

A property owner can transfer the entire interest she owns or she can carve out and transfer a smaller interest. The following is a list of estates from the largest to the smallest:

Fee simple absolute
Fee simple defeasible   *estates from largest to smallest*
Fee tail
Life estate
Leasehold

Explanatory Examples

(1) **A owns a fee simple absolute interest in Blackacre. A transfers a present life estate in Blackacre to B.** This is permissible because a life estate is a smaller or lesser estate than a fee simple absolute estate. When A transfers the life estate to B she has only transferred part of her estate so subsequent to the transfer A still owns an interest in Blackacre. That interest is a future interest because A will only have the right to present possession of Blackacre after B dies. The future interest retained by A is a reversion in Blackacre in fee simple absolute.

(2) **A owns a fee simple absolute interest in Blackacre. A transfers a five year estate for years leasehold to B.** This is permissible because a leasehold estate is a smaller or lesser estate than a fee simple absolute estate. As in the previous example, when A makes the transfer of the smaller estate to B she still retains the rest of the estate. A retains a reversion in Blackacre in fee simple absolute which will only become a present possessory estate when B's five year lease term ends.

(3) **A owns a fee simple subject to a condition subsequent interest in Black-acre. A conveys a life estate in Blackacre to B.** A life estate is a smaller or lesser estate than a fee simple defeasible estate. B now owns a life estate measured by his life. However, the original estate owned by A was subject to termination if the applicable condition was violated. Therefore, the interest owned by B must also be subject to that same condition to avoid B's interest being greater than the original interest owned by A. B owns a life estate subject to the same condition subsequent that applies to A's original estate.

(4) **A owns a life estate in Blackacre. A leases Blackacre to B for ten years.** A leasehold interest is a smaller or lesser estate than a life estate so A can convey a ten year estate for years leasehold to B. A's conveyance cannot increase the size of the estate owned by A. Therefore, B's ten year estate for years lease must be subject to premature termination in the event A dies before the ten year leasehold term ends. This is necessitated by the fact that A's interest is a life estate so it naturally ends upon A's death. A purportedly conveyed a ten year estate for years leasehold to B that was not subject to premature termination in light of A's death. B must have a defeasible ten year estate for years leasehold. B's lease lasts for ten years or until A's death, whichever happens first.

(5) **O leases Blackacre to A for twenty-five years. Ten years into the lease A conveys a five year leasehold interest in Blackacre to B.** O transfers to A a twenty-five year present possessory estate for years leasehold. A can convey the five year leasehold to B because it is a smaller estate than the estate owned by A. Essentially, A has carved a five year estate for years leasehold interest out of her twenty-five year estate for years leasehold (it is a sublease because A did not transfer her entire remaining interest in Blackacre). B has a present estate in Blackacre which is a five year estate for years leasehold. A has a reversion in Blackacre because A retained the portion of her estate that was not conveyed to B (the remaining ten years of the original leasehold). Additionally, O never conveyed all of her interest in Blackacre so she retains a reversion that becomes a present possessory interest at the end of A's twenty-five year leasehold.

> **Third general rule: The most a property owner can transfer is the particular property interest that she owns—a property owner cannot transfer more than she owns**

Explanatory Examples

(1) **A owns a life estate in Blackacre. A sells her life estate to B. Two days later A dies.** A originally had a life estate measured by her life. When A's estate is transferred to B it is still a life estate measured by A's life so the estate natu-

rally ends upon A's death (B has a life estate pur autre vie). The original estate was measured by A's life so that does not change even if the estate is transferred to another party. If the transfer of A's life estate caused it to be measured by B's life that would impermissibly enlarge the estate beyond its original size.

(2) **A owns a fee simple determinable estate in Blackacre. A conveys a fee simple absolute estate to B.** A cannot convey a fee simple absolute estate to B because she only owns a fee simple determinable estate which is a smaller estate than a fee simple absolute (a fee simple absolute is the largest estate that exists). If this transfer was permitted B would own more than A originally owned.

(3) **O conveys a life estate in Blackacre to A, remainder in B provided B graduates from law school. At A's death B is a first year law student. A week after A's death B conveys a present life estate in Blackacre to X.** O's original conveyance creates a present life estate in A followed by a remainder in B. B's remainder is subject to a condition precedent (graduation from law school) which must be satisfied before he is entitled to present possession of Blackacre so B's interest is a contingent remainder. B's interest in Blackacre cannot become a present possessory estate at the termination of the prior possessory estate because at A's death B has not satisfied the condition precedent, nor will B have satisfied the condition precedent a week later. Therefore, the transfer by B to X is not valid because at the time of the transfer B does not own a present estate in Blackacre.

(4) **O leases Blackacre to A pursuant to a defeasible ten year estate for years leasehold which provides that O shall have a right of entry to retake possession of Blackacre if A fails to perform all routine maintenance necessary for Blackacre to remain in a habitable condition. One year later A subleases Blackacre to B pursuant to a two year estate for years leasehold. The next day B conveys a life estate to C. A week later A fails to maintain Blackacre in a habitable condition. Can O retake possession of Blackacre?** O originally transfers a defeasible ten year estate for years leasehold to A. More specifically, it was a ten year estate for years leasehold subject to a condition subsequent. A's purported conveyance (sublease) of a two year estate for years leasehold to B is problematic because A is attempting to convey a larger estate to B than A owns. A could convey a defeasible two year estate for years leasehold to B because the original lease is subject to a right of entry. Therefore, any subsequent conveyance of all or part of the original lease must also be subject to this right of entry. A's conveyance to B purports to convey a two year estate for years leasehold rather than a defeasible two year estate for years leasehold. Nevertheless, the most B could have is a defeasible two year estate for years leasehold since removing the defeasible condition would amount to enlarging the interest owned by A. B's subsequent purported conveyance of a life estate to C is problematic. A life estate is larger than a leasehold estate. Therefore, B cannot con-

vey a life estate to C. The largest estate B could transfer to C would be the remaining term of B's defeasible two year estate for years lease. When A fails to maintain Blackacre in a habitable condition O has the immediate right to exercise his right of entry to retake possession of Blackacre.

> **Fourth general rule: A future interest is still a property interest even though the right to possession is postponed until the future**

This is a conceptually difficult rule because it essentially means that you can currently own a property interest even though you do not actually get the right to possess or use the property until a future date.

Explanatory Examples

(1) **O conveys Blackacre to A for life, remainder to B.** O's original conveyance creates ownership interests in Blackacre in both A and B. A's interest is a present life estate which gives A the right to immediate present possession of Blackacre until his death. Additionally, at the time O made the conveyance to A she transferred a property interest in Blackacre to B. B's right to possession of Blackacre is postponed until the death of A but B owns an interest in Blackacre as soon as O makes the conveyance. Subsequent to the conveyance O cannot convey any future interest in Blackacre to someone else because O has already conveyed all of her interest in Blackacre. B's interest in Blackacre is owned immediately after the conveyance by O despite the fact that B's right to present possession of Blackacre is postponed until after A's death.

(2) **O leases Blackacre to A for twenty years. Five days later, O conveys all of her interest in Blackacre to B.** O's original conveyance creates a twenty year estate for years lease in Blackacre in A. O retains any interest in Blackacre not transferred to A. Therefore, O retains a future interest (reversion) in Blackacre that will become a present possessory interest in Blackacre when A's twenty year lease term ends. When O transferred her interest in Blackacre to B she could only convey to B what she owned. Therefore, B now owns an interest in Blackacre but his right to present possession of Blackacre is postponed until A's twenty year leasehold ends.

> **Fifth general rule: A contingent future interest that may or may not become a present possessory interest is still a property interest**

The likelihood or unlikelihood that a future interest will become a present possessory interest does not effect whether it is property (although it may affect the economic value of the property). This is often a confusing concept because essentially it means that someone can own a property interest which in effect is no more than a possible right to gain present possession of the property at some future date. In many cases it is not clear if such present possession will ever be gained. Nevertheless, such a contingent future interest is considered property that is owned by the transferee upon its creation. Additionally, a future interest conveyed to someone who does not exist at the time of the conveyance is also a recognized property interest even though it is unknown if that person will ever exist.

Explanatory Examples

(1) **O conveys Blackacre to A for life, then a contingent remainder in B if B reaches twenty-one during A's lifetime. B is ten years old at the time of the conveyance. B sells his interest in Blackacre to C.** O's original conveyance creates a present life estate in A followed by a remainder in B. B's remainder is subject to a condition precedent, (B must reach twenty-one during A's lifetime) so it is a contingent remainder. If B reaches twenty-one during A's lifetime his interest will be converted into a vested remainder because the condition will have been satisfied. If A dies before B reaches twenty-one it will now be impossible for B to ever satisfy the condition. At the time of O's original conveyance it is unknown if B's future interest will ever become a present possessory estate. Nevertheless, despite this uncertainty, B's contingent remainder is property which can be conveyed to C. Although C may now own a future interest in Blackacre, whether C will ever have a right to present possession is unknown. Despite this uncertainty C owns a recognized property interest in Blackacre.

(2) **O conveys a fee simple determinable in Blackacre to A subject to the condition that alcohol can never be sold on Blackacre.** O does not convey all of her interest in Blackacre to A so O retains an interest in Blackacre. That retained interest is a future interest called a possibility of reverter. The possibility of reverter is a property interest owned by O even though it may never become a present possessory interest in Blackacre if the condition is never violated. Nevertheless, the law considers the possibility of reverter to be a presently owned property interest despite the fact that it may or may not become a present possessory estate.

(3) **O conveys a life estate in Blackacre to A, then a contingent remainder to A's first child. A has no children at the time of the conveyance.** O conveys a life

estate to A followed by a contingent remainder in A's first child. O, by operation of law, retains a reversion in Blackacre. The contingent remainder is considered a property interest even though it is unknown if anyone will ever exist to take the property interest. If A has a child that child will get the remainder interest in Blackacre. If A never has children no one will get the remainder.

Review Questions

(1) Is the modern trend to allow all estates to be freely transferable?

(2) What is an assignment of a lease?

(3) What is a sublet or sublease?

(4) Is the modern trend to allow all future interests to be freely transferable?

(5) O conveys Blackacre to A for life. A subsequently makes an inter vivos conveyance of Blackacre to X for a term equal to X's lifetime. A predeceases X. Does X own Blackacre until her death?

(6) Which of the following is incorrect?

  (a) It is possible to devise a life estate pur autre vie

  (b) It is possible to devise an ordinary life estate

  (c) It is possible to devise a fee simple defeasible estate

  (d) It possible to devise a fee simple absolute estate

(7) Name the estates in order from largest to smallest.

(8) O conveys a fee simple absolute estate in Blackacre to A. A subsequently conveys a life estate in Blackacre to B. B then leases Blackacre to C for one year. What interest in Blackacre does B own? What interest in Blackacre does C own?

(9) O conveys a life estate in Blackacre to A followed by a remainder in Blackacre in B in fee simple absolute. Does B own a property interest in Blackacre at the time of the original conveyance by O?

(10) O conveys a life estate in Blackacre to A, but if A becomes an attorney Blackacre shall automatically go to B in fee simple absolute. A is not an attorney at the time of O's conveyance. Which of the following is correct?

  (a) B does not own a property interest in Blackacre because it is possible A will never become an attorney

  (b) B will only own a property interest in Blackacre if A becomes an attorney

  (c) B owns a property interest in Blackacre

(11) O conveys Blackacre to A for life, then to A's children. A has no children. Did O's conveyance create a remainder in A's children even though no children currently exist?

Review Questions: Answers

(1) Yes. Fee simple absolute estates, fee simple defeasible estates, fee tail estates (where they exist), life estates and leaseholds are generally freely transferable. (See the first general rule discussed in this chapter).

(2) The transfer by a lessee of an entire leasehold estate (or the entire remaining interest in the estate).

(3) The transfer by a lessee of only a portion of the leasehold which ends prior to the end of the lease term.

(4) Yes. However, some states restrict certain transfers of a possibility of reverter. Furthermore, some states restrict inter vivos transfer of a right of entry and inter vivos transfer of a contingent remainder. (See the first general rule discussed in this chapter).

(5) No. The third general rule discussed in this chapter states that a property owner cannot transfer more than she owns. A owns an ordinary life estate that lasts for A's lifetime. Therefore, the estate naturally ends at A's death even though X is still alive.

(6) (b). It is impossible to devise an ordinary life estate because it naturally ends at the owner's death. A life estate pur autre vie can continue to exist after the death of the life estate owner because it is based on the lifetime of a third party who could outlive the owner of the life estate pur autre vie. Fee simple defeasible estates and fee simple absolute estates are freely transferable via inter vivos or testamentary transfer.

(7) Fee simple absolute; fee simple defeasible; fee tail; life estate; leasehold

(8) B owns an ordinary life estate. C owns a defeasible one year estate for years leasehold. The defeasible condition which can prematurely terminate the leasehold is A dying before the one year lease ends. The second general rule discussed in this chapter states that a property owner can transfer less than she owns. A life estate is smaller than a fee simple absolute. Likewise, a leasehold is smaller than a life estate. However, C's leasehold cannot last longer than B's life estate because if it lasts longer C would have a larger interest than B transferred. (See third general rule discussed in this chapter).

(9) Yes. B owns an indefeasibly vested remainder in Blackacre at the time of the original conveyance. B will not get present possession of Blackacre until A dies. However, B still has a recognized property interest in Blackacre despite this delay in possession. The fourth general rule discussed in this chapter states that a future interest is still a property interest even though the right to possession is postponed to the future.

(10) (c). The fifth general rule discussed in this chapter states that a contingent future interest that may or may not become a present possessory interest

is still a property interest. Therefore, B owns a recognized property interest (a shifting executory interest in Blackacre in fee simple absolute) despite the fact that it is unknown whether the interest will ever become a present possessory estate.

(11) Yes. O's conveyance creates a contingent remainder in the class of A's children. A currently does not have any children so there is no one to own the contingent remainder. If A never has children no one will ever exist who can own the interest. Nevertheless, the contingent remainder in A's children is recognized as a property interest at the time of O's original conveyance.

Summary of Main Points

A. Transferability of present estates—All present estates are freely transferable
   1. Fee simple absolute and fee simple defeasible estates are freely transferable via an inter vivos transfer, via a will or via intestate succession
   2. Fee tail estates are freely transferable via an inter vivos transfer but not via a will or intestate succession since a fee tail is essentially a series of life estates and therefore there is no property interest left to be transferred at the death of the fee tail owner
   3. Life estates are freely transferable via an inter vivos transfer but not via a will or intestate succession since an ordinary life estate ends at the estate owner's death
   4. Life estates pur autre vie are freely transferable via an inter vivos transfer; and may be transferable via a will or intestate succession if the life estate owner predeceases the person who is the measuring life
   5. Leaseholds are generally freely transferable via an inter vivos transfer, via a will or via intestate succession unless the lease contains a valid restriction on transferability
B. Transferability of future interests retained by grantor—Modern trend is freely transferable
   1. Reversions are freely transferable inter vivos, via will or via intestate succession
   2. Possibility of reverter freely transferable inter vivos, via will or via intestate succession in most jurisdictions although some states restrict some transfers
   3. Right of entry freely transferable via will or via intestate succession but some states only allow inter vivos transfers in the following situations:
      a. Inter vivos transfer allowed if granting a release of the condition to the holder of the present estate subject to the condition; or
      b. Inter vivos transfer allowed if it is incident to or accompanied by a reversion
C. Transferability of future interests conveyed to third parties—Modern trend is freely transferable
   1. All vested remainders freely transferable inter vivos, via will or via intestate succession
   2. Contingent remainder freely transferable via will or via intestate succession but some jurisdictions restrict inter vivos transfers
      a. It may be impossible to transfer a contingent remainder if the owner of the remainder does not exist

    3.   Executory interests freely transferable inter vivos, via will or via intestate succession but some jurisdictions restrict transfers

        a.   It may be impossible to transfer an executory interest if the owner of the executory interest does not exist

D. A property owner cannot transfer an interest that is larger or greater than the interest owned

    1.   List of interests from largest to smallest:

        a.   Fee simple absolute

        b.   Fee simple defeasible

        c.   Fee tail

        d.   Life estate

        e.   Leasehold

E. A property owner can transfer a smaller interest than she owns

    1.   For example, an owner of an estate (fee simple) can carve a smaller estate (life estate) out of her estate and transfer that smaller estate to a third party

F. A future interest is a presently owned property interest despite any of the following:

    1.   Present possession is postponed to the future;

    2.   The future interest may never become a present interest; or

    3.   No person exists at the time of the conveyance to own the future interest

Transferability of Present Estates

Type of Interest	Transferability
Fee simple absolute	Freely transferable
Fee simple defeasible	Freely transferable
Fee tail	Transferable inter vivos but not via will or via intestate succession
Life estate	Transferable inter vivos but not via will or via intestate succession
Life estate pur autre vie	Transferable inter vivos; transferable via will or via intestate succession if owner predeceases person who is measuring life
Leasehold	Freely transferable absent restriction in lease limiting or prohibiting transfer

Transferability of Future Interests

Type of Interest	Transferability
Reversion	Freely transferable
Possibility of reverter	Generally freely transferable; some states restrict some transfers
Right of entry	Generally freely transferable but some states may restrict inter vivos transfers except in the following situations: (1) Release of condition to owner of present estate subject to the condition; or (2) If inter vivos transfer is incident to or accompanied by a reversion
Vested remainder (all types)	Freely transferable
Contingent remainder	Generally transferable but some states restrict inter vivos transfers; transfer not possible if owner of remainder does not exist
Executory interest	Freely transferable in some states; some states restrict transfers; transfer not possible if owner of executory interest does not exist

Chapter Ten

Creating and Analyzing Estates and Future Interests

This chapter will explain the specific words of art and rules of construction that have developed over time for analyzing what type of estate or future interest is created by a document purporting to transfer an interest in property. Often these rules are applied in an overlying formalistic manner because determining what a document drafter intended, in many transfers, is difficult.

When attempting to determine what type of estate or future interest is created you should consider the following:

(1) How is the estate or future interest obtained (via will, intestate succession, inter vivos transfer or gift)?

(2) Who specifically gets the estate or future interest (existing person, unborn person or class of people)?

(3) How long does the estate or future interest last (lifetime, forever, fixed time period or unknown duration)?

(4) Does the transfer provide for an immediate or future right to possession?

(5) Must any condition be satisfied before the transferee has a right to present possession of the estate?

(6) Can ownership of the estate or future interest be lost by being terminated due to a condition being violated? (See charts on next page.)

The following rules govern creation of a fee simple absolute estate:

Historically, a fee simple absolute estate was created by the following language:

To A and his heirs

To A, his heirs and assigns

The wording *to A* are the words of purchase because they identify A as the transferee.

The wording *and his heirs* (or *his heirs and assigns*) are the words of limitation because they signify that a fee simple absolute estate was transferred. The words of limitation do not create a property interest in A's heirs.

General Rules of Construction

(1) Analyze the property interests transferred at the time of an original transfer and under the facts that exist at that time

(2) The original transferor's intent is controlling. Words of art used in the relevant deed, will or other document actually transferring the property interests are typically viewed as indicative of the transferor's intent

(3) If the original transferor's intent is unclear or ambiguous based on the relevant documentation the following rules are often applied:

   (a) It is presumed that the transferor transferred the largest estate possible under the circumstances

   (b) The transfer is interpreted to favor the transferee

   (c) A fee simple subject to a condition subsequent is preferred over a fee simple determinable

   (d) A remainder is preferred over an executory interest

   (e) A vested remainder is preferred over a contingent remainder

---

Basic Vocabulary

"Words of purchase" are the words in a property transfer that identify the transferee

"Words of limitation" are the words in a property transfer that identify the type of estate transferred

---

Formalities for Creating Specific Estates

Today, the words of limitation can be omitted when creating a fee simple absolute, so the following language will give A a fee simple absolute interest:

To A

Explanatory Examples

(1) **O conveys Blackacre to A and his heirs.** The wording "to A" are words of purchase indicating the estate goes to A. The wording "and his heirs" are the words of limitation which indicate the creation of a fee simple absolute.

(2) **O devises Blackacre to X.** The wording "to X" are words of purchase indicating X gets the estate. In the absence of any words of limitation a fee simple absolute estate is devised to X.

The following rules govern creation of a fee tail estate.
The following wording will create a fee tail:

> *To A and the heirs of his body*
> *To A and her issue*
> *To A and the heirs male of her body*
> *To A and the heirs female of her body*
> *To A and the heirs of his body by his spouse X*

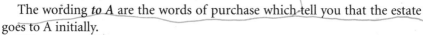

The wording *to A* are the words of purchase which tell you that the estate goes to A initially.

The wording *the heirs of his body* or *her issue* are the words of limitation because they indicate the creation of a fee tail estate which initially goes to A and then to the lineal descendants of A for as long as lineal descendants exist. This type of fee tail is more specifically called a *fee tail general*. It is not limited to specific lineal descendants.

However, a fee tail can include a limitation that dictates which lineal descendants a property passes to. For example, the wording *the heirs male of her body* restricts the fee tail to male lineal descendants. Likewise, the wording *the heirs female of her body* restricts the fee tail to female lineal descendants. Finally, the wording *the heirs of his body by his spouse X* restricts the fee tail to his lineal descendants by X. This type of fee tail is more specifically called a *fee tail special*.

Explanatory Examples

(1) **O conveys Blackacre to A and the heirs of his body.** The wording "to A" are words of purchase indicating the estate goes to A. The wording "and the heirs of his body" are words of limitation which indicate the creation of a fee tail general.

(2) **O devises Blackacre to A and the heirs female of her body.** The wording "to A" are words of purchase indicating the estate goes to A. The wording "and the heirs female of her body" are words of limitation which indicate the creation of a fee tail special which provides that only female heirs have future interests in Blackacre.

The following rules govern the creation of a fee simple determinable estate. A fee simple determinable is generally created by the following language:

> *To A so long as A only uses Blackacre for residential purposes*
> *To A as long as A only uses Blackacre for residential purposes*
> *To A while A only uses Blackacre for residential purposes*
> *To A until A ceases using Blackacre for residential purposes*

To A during the time that A uses Blackacre for residential purposes

In the above, the wording *to A* are the words of purchase which tell you that the estate initially goes to A. The above wording—*so long as, as long as, while, until, during, automatically*—are words of limitation because they indicate the creation of a fee simple determinable estate.

Additionally, any language in a transfer that makes it clear that upon the happening of an event or upon violation of a condition the estate will *automatically* terminate and return to the transferor creates a fee simple determinable.

Explanatory Examples

(1) **O devises Blackacre to A so long as A only uses Blackacre for farming.** The wording "to A" are words of purchase that indicate the estate goes to A. The wording "so long as A only uses Blackacre for farming" are words of limitation that indicate A received a fee simple determinable estate from O.

(2) **O conveys Blackacre to A, but A's estate in Blackacre shall automatically terminate if Blackacre is used for commercial purposes, and upon such termination Blackacre shall automatically re-vest in the grantor or his heirs.** The wording "to A" are words of purchase that indicate the estate goes to A. The conveyance does not use the typical wording for creating a fee simple determinable estate. But the wording indicates that if Blackacre is used for commercial purposes A's estate will automatically terminate and the estate will automatically go back to the grantor. This language indicates O conveyed a fee simple determinable estate in Blackacre to A.

The following rules govern creation of a fee simple subject to a condition subsequent estate.

A fee simple subject to a condition subsequent is generally created by the following language:

> *To A on condition that A only uses Blackacre for residential purposes*
> *To A provided that A continues using Blackacre for residential purposes*
> *To A, but if A uses Blackacre for commercial purposes A shall lose her right to Blackacre*
> *To A provided that A continues using Blackacre for residential purposes but if she ceases to use Blackacre for residential purposes the grantor, O, shall have the right to retake Blackacre*
> *To A provided that A continues using Blackacre for residential purposes but if she ceases to use Blackacre for residential purposes the grantor, O, shall have the right to re-enter and retake Blackacre*

In the above, the wording *to A* are words of purchase which tell you that the estate goes to A initially. The above wording—*on condition that, provided that, but if, right to retake, right to re-enter and retake*—are words of limitation because they indicate the creation of a fee simple subject to a condition subsequent estate.

Additionally, any language in a transfer that makes it clear that upon the happening of an event or upon violation of a condition the original transferor will have the *right to retake* (or the "right to re-enter and claim," "right to enter and reclaim," "right to re-enter and reclaim") possession of Blackacre will create a fee simple subject to a condition subsequent estate.

Explanatory Examples

(1) **O devises Blackacre to A on condition that A only uses Blackacre for farming.**

The wording "to A" are words of purchase that indicate the estate goes to A. The wording "on condition that A only uses Blackacre for farming" are words of limitation that indicate A received a fee simple subject to a condition subsequent estate.

(2) **O conveys Blackacre to A, but if A engages in commercial use of Blackacre the grantor shall have the right to take appropriate action to recover possession of Blackacre.** The phrase "to A" are words of purchase that indicate the estate goes to A. The conveyance does not use the typical language for creating a fee simple subject to a condition subsequent estate. Nevertheless, the language of the conveyance provides that if Blackacre is used for commercial purposes the original grantor, O, will have the right to recover possession of Blackacre. This conveyance transfers a fee simple subject to a condition subsequent estate in Blackacre.

The following rules govern the creation of a fee simple subject to an executory limitation estate:

A fee simple subject to an executory limitation is the easiest type of fee simple defeasible estate to identify. It must be subject to a condition or event that would prematurely end the transferee's estate and give it to someone other than the original transferor or her heirs.

Explanatory Examples

(1) **O devises Blackacre to A on condition that A only uses Blackacre for residential purposes, and if A uses Blackacre for non-residential purposes then it shall automatically go to B.** The wording "to A" are words of purchase which tell you that the estate initially goes to A. The additional language in the devise are words of limitation which provide for termination of the estate and transfer of Blackacre to a third party, B, if the residential condition is violated by A. A has a fee simple subject to an executory limitation.

(2) **O conveys Blackacre to A, but if A engages in commercial use of Blackacre A shall lose all interest in Blackacre and B shall have the right to take present possession of Blackacre.** The wording "to A" are words of purchase which initially tell you that the estate goes to A. The additional language in the conveyance are words of limitation which give a third party, B, the right to retake possession of Blackacre if the commercial use condition is violated by A. A has a fee simple subject to an executory limitation.

> Any estate can be made defeasible. Therefore, any of the above wording and rules relating to the creation of a fee simple determinable, fee simple subject to a condition subsequent or fee simple subject to an executory limitation estate apply equally to other defeasible estates (such as a determinable life estate, a life estate subject to an executory interest, a leasehold subject to a condition subsequent, etc.)

The following rules govern the creation of a life estate.

A life estate is created by clear language that indicates its duration shall be measured by a natural person's lifetime. The following are examples of specific language used to create a life estate:

To A for life
To A until her death
To A until she dies
To A for her natural life
To A for and during her natural life
To A for the life of B

In the above, the wording *to A* are the words of purchase which tell you that the estate goes initially to A. The above wording—*until her death, until*

she dies, for her natural life, for and during her natural life, for the life of B—
are words of limitation because they indicate the creation of a life estate.

The duration of an ordinary life estate is measured by the life of the life estate owner. A life estate can also be measured by the life of a natural person other than the life estate owner (for example *to A for the life of B*). This type of life estate is called a *life estate pur autre vie.*

Explanatory Examples

(1) **O conveys Blackacre to A for so long as A shall live.** The wording "to A" are words of purchase which tell you that the estate initially goes to A. The additional language—"for so long as A shall live"—are words of limitation which indicate the estate will last for A's natural lifetime. A has an ordinary life estate.

(2) **O devises Blackacre to A for so long as B shall be alive.** The wording "to A" are words of purchase which tell you that the estate initially goes to A. The additional language—"for so long as B shall be alive"—are words of limitation which indicate the estate will last for B's natural lifetime. A has a life estate pur autre vie based on B's life.

 | Formalities for Creating Specific Future Interests |

After determining which present estate, if any, is transferred by a transferor, you must determine if another person will have a right to present possession of the property in the future. When analyzing such future interests you must determine the following:

(1) What present estate the future interest holder may obtain in the future; and

(2) When and how the future interest holder will obtain that present estate in the property.

Keep in mind that the type of future interest created (vested remainder, contingent remainder, executory interest, possibility of reverter, right of entry or reversion) determines when and how a future interest will become a present possessory estate at a future date. The same words of art and rules of construction used for the creation of estates are used to determine what type of estate a future interest owner will get if the future interest subsequently becomes a present possessory estate.

Reversionary future interests (reversion, possibility of reverter and right of entry) do not have to be expressly mentioned in a transfer. These interests are automatically created by operation of law whenever an original transferor makes a transfer but retains some interest in the transferred property (see Chapter Six).

The determination of what type of future interest is created depends upon the following factors:

(1) Will the future interest definitely become a present possessory interest at some future time?

(2) If the future interest will become a present possessory interest in the future, will it be at the natural end of the prior possessory estate or by prematurely terminating the prior possessory estate?

(3) Will the future interest potentially never become a present possessory interest?

(4) Is the future interest owner the original transferor or a third party?

Explanatory Examples

(1) **O conveys Blackacre to A for life, then to B for life.** O's conveyance creates a present life estate in A followed by a future interest in B. B's interest will become a present possessory estate at the natural end of the prior possessory estate (A's life estate). No condition precedent exists. B's future interest is a vested remainder. Next, it must be determined what present estate B will own in the future after A dies. The language "to B for life" clearly creates a life estate. B has a vested remainder in a life estate in Blackacre. However, B could predecease A which means at the time of O's original conveyance it is not a certainty that B will ever get a present possessory estate in Blackacre. B has a vested remainder subject to complete defeasance in a life estate in Blackacre. O has retained a reversion in Blackacre because he only conveyed two successive life estates. The future interest in the grantor is implied in law so it does not have to be specifically mentioned in the original conveyance. O's future interest is a reversion in a fee simple absolute in Blackacre.

(2) **O conveys Blackacre to A for life, then to B.** Analogous to the prior example, B has a vested remainder in Blackacre. The language "to B" creates a fee simple absolute estate. B has a vested remainder in a fee simple absolute estate in Blackacre. Unlike example (1), B's death will not prevent B's remainder from becoming a present possessory estate at A's death. It can be said with absolute certainty that B's vested remainder will become a present possessory estate in the future. B has an indefeasibly vested remainder in a fee simple absolute in Blackacre.

O has not retained any interest in Blackacre because her conveyance transferred all of her interest.

(3) **O conveys Blackacre to A for life.** O's conveyance creates a present life estate in A. However, by only conveying a life estate O retains the remaining interest in Blackacre. O has a reversion and the present estate she will obtain via the reversion (upon A's death) is a fee simple absolute estate. At the time of O's original conveyance O retained a reversion in fee simple absolute in Blackacre.

(4) **O conveys Blackacre to A, but if alcohol is ever sold on Blackacre during B's lifetime then to B for life.** O's original conveyance creates a present estate in A that is a fee simple based on the language "to A." A divesting condition follows the grant of the estate to A. The condition provides that Blackacre shall go to B for life if the condition is violated. A has a present estate in Blackacre in fee simple subject to an executory limitation. B only obtains present possession of Blackacre if alcohol is sold on Blackacre. If alcohol is never sold on Blackacre B will never obtain a present possessory estate in Blackacre. B has a contingent future interest, or more specifically, a shifting executory interest. If B obtains present possession of Blackacre he will only have a life estate in Blackacre. B has a shifting executory interest in a life estate in Blackacre. O has retained a reversion in Blackacre in fee simple absolute which will only become a present estate at the natural end of B's estate (at B's death) if B obtains present possession of Blackacre during his lifetime due to A selling alcohol on Blackacre.

> ## Future Interests Can Change Subsequent to the Original Transfer

As facts change subsequent to the original conveyance the types of interests originally created may change.

A future interest is *vested* when the owner of the future interest has a right to present possession of the property at some future date, after the prior estates have naturally ended, without having to satisfy any precedent conditions. This means, for example, that a contingent remainder can become a vested remainder if an applicable condition precedent is satisfied. Once an interest is vested it cannot be destroyed due to the death of the owner of the vested future interest. If the owner dies, the future interest is simply considered property which is transferred via will or intestate succession along with the other property.

Historically, a possibility of reverter, a right of entry and a reversion are all considered vested interests. In contrast, a contingent future interest (contingent remainder or executory interest) may or may not be destroyed upon the death of the interest owner prior to the interest vesting.

Explanatory Examples

(1) **O conveys Blackacre to A for life, then to B once B attains the age of twenty-one. At the time of the conveyance B is fifteen.** O's conveyance creates a life estate in Blackacre in A followed by a remainder in B. B's interest is a remainder because it will only become a present possessory estate at the natural end of the prior possessory estate (at A's death). It is subject to a condition precedent (B must reach twenty-one) which must be satisfied before B's interest will vest. B has a contingent remainder in Blackacre at the time of O's original conveyance. If B subsequently reaches twenty-one while A is still alive, B's interest will immediately vest because B has satisfied the condition precedent. Upon such vesting, B's future interest becomes an indefeasibly vested remainder in fee simple absolute.

(2) **In example (1), assume that B dies when he is twenty-two years old, and at the time of his death A is still alive. At B's death his will leaves all of his property to X.** B's contingent remainder became a vested remainder when he reached twenty-one. At his subsequent death, his vested remainder is transferred to X via B's will. At A's death, X becomes the present possessory owner of Blackacre.

(3) **In example (1), assume that B dies when he is twenty years old, and at the time of his death A is still alive. At B's death his will leaves all of his property to X.** B has a contingent remainder in Blackacre at his death because he did not satisfy the condition of reaching twenty-one. Additionally, because he is dead he can never satisfy the condition so his interest is destroyed because it will never vest. At B's death his contingent future interest is not inherited by X because there is no future interest to transfer to X via B's will. This is an example of a contingent future interest that is destroyed prior to vesting.

(4) **O conveys Blackacre to A for life, but if A graduates from law school all interests in Blackacre shall immediately go to B. At the time of the conveyance A is in high school. Ten years later A graduates from law school. However, he is killed in an airplane accident one year after graduation. A leaves a will which gives everything to Z.** O's original conveyance creates a life estate in A subject to a shifting executory interest in B. B's future interest is an executory interest because it will only become a present possessory interest if A's life estate is prematurely terminated due to A graduating from law school. If A does not graduate from law school, at A's death (the natural end of the estate), B does not become the present possessor of Blackacre. O retained a reversion in Blackacre because he made no provision for who would own Blackacre if A died without graduating from law school. When A graduates from law school his life

estate is prematurely terminated and B becomes the owner of the present possessory estate in Blackacre. B's shifting executory interest, upon A's graduation, becomes a present estate. O's reversion is destroyed because it will now be impossible for A to die without having graduated from law school. A's will does not convey any interest in Blackacre to Z because A lost all of his interest in Blackacre upon his graduation from law school.

(5) **O conveys Blackacre to A for life, but if A graduates from law school all interest in Blackacre shall immediately go to B. At the time of the conveyance A is in high school. O dies intestate two days after the conveyance leaving Y as his only heir. Ten years later A graduates from law school. However, A is killed in an airplane accident one year after graduation. A leaves a will which gives everything to Z.** This is the same as example (4) except that O dies subsequent to the conveyance but before A graduates from law school. At O's death his interest in Blackacre (a reversion) passes by intestate succession to Y, his only heir. When A subsequently graduates from law school his life estate is immediately terminated and B becomes the owner of the present possessory estate in Blackacre. Y's reversion is destroyed because it will now be impossible for A to die without having graduated from law school.

(6) **O conveys Blackacre to A for life, but if A graduates from law school all interests in Blackacre shall immediately go to B. At the time of the conveyance A is in high school. O dies intestate two days after the conveyance leaving Y as his only heir. Ten years later, A, who never graduated from law school, is killed in an airplane accident. A leaves a will which gives everything to Z.** This is the same as example (5) except that A dies without having graduated from law school. At O's death his interest in Blackacre (a reversion) passes by intestate succession to Y, his only heir. When A dies testate without graduating from law school B's shifting executory interest is destroyed because it will now be impossible for A to graduate from law school. A's will does not convey any interest in Blackacre to Z because A's life estate naturally ends at A's death. Upon A's death, Y, the owner of the reversion in Blackacre, becomes the owner of a present estate in Blackacre.

(7) **O conveys Blackacre to A for life, but if A graduates from law school all interest in Blackacre shall immediately go to B. At the time of the conveyance A is in high school. B dies one year after the conveyance with a will leaving everything to W. Ten years later A graduates from law school.** This is the same as example (6) except that B dies while A is alive but prior to A graduating from law school. At B's death his will leaves everything to W, so at B's death W owns a shifting executory interest in Blackacre. Ten years later A's life estate is prematurely terminated when A graduates from law school. W's executory interest then becomes a present possessory estate in Blackacre.

Review Questions

(1) What are "words of purchase"?

(2) What are "words of limitation"?

(3) Must a conveyance or grant expressly mention a possibility of reverter or right of entry in order for such future interests to be created?

(4) Can all estates be made defeasible?

(5) What are the three types of defeasible estates?

(6) O devises Blackacre to A and her heirs. What interest do A's heirs own in Blackacre?

(7) O conveys a life estate in Blackacre to Suffolk Law School for the life of B. What estate does Suffolk Law School own?

(8) O conveys Blackacre to State University so long as A never uses Blackacre as a soccer stadium. What interests are created by this conveyance?

(9) O conveys Blackacre to State University, but if State University uses Blackacre as a soccer stadium, State University shall lose its right to Blackacre. What interests are created by this conveyance?

(10) O conveys Blackacre to State University, but if State University uses Blackacre as a polo field, State University shall lose its right to Blackacre and Blackacre shall automatically go to the Society to Oppose Polo (STOP). What interests are created by O's conveyance?

(11) O leases Blackacre to Acme Enterprises for a fixed twenty year term. The lease provides that Blackacre shall automatically go to A for A's lifetime if Acme uses the property for residential purposes. What interests are created by O's conveyance?

(12) O conveys Blackacre to A for life so long as A only uses Blackacre for farming. Twenty years after the conveyance A ceases all farming operations and begins building homes on Blackacre.

> (a) What estate does A own in Blackacre immediately after the conveyance by O?

> (b) What estate does A own after he ceases all farming operations?

(13) O conveys Blackacre to A for life on condition that A only uses Blackacre for farming; and if A marries X Blackacre shall automatically go to B.

> (a) What interests does O's conveyance create?

> (b) What estate does A own if she ceases all farming operations on Blackacre?

O ⸻ BA life ⟶ A for farming

Review Questions: Answers

(1) The words in a transfer that identify the transferee.

(2) The words in a transfer that identify the specific type of estate transferred.

(3) No. A possibility of reverter and a right of entry are future interests created by operation of law whenever a determinable estate or an estate subject to a condition subsequent is created, respectively.

(4) Yes.

(5) Determinable, on condition subsequent, and subject to an executory limitation.

(6) No interest. This language indicates O conveyed a fee simple absolute estate to A. The phrase "and her heirs" are words of limitation not words of purchase.

(7) A life estate pur autre vie. The life estate must be measured by the life of a natural person. If the life estate was measured by the life of Suffolk Law School it would be an invalid life estate because the Law School is not a natural person. However, it is measured by the life of a third party (B) who is a natural person.

(8) State University has a fee simple determinable in Blackacre. O has a possibility of reverter in Blackacre in fee simple absolute. The phrase "to State University" are the words of purchase indicating Blackacre goes to State University. The remaining words are the usual words of limitation ("so long as") that indicate State University received a fee simple determinable. The creation of a fee simple determinable means that State University will automatically lose its estate if Blackacre is ever used as a soccer stadium. The grantor, O, retains a possibility of reverter. The possibility of reverter is created by operation of law. It does not have to be expressly mentioned in the conveyance.

(9) State University has a fee simple subject to a condition subsequent in Blackacre. O has a right of entry in Blackacre in fee simple absolute. The phrase "to State University" are the words of purchase indicating Blackacre goes to State University. The remaining words ("but if") are the usual words of limitation that indicate State University received a fee simple subject to a condition subsequent. The creation of a fee simple subject to a condition subsequent means that State University may lose its estate if Blackacre is ever used as a soccer stadium and the grantor, O, exercises her right to retake possession of Blackacre. The grantor retains a right of entry which is created by operation of law. It does not have to be expressly mentioned in the conveyance.

(10) State University has a fee simple subject to an executory limitation. STOP has a shifting executory interest in Blackacre in fee simple absolute. O has not retained any interest in Blackacre. State University will lose Blackacre

if it is ever used as a polo field. If State University uses Blackacre as a polo field Blackacre will automatically be transferred to STOP.

(11) Acme has a twenty year estate for years leasehold subject to an executory limitation. A has a shifting executory interest in a defeasible twenty year leasehold. O has a reversion in Blackacre in fee simple absolute. Acme's lease is subject to an executory limitation because it will prematurely terminate and go to a third party, A, if Acme violates the condition (use Blackacre for residential purposes). If the condition is violated A will get the lease for the remaining term. However, if A gets the lease it can be cut off or prematurely terminated before the end of the term if A dies before the end of the lease term. Therefore, any lease A gets will be defeasible. O will get possession of Blackacre at the end of the twenty year lease term, or she will get it earlier if Acme violates the condition and A subsequently dies before the lease term ends.

(12) (a) A owns a determinable life estate in Blackacre. The language "so long as" makes the life estate determinable. If A violates the condition (ceases farming) his life estate will be cut off and Blackacre will automatically go to O in fee simple absolute. (B) No estate. A has a determinable life estate, so O, by operation of law, retains a possibility of reverter in Blackacre. Once A ceased farming O automatically became the present possessory owner of Blackacre in fee simple absolute.

(13) (a) A has a life estate subject to both a condition subsequent (continue farming) and to an executory limitation (Blackacre goes to B if A marries X). The language "on condition that" indicates the creation of an estate subject to a condition subsequent. B has a shifting executory interest in Blackacre in fee simple absolute. O has both a reversion (if A dies without ceasing to farm Blackacre and without marrying X) and a right of entry in Blackacre (if A is not married to X and ceases to farm Blackacre). (B) If A ceases all farming operations on Blackacre it will not affect her interest in Blackacre. O has a right of entry so A's interest is unaffected by violation of the condition until O affirmatively exercises her right of entry by taking possession of Blackacre.

Summary of Main Points

A. General rules for analyzing a transfer
   1. Analyze interests at the time of the original transfer
   2. Ascertain how a transfer is accomplished (will, intestate succession, inter vivos transfer or gift)
   3. Ascertain who the transferee is (existing person, unborn person or class of persons)
   4. Ascertain how long the interest lasts (lifetime, forever, fixed time or unknown duration)
   5. Determine if the interest can terminate prematurely (violation of a condition)
   6. Determine if the transferee gets an immediate right to possession or a future right to possession
   7. Determine if a condition must be satisfied before the transferee has a right to present possession
   8. Determine intent of the original transferor which is controlling (intent of original transferor typically ascertained by looking at the written document which accomplishes the transfer)
   9. If the original transferor's intent is unclear or ambiguous the following rules of construction are often used:
      a. It is presumed the original transferor intended to transfer the largest estate she could transfer
      b. A transfer is interpreted to favor a transferee
      c. A fee simple subject to a condition subsequent is preferred over a fee simple determinable
      d. A remainder is preferred over an executory interest
      e. A vested remainder is preferred over a contingent remainder
B. Basic vocabulary
   1. Words of purchase are the words in a transfer that identify the transferee
   2. Words of limitation are the words in a transfer that identify the type of estate transferred
C. Formalities for creating specific estates (commonly used wording)
   1. Fee simple absolute
      a. Historically, typical language to create a fee simple at common law: *To A and his heirs*
         i. *To A* are words of purchase
         ii. *and his heirs* are words of limitation
      b. Today, *To A* will also create a fee simple absolute
   2. Fee tail

    a. Typical language to create a fee tail general: *To A and the heirs of his body*

        i. *To A* are words of purchase

        ii. *and the heirs of his body* are words of limitation

    b. Typical language to create a fee tail special: *To A and the heirs female of her body*

        i. *To A* are words of purchase

        ii. *and the heirs female of her body* are words of limitation

3. Fee simple determinable

    a. Typical language to create a fee simple determinable: *To A so long as A only uses Blackacre for residential purposes*

        i. *To A* are words of purchase

        ii. *and so long as A only uses Blackacre for residential purposes* are words of limitation

    b. The following terms are typically construed to create a fee simple determinable:

        i. So long as

        ii. As long as

        iii. While

        iv. Until

        v. During

    c. Additionally, any language which clearly expresses transferor's intent that upon violation of the specified condition the estate automatically terminates and reverts to the transferor

4. Fee simple subject to a condition subsequent

    a. Typical language to create a fee simple subject to a condition subsequent: *To A provided that A continues using Blackacre for residential purposes*

        i. *To A* are words of purchase

        ii. *provided that A continues using Blackacre for residential purposes* are words of limitation

    b. The following terms are typically construed to create a fee simple subject to a condition subsequent:

        i. On condition that

        ii. Provided that

        iii. But if

    c. Additionally, any language which clearly expresses transferor's intent that upon violation of the specified condition the original transferor shall have the right to retake possession of Blackacre

5. Fee simple subject to an executory limitation

      a. Typical language to create a fee simple subject to an executory limitation: *To A provided that A continues using Blackacre for residential purposes, and if A fails to use Blackacre for residential purposes then Blackacre shall go to B*

        i. *To A* are words of purchase

        ii. *provided that A continues using Blackacre for residential purposes, and if A fails to use Blackacre for residential purposes then Blackacre shall go to B* are words of limitation

      b. Additionally, any language which clearly expresses transferor's intent that upon violation of the specified condition the property shall go to a third party

      c. A fee simple subject to an executory limitation is essentially the same as a fee simple determinable or a fee simple subject to an executory limitation except that upon violation of the specified condition the property goes to a third party rather than to the transferor

  6. Life estate

      a. Typical language to create an ordinary life estate: *To A for life*

      b. Typical language to create a life estate pur autre vie: *To A for the life of B*

      c. The duration of a life estate must be based on the life of a natural person

D. All estates can be made determinable, subject to a condition subsequent or subject to an executory limitation, in accordance with the above rules for fee simple estates

E. Creation of future interests

  1. A future interest is a presently owned property interest for which the right to present possession is delayed until a future time

  2. Analyzing a future interest requires:

      a. Determining when and under what conditions the future interest will become a present possessory estate (reversion, possibility of reverter, right of entry, remainder or executory interest); and

      b. If the future interest becomes a present possessory estate what will that estate be (fee simple absolute, fee simple defeasible, fee tail, life estate or leasehold)

      c. Some future interests may never become present possessory estates

F. Some future interests can change subsequent to the original transfer

  1. Vested future interests

      a. A future interest is vested when:

        i.   Owner of a future interest has a right to present possession of the estate at some future date after the prior estate has naturally ended; and

        ii. No condition precedent must be satisfied

    b. A vested future interest continues to exist if the owner of the interest dies before she is entitled to present possession of the interest (it simply passes via the decedent's will or via intestate succession)

    c. The following are considered vested future interests:

        i.   Possibility of reverter

        ii. Right of entry

        iii. Reversion

        iv. Vested remainder (indefeasibly vested, vested subject to complete defeasance and vested subject to open)

2.   Unvested (contingent) future interests

    a. An unvested (contingent) future interest can become a vested future interest in light of changing facts subsequent to the original transfer

    b. A contingent future interest may or may not be destroyed if the owner of the future interest dies before a right to present possession of the interest occurs

    c. The following are considered contingent future interests:

        i.   Contingent remainder

        ii. Executory interest (both springing and shifting executory interests)

Words of Art for Creating Estates

Estate	Typical Words of Art
Fee simple absolute	(1) To A & her heirs (2) To A
Fee tail general	To A & the heirs of his body (conveys interest to all lineal descendants)
Fee tail special	To A & the heirs female of her body (conveys interest only to female lineal descendants)
Fee simple determinable	(1) To A so long as Blackacre is used for residential purposes (2) The following terms typically signify a determinable estate: - so long as - as long as - while - until - during (3) Language that indicates violation of a condition automatically transfers Blackacre back to the original transferor All estates can be made determinable A possibility of reverter (owned by the original transferor) is created by operation of law when a determinable estate is created
Fee simple subject to a condition subsequent	(1) To A provided that A continues using Blackacre for residential purposes (2) The following terms typically signify an estate subject to a condition subsequent: - on condition that - provided that - but if (3) Language that indicates violation of a condition gives the original transferor the right to re-enter and retake possession of Blackacre All estates can be made subject to a condition subsequent A right of entry (owned by the original transferor) is created by operation of law when an estate subject to a condition subsequent is created

Fee simple subject to an executory limitation	(1) To A provided that A continues using Blackacre for residential purposes, and if A fails to use Blackacre for residential purposes then Blackacre shall go to B (2) Language that indicates violation of a condition transfers Blackacre back to a third party other than the original transferor All estates can be made subject to an executory limitation
Life estate (ordinary)	To A for life
Life estate pur autre vie	To A for the life of B

Chapter Eleven

Distinguishing between a Condition Precedent and a Condition Subsequent

This chapter will explain how to distinguish a condition precedent from a condition subsequent. It is often difficult to distinguish between the two. Nevertheless, the distinction is important because it can affect the type of interest created. Determining the type of condition is particularly relevant as it distinguishes a contingent remainder from a vested remainder subject to complete defeasance. (Remainders are discussed in Chapter Seven.)

> A "condition precedent" is a condition that must be met before a future interest can vest

A condition precedent is usually associated with a contingent remainder or an executory interest.

The distinction between a contingent remainder and an executory interest is based on when the future interest can potentially become a present possessory interest. If this can only happen at the natural end of the prior estate a contingent remainder is created. If this can only happen due to the prior estate being prematurely terminated or cut off it is an executory interest.

A condition precedent may also be associated with some types of vested remainders subject to open. For example, a vested remainder subject to open where all class members are subject to a condition precedent but only some class members have satisfied the condition.

> A "condition subsequent" is a condition that prematurely terminates, cuts off or divests a future interest that is already vested

A condition subsequent is usually associated with a vested remainder subject to complete defeasance or a defeasible estate.

If a condition makes it possible for a vested remainder to be divested either prior to the time it becomes a present possessory estate or after it becomes a present possessory estate then a vested remainder subject to complete defeasance is created. In this situation, the conditional language defines the type of vested remainder created.

If the condition makes it possible to prematurely terminate or cut off a present possessory estate a defeasible estate is created. In this situation, the condition can be considered words of limitation that define the estate as a defeasible estate (for example, a determinable life estate, a fee simple subject to a condition subsequent or a fee simple subject to an executory limitation).

General Rules of Construction

The location of the condition relative to the rest of the transfer language can be an important aid in determining if the condition is a condition precedent or a condition subsequent:

(a) If the condition is in a clause that is set off by a comma and which follows the transferring language it typically creates a condition subsequent

(b) If the condition is contained in the same clause that contains the transferring language it typically creates a condition precedent

(c) If the conditional language is before the clause that contains the transferring language it typically creates a condition precedent

---

Explanatory Examples

(1) **O conveys Blackacre to A for life, then to B for B's lifetime.** O's conveyance creates a present life estate in A and a future interest in B. B's future interest will only become a present possessory estate at the natural end of the prior possessory estate (at A's death). B's future interest is a remainder. B is alive and therefore whether B's future interest is a vested remainder or a contingent remainder depends upon the existence or non-existence of a condition precedent. The language "for B's lifetime" are words of limitation rather than a condition. These words make B's future interest a life estate. B has a vested remainder in a life estate in Blackacre. The next issue is whether B has an indefeasibly vested remainder or a vested remainder subject to complete defeasance. At the time of O's original conveyance, it cannot be said that B's future interest will definitely become a present possessory estate in the future because

B could predecease A. Therefore, B has a vested remainder subject to complete defeasance in a life estate in Blackacre.

(2) **O conveys Blackacre to A for life, then to B provided B is alive at A's death.** O's conveyance creates a present life estate in A and a future interest in B. B's future interest can only become a present possessory estate at the natural end of the prior present estate (at A's death) so B's future interest is a remainder. B must be alive at A's death as a precondition to B's future interest becoming a present possessory estate. The language "provided B is alive at A's death" are not words of limitation. Instead, they state a condition. The condition must be met before B can obtain a present possessory interest in Blackacre so it is a condition precedent. B has a contingent remainder. The language "then to B" indicates B was given a fee simple absolute estate. B's future interest can be fully described as a contingent remainder in a fee simple absolute estate in Blackacre.

(3) **O conveys Blackacre to A for life, then to B, but if B predeceases A to C.** O's conveyance in this example is very similar to example (2). In both examples, B has a remainder that follows the natural end of the prior present estate (A's life estate) and B must survive A in order for B's future interest to become a present possessory estate at A's death. In the prior example, B has a contingent remainder because the requirement to be alive at A's death is a condition precedent based on the way the grant is written. Note the wording in example (2) which states "to B provided B is alive at A's death." The grant to B and the condition are all stated in the same clause. This wording generally indicates the condition must be satisfied before B's remainder can vest. In contrast, this example states "then to B" immediately following A's life estate. The condition that applies to B's interest is in a separate clause which both follows and is set off from the grant to B by a comma. This construction typically indicates that O gave B a vested remainder in Blackacre but intended for this vested remainder to able to be divested if B predeceases A. Therefore, in this example O's original conveyance gave B a vested remainder subject to complete defeasance in a fee simple defeasible estate (more specifically a fee simple subject to an executory limitation) in Blackacre. If B is alive at A's death, B will obtain a present possessory estate in Blackacre in fee simple absolute because the divesting condition cannot occur once A predeceases B. C has a shifting executory interest in Blackacre in fee simple absolute.

(4) **O conveys Blackacre to A for life, then to B, but if B marries, then Blackacre shall go to C.** O's conveyance creates a present life estate in A. The wording "to B" indicates B has been given a fee simple estate. B is known and ascertained and no condition precedent exists. B will only obtain present possession of Blackacre, if at all, upon A's death which is the natural end of her

life estate. B has a vested remainder in fee simple. However, the final clause of O's conveyance contains a condition which follows the grant to B and is setoff by a comma. This construction of the wording generally indicates that the condition is a condition subsequent. This condition subsequent has the potential to divest B's future interest if B marries. B could marry before or after A dies. Therefore, B's future interest could be destroyed or divested prior to B obtaining a present possessory estate in Blackacre. The condition subsequent will continue to apply to B's estate even after it becomes a present possessory estate. B's interest, at the time of O's original conveyance, can be fully described as a vested remainder subject to complete defeasance in Blackacre in a fee simple subject to an executory limitation. C has a shifting executory interest in fee simple absolute in Blackacre.

(5) **O conveys Blackacre to A for life, then to B, but if B should ever sell alcohol on Blackacre, then to C.** This example is very similar to example (4). However, one distinction exists. The condition subsequent in this example can only prematurely terminate or cut off B's future interest after it has become a present possessory estate because B cannot sell alcohol on Blackacre until he has a present possessory interest in Blackacre. The condition cannot cut off B's future interest. Nevertheless, the fact that B's interest can potentially be cut off even after it becomes a present possessory estate prevents B's future interest from being an indefeasibly vested remainder. B's interest is a vested remainder subject to complete defeasance in Blackacre in a fee simple subject to an executory limitation. C's interest is a shifting executory interest.

(6) **O conveys Blackacre to A for life, then if B never drinks alcohol during A's lifetime to B.** The conveyance by O creates a present life estate in A followed by a future interest in B. B's future interest can only become a present possessory interest at the natural end of the prior present estate (A's life estate) so B has a remainder. However, a condition must be satisfied (B cannot drink alcohol during A's lifetime) before B's future interest can vest. This condition is a condition precedent so B's future interest is a contingent remainder. The wording in the conveyance "to B" indicates that B has a future interest in Blackacre in fee simple absolute so B has a contingent remainder in a fee simple absolute. This result is consistent with the rules of construction which generally hold that if a condition is contained in the same clause that contains the transferring language a condition precedent is typically created.

(7) **O conveys Blackacre to A for life, then to B, but if B graduates from law school, then to C.** O's conveyance creates a present life estate in A followed by a future interest in B. B's future interest is a remainder because it can only become a present possessory estate at the natural end of A's life estate. The grant "to B" by itself would be construed as an indefeasibly vested remainder in fee

simple absolute. However, the grant "to B" is followed by a condition which is in a separate clause setoff from and following the grant to B. Consistent with the rules of construction the condition is a condition subsequent which can divest B's interest before or after A dies. B's interest can be fully described as a vested remainder subject to complete defeasance in Blackacre in fee simple subject to an executory limitation. C has a shifting executory interest in Blackacre in fee simple absolute.

(8) **O conveys Blackacre to A for life, then to B, but if B does not provide a proper funeral for A, then to C.** O's conveyance creates a present life estate in A followed by a future interest in B. B's future interest will become a present possessory estate at the natural end of A's life estate (at A's death) so B has a remainder. No condition precedent exists so B's interest is a vested remainder. However, a condition subsequent exists (B must provide a proper funeral) which can divest B's interest after it becomes a present possessory estate. O's conveyance grants B a vested remainder subject to complete defeasance in a fee simple subject to an executory limitation in Blackacre. C has a shifting executory interest in Blackacre in fee simple absolute.

(9) **O conveys Blackacre to A for life, then if B gives A a proper funeral to B.** O's conveyance creates a present life estate in A followed by a future interest in B. This grant is very similar to example (8). However, the condition precedes the grant to B and it is contained in the same clause that creates B's interest. The condition must be satisfied before B's interest can vest. The condition is a condition precedent which appears to make B's future interest a contingent remainder. However, B will be unable to satisfy the condition until after A is dead. B's interest cannot be a remainder because it will not become a present possessory estate immediately at the natural end of the prior possessory estate (at A's death). Due to this time gap B's contingent future interest must be an executory interest. Since B cannot take immediate possession of Blackacre upon A's death it goes back to O (O retained a reversion in Blackacre) who would have a fee simple subject to an executory limitation in Blackacre. B would have a springing executory interest in Blackacre which would become a present possessory estate once B gave A a proper funeral.

(10) **O conveys Blackacre to A, but if A shall ever use Blackacre for commercial purposes Blackacre shall automatically revert to O who retains a possibility of reverter in Blackacre.** O's grant gives A a present estate in Blackacre. The estate can be subsequently divested if A violates the condition (use restriction) so the condition is a condition subsequent. The existence of this condition subsequent defines A's present estate as a defeasable estate. The type of future interest retained by the grantor determines the type of defeasible estate created by O. This grant provides for the estate to automatically revert to O

upon violation of the condition so A's estate is a determinable fee simple in Blackacre.

(11) **O conveys Blackacre to A, but if A shall ever use Blackacre for commercial purposes O shall have a right of entry which allows O to retake possession of Blackacre.** This example is very similar to example (10). In both examples O's grant gives A a present estate in Blackacre subject to a condition subsequent. Unlike example (10) however, the grant in this example indicates that O has a right of entry which gives O the right to retake possession of Blackacre upon violation of the condition. This is a right which O may or may not exercise unlike example (10) where violation of the condition automatically divested A of all rights in Blackacre in favor of O. The condition subsequent in this example creates a present fee simple defeasible estate. The defeasible estate is a fee simple subject to a condition subsequent.

(12) **O conveys Blackacre to A for life, then to A's children, but if any of A's children ever use Blackacre for residential purposes, Blackacre shall automatically revert back to O. At the time of the conveyance A has one child, C1.** O's grant creates a present life estate in A followed by a class gift in A's children. The divesting condition (residential use) is located in a clause following the language granting an interest to A. Additionally, it is separated from the granting language by a comma. In accordance with the rules of construction the condition is a condition subsequent. However, because one child, C1, is alive and no condition precedent exists, A's children have a vested remainder subject to open. The condition subsequent makes the estate defeasible. Furthermore, the fact that violation of the condition automatically causes Blackacre to revert to O makes it more specifically a determinable estate. The children's future interest can be fully described as a vested remainder subject to open in a fee simple determinable estate in Blackacre.

(13) **O conveys Blackacre to A for life, then to A's children who reach fifteen years of age, but if any of A's children ever use Blackacre for residential purposes, Blackacre shall automatically revert back to O. At the time of the conveyance A has one child, C1, who is thirteen years old.** O's conveyance creates a present life estate in A followed by a class gift in A's children. The class gift is subject to a condition precedent (A's children must reach fifteen) before it can become a vested interest. No child has satisfied the condition at the time of O's original conveyance. The children will take a present possessory interest at the end of the prior estate if they satisfy the condition precedent. The future interest in A's children can be described as a contingent remainder in a class of children. The children's interest is also subject to a divesting condition (residential use) which automatically causes Blackacre to revert back to O if the condition is violated. The divesting condition is located in the clause follow-

ing the language that grants an interest to A's children and it is separated from the granting language by a comma. Hence, the condition is a condition subsequent which makes the estate defeasible. The fact that violation of the condition subsequent automatically causes Blackacre to revert to O makes it more specifically a determinable estate. The children's future interest can be fully described as a contingent remainder in a class gift in a fee simple determinable estate in Blackacre.

Review Questions

(1) What is the definition of a condition precedent?

(2) What is the definition of a condition subsequent?

(3) The presence of a condition precedent often indicates the existence of what type of future interest?

(4) The presence of a condition subsequent typically indicates the existence of what type of future interest?

(5) The presence of a condition subsequent typically indicates the existence of what type of estate?

(6) What do the rules of construction for distinguishing a condition precedent from a condition subsequent focus on?

Review Question: Answers

(1) A condition that must be satisfied before a future interest can become a vested interest.

(2) A condition that prematurely terminates, cuts off or divests a future interest that is already vested.

(3) A contingent remainder or executory interest.

(4) A vested remainder subject to complete defeasance.

(5) A defeasible estate.

(6) The location of the conditional language relative to the granting language.

Summary of Main Points

A. Distinguishing between a condition precedent and a condition subsequent
    1. Condition precedent—A condition that must be satisfied before a future interest can become a vested interest
        a. A condition precedent is typically associated with one of the following:
            i.   A contingent remainder
            ii. An executory interest
        b. A condition precedent may also be associated with certain vested remainders subject to open
    2. Condition subsequent—A condition that prematurely terminates, cuts off or divests a future interest that is already vested
        a. A condition subsequent is typically associated with one of the following:
            i.   A defeasible estate (which includes a determinable estate, an estate subject to a condition subsequent and an estate subject to an executory limitation)
            ii. A vested remainder subject to complete defeasance if the condition makes it possible for a vested remainder to be prematurely terminated, cut off or divested either prior to the time it becomes a present possessory estate or after it becomes a present possessory estate
B. Rules of construction for interpreting conditional language
    1. If the conditional language is in a clause that is set off by a comma and it follows the transferring language it is most likely a condition subsequent
    2. If the conditional language is contained in the same clause that contains the transferring language it is most likely a condition precedent
    3. If the conditional language is before the clause that contains the transferring language it is most likely a condition precedent

Overview of Conditions

Types of Conditions	Effect of Condition	Relevance of Condition	Rules of Construction
Condition precedent	A condition precedent is a condition that must be satisfied before an interest can vest	Existence of a condition precedent typically indicates a future interest is a contingent remainder or an executory interest	Conditional language preceding the granting language or contained within the granting language is usually a condition precedent
Condition subsequent	A condition subsequent is a condition which can prematurely terminate, cut off or divest a present possessory estate or a vested remainder	Existence of a condition subsequent typically indicates a present estate is a defeasible estate; and a future interest is a vested remainder subject to complete defeasance rather than an indefeasibly vested remainder	Conditional language that follows the granting language and is separated by a comma from the granting language is usually a condition subsequent

Chapter Twelve

Alternative Contingent Remainders

Contingent remainders were discussed in general terms in Chapter Seven. This chapter will examine transfers that create multiple contingent remainders. Under certain circumstances such multiple remainders are commonly called *alternative contingent remainders.*

> "Alternative contingent remainders" are created when:
> (1) Multiple contingent remainders are created by a transfer;
> (2) At the time of the original transfer it can be said that only one of the contingent remainders can become a present estate, if at all, at the end of the prior possessory estate; and
> (3) If one contingent remainder becomes a present estate it is impossible for the other contingent remainder to ever become a present estate

It is sometimes difficult to determine the existence of alternative contingent remainders. They are often confused with executory interests, vested remainders subject to complete defeasance or defeasible interests. (See chart on next page.)

> **General Rules**
> (1) A nonreversionary future interest that follows a fee simple defeasible estate is an executory interest
> (2) A nonreversionary future interest that follows a vested remainder in fee simple subject to complete defeasance is an executory interest
> (3) A nonreversionary interest that will vest immediately at the natural end of a prior present estate, if at all, is a remainder (either a vested or a contingent remainder)
> (4) A reversionary future interest is a reversion, a right of entry or a possibility of reverter

Explanatory Examples

(1) **O conveys Blackacre to A for life, then to B if B is alive and at least twenty-one years old at A's death, but if B is deceased or younger than twenty-one years old at A's death to C.** O's conveyance creates a present life estate in Blackacre in A followed by two future interests, one in B and one in C. B's future interest is subject to two conditions precedent (B must be alive and at least twenty-one at A's death). B's future interest can only become a present possessory estate at the natural end of the prior present estate (at A's death). B has a contingent remainder in Blackacre. Likewise, C's future interest is also subject to a condition precedent (B must be deceased or younger than twenty-one at A's death). C's future interest can only become a present possessory estate at the natural end of the prior present estate (at A's death). C also has a contingent remainder in Blackacre. At A's death only one of the two contingent remainders will become a present possessory estate. The other contingent remainder will never become a present estate. These contingent remainders are essentially alternatives—one will vest and the other will never vest—referred to as alternative contingent remainders.

(2) **O devises Blackacre to A for life, then to the first child of B to reach nineteen years of age. B predeceased O leaving three children, C1, C2 and C3, who are between the ages of three and nine at the time of O's death.** O's will creates a present life estate in A. The future interest, following the natural end of A's life estate, is not a class gift since no additional children of B can be born in light of the fact that B is dead. The future interest is subject to a condition precedent (first child to reach nineteen) so it is a contingent remainder. At the time of O's death all of the children are younger than nineteen. It is unknown which child

will reach nineteen first since a child could die before reaching nineteen. Nevertheless, the first child to reach nineteen will get an interest in Blackacre and the other children will receive nothing. Therefore, C1, C2 and C3 each have an alternative contingent remainder in Blackacre in fee simple absolute.

(3) **O drafts a valid will which leaves Blackacre to A for life, then to the first child of B to reach nineteen years of age. At the time O drafted her will B was dead and B's children, C1, C2 and C3, were three, nine and seventeen, respectively. At O's death, two years later, C1, C2 and C3 were five, eleven and nineteen, respectively.** O's will creates a present life estate in A. The future interest, following A's life estate, is not a class gift since no additional children of B can be born. The future interest is a remainder subject to a condition precedent (first child to reach nineteen). O's will has no effect until his death. At O's death C3 has already satisfied the condition precedent (C3 is nineteen). Therefore, O's will creates a present life estate in A followed by an indefeasibly vested remainder in fee simple in Blackacre in C3. C1 and C2 have no interest in Blackacre.

(4) **O conveys Blackacre to A for life, then to B, but if B does not graduate from law school during A's lifetime then to C.** O's conveyance creates a present life estate in Blackacre in A and a future interest in both B and C. B's future interest will become a present estate at the natural end of A's present estate (at A's death) so B has a remainder. B is known and ascertained and no condition precedent exists so his interest is a vested remainder. Following the grant to B, and setoff by a comma, is a condition which can divest B's interest (failure to graduate from law school during A's lifetime). This is a condition subsequent. B has a vested remainder subject to complete defeasance in Blackacre in a fee simple subject to an executory limitation (it is an executory limitation because violation of the condition transfers B's interest to a third party rather than back to the original grantor). If B has completed law school prior to A's death B's interest cannot be subsequently terminated or divested. If B has not completed law school at A's death the condition subsequent will divest B's interest in favor of C. C has a shifting executory interest in Blackacre in fee simple absolute.

(5) **O conveys Blackacre to A for life, then if B graduates from law school during A's lifetime to B, but if B does not graduate from law school during A's lifetime then to C.** O's conveyance creates a present life estate in A followed by future interests in both B and C. Either future interest can only become a present possessory interest, if at all, at the natural end of A's life estate (at A's death) so both future interests are remainders. B's future interest is a contingent remainder because it is subject to a condition precedent (B must graduate from law school during A's lifetime) which must be satisfied before B's interest can vest. C's future

interest is also a contingent remainder because it is subject to a condition precedent (B must not graduate from law school during A's lifetime) which must be satisfied before C's interest can vest. At A's death either B's contingent remainder or C's contingent remainder will become a present possessory estate depending upon whether B has completed law school prior to A's death. B and C have alternative contingent remainders in Blackacre in fee simple absolute. Although the wording of the conveyances in example (4) and this example are very similar the slight difference in wording produces significantly different results.

(6) **O conveys Blackacre to A for life, remainder to B if B survives A, but if B does not survive A, then to C.** O's conveyance creates a present life estate in A followed by future interests in B and C. B's future interest is subject to a condition precedent (B must survive A) which must be satisfied before B's interest can vest. C's future interest is also subject to a condition precedent (B does not survive A). The future interest in either B or C will only become a present possessory estate, if at all, at the natural end of the prior present estate (at A's death) which means B and C have remainders. The existence of a condition precedent makes them contingent remainders. At A's death either B's contingent remainder or C's contingent remainder will become a present possessory estate depending upon whether B is alive at A's death. If B is alive at A's death, B will take a present possessory estate in Blackacre in fee simple absolute. If B is not alive at A's death, C will take a present possessory estate in Blackacre in fee simple absolute. B and C have alternative contingent remainders in Blackacre in fee simple absolute.

(7) **O conveys Blackacre to A for life, remainder to B, but if B predeceases A, then to C.** O's conveyance creates a present life estate in A in Blackacre and future interests in both B and C. B's future interest will only become a present possessory estate at the natural end of the prior estate (at A's death), if at all. It is not subject to a condition precedent so B has a vested remainder in Blackacre in fee simple. Following the grant to B and setoff from the grant language by a comma is a divesting condition (if B predeceases A). This condition is a condition subsequent which can divest B's vested remainder. B's future interest is a vested remainder subject to complete defeasance in Blackacre in fee simple absolute. C's interest can only become a present possessory interest if B's vested remainder is cut off or divested due to B predeceasing A. Therefore, C has a shifting executory interest in Blackacre in fee simple absolute.

(8) **O devises Blackacre to A for life and all her other property to B, then sixty days after A's death Blackacre shall go to C if C has provided a proper funeral for A, but if C fails to provide a property funeral for A within the sixty day period then Blackacre shall go to D.** O's will creates a present life estate in A in Blackacre and a present estate in B in all of her other property. It also creates future interests in C and D. C's future interest is subject to a condition

precedent (C must provide a proper funeral for A within sixty days of A's death) which must be satisfied before her interest can become a present possessory estate. D's interest is also subject to a condition precedent (failure of B to provide a proper funeral for A in the sixty day period). Both C and D have contingent future interests in Blackacre which look like contingent remainders. However, neither future interest can become a present possessory estate at the natural end of A's life estate due to the sixty day time period or gap following A's death. Due to this gap neither interest can be a remainder. If the interests are not remainders they must be executory interests. C and D have alternative executory interests in Blackacre in fee simple absolute. Absent the sixty day gap following A's death C and D would have alternative contingent remainders in Blackacre.

Review Questions

(1) What are alternative contingent remainders?

(2) Which of the following statements are true?

(a) A contingent remainder will become a present possessory estate

(b) If a conveyance creates two alternative contingent remainders it is possible that neither contingent remainder will become a present possessory estate

(c) If a conveyance creates two alternative contingent remainders at least one contingent remainder will become a present possessory estate in the future

(3) O devises Blackacre to A for life, then to B if B is alive at A's death, but if B is not alive at A's death then to C. Did O create alternative contingent remainders?

(4) O conveys Blackacre to A for life, then to B at A's death if A first marries X but if A first marries Y then to C at A's death. Did O create alternative contingent remainders?

(5) O conveys Blackacre to A for life, but it shall immediately go to B if A first marries X and it shall immediately go to C if A first marries Y. Did O create alternative contingent remainders?

Review Questions: Answers

(1) Alternative contingent remainders exist when a transfer creates multiple contingent remainders. When alternative contingent remainders are created, it is unknown at the time of an original transfer which, if any, of the contingent remainders will ultimately become a present possessory estate, and if one of the remainders becomes a present possessory estate the other remainders can never become present possessory estates.

(2) (b). A contingent remainder may never become a present possessory interest because an applicable condition precedent may never be satisfied. Alternatively, the remainder may be given to an unascertained person who may never come into existence.

(3) Yes. O created alternative contingent remainders. Both B and C have remainders because their respective future interests can only become present possessory estates, if at all, at the end of the prior possessory estate (at A's death). B's remainder is subject to a condition precedent (B must be alive at A's death). C's remainder is also subject to a condition precedent (B must not be alive at A's death). At A's death if B is alive his interest becomes a present possessory estate and C's interest can never become a present estate. Likewise, if B predeceases A, C's interest will become a present possessory estate and B's interest will never become a present estate.

(4) Yes. O created alternative contingent remainders. Both B and C have remainders because their future interests can only become present possessory estates, if at all, at the natural end of the prior present estate (at A's death). Each remainder is a contingent remainder because it is subject to a condition precedent. If B's interest becomes a present estate at A's death, C's interest will never become a present possessory estate. Likewise, at A's death if C's interest becomes a present possessory estate, B's interest will never become a present possessory estate. If A dies without every marrying Blackacre will revert to O via a reversion.

(5) No. O did not create alternative contingent remainders. Both X and Y have future interests that can only become present possessory estates by prematurely terminating or cutting off A's life estate if A violates either condition by marrying either X or Y. These future interests are not remainders because they will not become present possessory interests, if at all, at the natural end of the prior present estate (at A's death). X and Y have shifting executory interests.

Summary of Main Points

A. Alternative contingent remainders are created when:
1. Multiple contingent remainders are created by a transfer;
2. At the time of the original transfer it can be said that only one of the contingent remainders can become a present estate at the end of the prior possessory estate, if at all; and
3. Once one contingent remainder becomes a present estate it is impossible for the other contingent remainders to ever become present estates

B. Identifying alternative contingent remainders
1. Identify the existence of multiple third party future interests (nonreversionary interests) which can only be:
    a. Remainders; or
    b. Executory interests
2. Categorize any remainders as vested or contingent
    a. Determine if any condition that exists is a condition precedent or a condition subsequent
        i.   If a condition precedent exists then it is a contingent remainder
    b. Determine if any parties named in remainders are known and ascertained (exist) at the time of the original transfer
        i.   If a party does not exist the remainder is a contingent remainder
    c. Determine if any gap exists between the end of the prior estate and when the contingent future interest can become a present possessory estate
        i.   If a gap exists then it is an executory interest

Chapter Thirteen

Limitations on Restricting Property Rights: Restraints on Alienation and Marriage

This chapter will examine restrictions on the transfer of property and on marriage which are contained in a real property transfer. The general rule states that a property owner can attach conditions or restrictions to a present estate or a future interest that may cause a transferee to lose rights in a property. The most common example of this is the creation of a defeasible estate (see Chapter Five). A defeasible estate can be lost if a stated condition is violated. This represents the right a property owner has to decide how a property is used. Nevertheless, some otherwise valid restrictions or conditions may be deemed void restraints that are contrary to public policy which favor transferability of land and marriage. When a condition or restriction is found to be a void restraint it is eliminated from the transfer by operation of law.

> **Direct Restraints on Alienation**
> Language in a transfer that expressly restricts a transferee's right to transfer a property is called a direct restraint on alienation (alienation is a word of art in property law which means a conveyance or transfer of property)

Direct restraints on alienation are divided into several categories. Restrictions that expressly prevent or restrict all transfers by a transferee are called *total direct restraints on alienation*. Restrictions that prevent or restrict only certain types or aspects of a transfer by a transferee are called *partial direct restraints on alienation*. For example, a restriction that limits a grantee from transferring an estate for a limited period of time or prohibits transfer to a specific person is a partial direct restraint on alienation.

Total and partial direct restraints on alienation are further classified as follows:

(a) *Disabling restraints* do not allow a transferee to transfer a property. A total direct disabling restraint on alienation does not allow the transferee to make any transfer of a property to anyone. A partial direct disabling restraint on alienation does not allow the transferee to make a transfer under certain conditions. For example, a transferee cannot convey a property to a specific person or for a specific period of time.

(b) *Forfeiture restraints* provide that if a transferee attempts to transfer a property to anyone the transferee's interest immediately terminates and it is forfeited to the original transferor or to another person. A total direct forfeiture restraint on alienation provides that a transferee forfeits her property interest to the original transferor or to another party if any attempt is made to transfer the property to anyone. A partial direct forfeiture restraint on alienation provides that a transferee's property is forfeited to the original transferor or to another party if any attempt is made to make a transfer that is specifically prohibited or restricted by the original transfer. For example, an original conveyance might state that a transferee shall lose all rights in the transferred estate and the rights automatically revert to the original transferor if any attempt is made to transfer the estate to an attorney.

(c) *Promissory restraints* provide that a transferee promises not to transfer a property. A total direct promissory restraint on alienation provides that a transferee promises not to transfer a property to anyone. A partial direct promissory restraint on alienation provides that a transferee promises not to transfer a property in contravention of the transfer restrictions in the original transfer. For example, a grantee could promise not to transfer a property interest to an attorney.

Direct restraints on alienation that do not fit within the above rules may or may not be valid. Typically, courts will uphold such restraints if they are reasonable with regard to how long the restraint lasts and who is affected by it. (See chart on next page.)

> **Restraints on Alienation—General Rules**
>
> Total and partial direct disabling restraints on alienation applicable to a fee simple estate are void
>
> Total direct forfeiture restraints and total direct promissory restraints on alienation applicable to a fee simple estate are void
>
> Total and partial direct disabling restraints on alienation applicable to a life estate are void
>
> Total and partial direct forfeiture restraints on alienation applicable to a life estate are valid
>
> Total and partial direct promissory restraints on alienation applicable to non-freehold estates (leases) are generally valid

Explanatory Examples

(1) **O conveys Blackacre to A, but thereafter Blackacre shall never be transferred.** O's original conveyance gives A a present fee simple estate in Blackacre. It further provides that Blackacre cannot be transferred. This transfer restriction is a total direct disabling restraint on alienation because A has no right to make any transfer of Blackacre to anyone. This restraint is void by operation of law so A has a present fee simple absolute estate in Blackacre.

(2) **O conveys Blackacre to A for life, then to B, but any attempt by B to transfer any interest in Blackacre shall be null and void.** O's original conveyance gives A a present life estate followed by a vested remainder in fee simple absolute in B in Blackacre. Under the terms of O's conveyance B cannot transfer any interest in Blackacre. This restriction is a total direct disabling restraint on alienation. This restraint is void so A has a present life estate followed by an indefeasibly vested remainder in fee simple absolute in B.

(3) **O conveys Blackacre to A, but if A shall ever attempt to sell, donate or transfer Blackacre it shall go to B in fee simple absolute.** O's conveyance purportedly creates a present estate in A which is a fee simple subject to an executory limitation followed by a shifting executory interest in B in fee simple absolute. The condition placed on A's estate provides that the estate shall be forfeited to B if A makes any attempt to sell or transfer Blackacre. Such a condition is a total direct forfeiture restraint on alienation which is void when it restricts a fee simple estate. Therefore, the condition is ignored and A has a fee simple absolute estate in Blackacre. B has no interest in Blackacre.

(4) O conveys Blackacre to A in fee simple, provided that A covenants and agrees for herself and her successors and assigns that Blackacre shall never be transferred or sold. O's conveyance creates a present fee simple estate in Blackacre which is subject to a restriction that prohibits the sale or transfer of Blackacre by A. Unlike the restrictions in the prior examples, the wording of this restriction reflects an agreement between the grantor, O, and the grantee, A, that A will not transfer or sell Blackacre. The restriction is a total direct promissory restraint on alienation which is void when it applies to a fee simple estate. A has a fee simple absolute estate in Blackacre.

(5) O leases Blackacre to A for two years. The lease includes a promise by A that she will not sublet, assign or transfer Blackacre. O's transfer creates a present possessory non-freehold estate (term of years lease) in A in Blackacre. The transfer includes a total direct promissory restraint on alienation. Such promissory restraints are valid when applicable to leaseholds. Therefore, A cannot transfer any interest in Blackacre to a third party.

(6) O leases Blackacre to A for two years subject to a promise that states that A can sublet Blackacre but she cannot assign Blackacre. O's transfer creates a present possessory non-freehold estate (term of years lease) in A in Blackacre. The transfer includes a partial direct promissory restraint on alienation because the lessee, A, has agreed that she can sublet Blackacre but she cannot assign Blackacre. (An *assignment* means A transfers her entire interest in the leasehold to another party; a *sublet* means A transfers only a portion of her leasehold to another party.) Such promissory restraints are valid when applicable to leaseholds. A is free to sublet Blackacre but she cannot assign Blackacre.

(7) O conveys Blackacre to A, but thereafter any attempt to transfer Blackacre to an attorney shall be null and void. O's original conveyance gives A a present fee simple estate in Blackacre accompanied by a restriction on transferring Blackacre to an attorney. This is a partial direct disabling restraint on alienation because A cannot transfer Blackacre to a specific class of persons (attorneys). This restraint is void because both total and partial direct disabling restraints on alienation applicable to freehold estates are void by operation of law. A has a fee simple absolute estate in Blackacre that she can freely transfer to anyone.

(8) O conveys Blackacre to A for life, but if A shall ever attempt to sell, donate or transfer Blackacre it shall go to B in fee simple absolute. O's conveyance purportedly creates a present defeasible life estate in A (life estate subject to an executory limitation) followed by a shifting executory interest in B in fee simple absolute. The condition placed on A's life estate which prohibits the attempted sale or transfer of Blackacre is a total direct forfeiture restraint on alienation because any attempted transfer by A terminates A's estate and automatically transfers it to B. This forfeiture restraint is valid because it restricts a life estate.

(9) **O conveys Blackacre to A for life, but any attempt by A to sell, donate or transfer Blackacre to B shall be null and void.** O's conveyance creates a present life estate in A which is subject to a restriction that prohibits A from transferring Blackacre to B. This restriction is a partial direct disabling restraint on alienation because it prohibits the transfer of Blackacre to B. This disabling restraint is void so A has a present life estate in Blackacre.

(10) **O conveys Blackacre to A for life, but if A shall ever attempt to sell, donate or transfer Blackacre to an attorney it shall go to B in fee simple absolute.** O's conveyance creates a present life estate in A which is subject to a restriction. If A attempts to transfer Blackacre to an attorney it automatically goes to B. A can freely transfer Blackacre to anyone other than an attorney without forfeiting her interest in Blackacre. This restriction is a partial direct forfeiture restraint. This forfeiture restraint is valid because it restricts a life estate.

> **Direct Restraints on Marriage**
> Language in a conveyance or other transfer that expressly restricts a transferee's right to marry is called a direct restraint on marriage

Historically, courts disfavored restraints on marriage. A total (also called *general* or *absolute*) direct restraint on marriage which prohibits marriage or which would result in forfeiture of property rights upon marriage is void as contrary to public policy. However, courts generally recognize an exception to this rule. Most courts will uphold a marriage restraint that terminates the transferee's property rights upon marriage if the intent of the transferor is to provide support to an unmarried transferee until she marries.

A partial direct restraint on marriage that is limited in time, limited to a specific person or limited to a class of persons is generally valid provided it is reasonable.

Explanatory Examples

(1) **O conveys Blackacre to A in fee simple, but if A marries said conveyance shall be null and void. Assume A is unmarried at the time of O's conveyance.** O's original conveyance creates a present possessory fee simple interest in Blackacre in A. It is subject to a condition that renders A's interest null and void if she marries. The condition is a total direct restraint on marriage which is void. A has a fee simple absolute interest in Blackacre.

(2) **O conveys Blackacre to A in fee simple, but if A gets married Blackacre shall automatically revert to O. Assume A is unmarried at the time of O's conveyance.** O's original conveyance creates a present possessory fee simple inter-

est in Blackacre. It is subject to a condition that causes A's estate to revert to the grantor if A marries. A's estate appears to be a fee simple determinable, and O appears to have a possibility of reverter in Blackacre in fee simple absolute. However, the condition, like in the prior example, is a total direct restraint on marriage and is therefore void. A has a fee simple absolute interest in Blackacre.

(3) **O conveys Blackacre (which is income generating commercial property) to A in fee simple for the purpose of supporting A, a single women, until such time as she marries, and upon her marriage Blackacre shall automatically revert to O. Assume A is unmarried at the time of O's conveyance.** O's original conveyance appears to create the same interests as example (2). Like the prior example, the condition appears to be a total direct restraint on marriage. However, the language used here, in O's conveyance indicates that the conveyance to A is for the purpose of supporting her until she is married. This conveyance, including the condition, is valid. It is an exception to the general rule that a total direct restraint on marriage is void. A has a present possessory fee simple determinable interest in Blackacre. O has a possibility of reverter in Blackacre in fee simple absolute. If A marries, her interest in Blackacre automatically reverts to O.

(4) **O conveys Blackacre to A in fee simple, but Blackacre shall automatically go to B if B marries. Assume B is unmarried at the time of O's conveyance.** O's original conveyance creates a present possessory fee simple estate in Blackacre in A. This estate is subject to a condition subsequent which can divest A's interest. Additionally, O's conveyance creates a shifting executory interest in B in fee simple absolute. In the event the condition is satisfied (B marries), A is divested of her interest in Blackacre. The interest would then go to B who would have a fee simple absolute interest in Blackacre. The condition is valid as it is not a restraint on marriage. Moreover, it encourages marriage because it rewards B for getting married. O's original conveyance creates a present fee simple subject to an executory limitation in A followed by a shifting executory interest in B in fee simple absolute.

(5) **O conveys Blackacre to A, a Roman Catholic, in fee simple, but Blackacre shall automatically go to B if A marries someone who is not Roman Catholic. Assume A is unmarried at the time of O's conveyance.** O's original conveyance creates a present fee simple estate in Blackacre in A which is subject to a condition subsequent that will divest her interest in Blackacre if she marries someone who is not Roman Catholic. However, if she marries someone who is a Roman Catholic she will retain her interest in Blackacre. The condition in this example is a partial direct restraint on marriage. It limits A to marrying someone within a large class of people (Roman Catholics). The partial direct restraint is arguably reasonable and therefore valid. A has a present

fee simple estate subject to an executory interest. B has a shifting executory interest in Blackacre in fee simple absolute.

(6) **O conveys Blackacre to A in fee simple, but Blackacre shall automatically go to B if A marries her third cousin, D. Assume A is unmarried at the time of O's conveyance.** O's original conveyance creates a present possessory fee simple estate in Blackacre in A. The estate is subject to a condition subsequent that terminates the estate if A marries D. B has a shifting executory interest in Blackacre in fee simple absolute. Like example (5), the condition in this conveyance is a partial direct restraint on marriage. It allows A to marry anyone other than D. A will only lose her interest in Blackacre if she marries one specific person. A is free to marry anyone else without it affecting her property rights in Blackacre. The partial direct restraint is arguably reasonable and therefore valid. A has a present possessory fee simple estate subject to an executory limitation.

(7) **O conveys Blackacre to A in fee simple, but Blackacre shall automatically revert to O if A marries an attorney. Assume A is unmarried at the time of O's conveyance.** O's original conveyance creates a present possessory fee simple estate in Blackacre in A. The estate is subject to a condition subsequent that terminates A's estate if she marries an attorney. Like example (6), the condition in this conveyance is a partial direct restraint on marriage because it only causes A to forfeit her interest in Blackacre if she marries an attorney. The majority of people are not attorneys, so a large pool of individuals exist from which she can choose a spouse. The restraint is arguably reasonable and therefore valid. A has a present possessory fee simple determinable estate in Blackacre. O has a possibility of reverter in Blackacre in fee simple absolute.

(8) **O conveys Blackacre to A in fee simple, but Blackacre shall automatically revert to O if A marries before she reaches the age of nineteen. Assume A is fifteen years old and unmarried at the time of O's conveyance.** O's original conveyance creates a present possessory fee simple estate in Blackacre in A. The estate is subject to a condition subsequent that will terminate A's estate if she marries before she is nineteen. Like the prior examples (5, 6 and 7), the condition in this conveyance is a partial direct restraint on marriage. Unlike the previous examples however, the limitation or condition in this example includes an age restriction on when A can marry. A must wait a minimum of four years from the time of the original conveyance before getting married. Although this is a long period of time it applies to A while she is between the ages of fifteen and nineteen, which is arguably reasonable and therefore valid. Once she reaches nineteen she is free to marry anyone without it affecting her property rights in Blackacre. The restraint is arguably a reasonable restraint so it is valid. A has a present possessory fee simple determinable estate in Blackacre, and O has a possibility of reverter in Blackacre in fee simple absolute.

Review Questions

(1) Are some restrictions placed on property rights void as contrary to public policy?

(2) What is a direct restraint on alienation?

(3) What is a total direct restraint on alienation?

(4) What is a partial direct restraint on alienation?

(5) What are the three types of direct restraints on alienation?

(6) Which of the following are true?

(a) Total and partial direct disabling restraints on alienation are void

(b) Total forfeiture and total promissory direct disabling restraints on alienation that are applicable to a fee simple estate are void

(c) Total and partial direct promissory restraints on alienation that are applicable to non-freehold estates are generally void

(d) Total and partial direct disabling restraints on alienation applicable to a life estate are void

(e) Total and partial direct disabling restraints on alienation applicable to a life estate are valid

(f) Total and partial direct forfeiture restraints on alienation applicable to a life estate are valid

(g) Total and partial direct promissory restraints on alienation that are applicable to non-freehold estates are generally valid

(7) What is a direct restraint on marriage?

(8) A total direct restraint on marriage is typically void. What is an exception to this general rule?

(9) Are partial direct restraints on marriage always valid?

Review Questions: Answers

(1) Yes. A restraint that prevents an estate owner from transferring his estate to another party may be void. A restriction on marriage attached to an estate may also be void.

(2) Language in a conveyance or other transfer that expressly restricts a transferee's right to convey or transfer her property is called a direct restraint on alienation (alienation is a word of art in property law which means a conveyance or transfer of property).

(3) A total direct restraint on alienation is an express restriction or condition in a property transfer that prevents or restricts all transfers by a transferee.

(4) A partial direct restraint on alienation is an express restriction or condition in a property transfer that prevents or restricts only certain types or aspects of a transfer by a transferee.

(5) (1) Disabling restraints (which can be either total or partial restraints) which expressly disallow a transferee from transferring her property; (2) Forfeiture restraints (which can be either total or partial restraints) which expressly provide that if a transferee attempts to transfer her property to anyone her interest immediately terminates and is forfeited to the original transferor or another person; and (3) Promissory restraints (which can be either total or partial restraints) that expressly provide that a transferee promises not to transfer her property.

(6) (a) (b) (d) (f) (g)

(7) Language in a conveyance or other transfer that expressly restricts a transferee's right to marry is called a direct restraint on marriage.

(8) If the intent of the transferor is to provide support to an unmarried transferee until the transferee marries. Most courts will uphold a marriage restraint that terminates the transferee's property rights upon marriage.

(9) No. A partial direct restraint on marriage that is limited in time, limited to a specific person or limited to a class of persons is generally valid provided it is reasonable.

Summary of Main Points

A. Restraints on Alienation
1. Direct restraints on alienation are defined as language in a conveyance or other transfer that expressly restricts a transferee's right to convey or transfer her property
   a. Total direct restraints on alienation are restraints which restrict or prevent all transfers by a transferee
   b. Partial direct restraints on alienation are restraints which restrict or prevent only certain types or aspects of a transfer by a transferee
2. Total and partial direct restraints on alienation are classified as follows:
   a. Disabling restraints on alienation
      i. Total direct disabling restraints on alienation do not allow a transferee to make any transfer of her property
      ii. Partial direct disabling restraints on alienation do not allow a transferee to make a transfer under certain conditions
      iii. Total and partial direct disabling restraints on alienation are void
   b. Forfeiture restraints on alienation
      i. Total direct forfeiture restraints on alienation provide that a transferee loses or forfeits her property interest to the grantor or a third party if she attempts a transfer
      ii. Partial direct forfeiture restraints on alienation provide that a transferee loses or forfeits her property interest to the grantor or a third party if she attempts a transfer that is prohibited or restricted by the original conveyance or transfer
      iii. Total direct forfeiture restraints on alienation applicable to a fee simple interest are void
      iv. Total and partial direct forfeiture restraints on alienation applicable to a life estate are valid
   c. Promissory restraints
      i. Total direct promissory restraints on alienation are a promise by a transferee that she will not transfer her property interest under any conditions to anyone
      ii. Partial direct promissory restraints on alienation are a promise by a transferee not to violate any transfer restrictions contained in an original transfer
      iii. Total direct promissory restraints on alienation applicable to a fee simple are void

   iv. Total and partial direct promissory restraints on alienation applicable to non-free hold estates (leases) are generally valid

B. Restraints on marriage

 1. Total direct restraints on marriage are express conditions or restrictions which either prohibit marriage or provide for forfeiture of property rights upon marriage

  a. General rule—total direct restraints on marriage are void

  b. Exception—total direct restraints on marriage that terminate a transferee's property rights are valid if intent of transferor is to provide support to an unmarried transferee until she marries

 2. Partial direct restraints on marriage which are limited in time, limited to a specific person or limited to a class of persons are valid if reasonable

Direct Restraints on Alienation

Type of Restraint	Valid or Void	Example of Restraint
Total disabling	Void	O conveys Blackacre to A, but thereafter Blackacre shall never be transferred
Partial disabling	Void	O conveys Blackacre to A, but thereafter any attempt to transfer Blackacre to an attorney shall be null and void
Total forfeiture	(1) Void when applicable to a fee simple estate (2) Valid when applicable to a life estate	(1) O conveys Blackacre to A, but if A shall ever attempt to transfer Blackacre it shall go to B in fee simple absolute (2) O conveys Blackacre to A for life, but if A shall ever attempt to transfer Blackacre it shall go to B in fee simple absolute
Partial forfeiture	Valid when applicable to a life estate	O conveys Blackacre to A for life, but if A shall ever attempt to transfer Blackacre to an attorney it shall go to B in fee simple absolute
Total promissory	(1) Void when applicable to a fee simple estate (2) Valid when applicable to a non-freehold (lease) estate	(1) O conveys Blackacre to A in fee simple provided A promises for herself, her successors and assigns that Blackacre shall never be transferred or sold (2) O leases Blackacre to A for a ten year term, provided A promises for herself, her successors and assigns she will not transfer Blackacre during the lease term

Direct Restraints on Alienation *continued*

Type of Restraint	Valid or Void	Example of Restraint
Partial promissory	Valid when applicable to a non-freehold (lease) estate	O leases Blackacre to A for a ten year term subject to A's promise she can sublet but she will not assign Blackacre

Direct Restraints on Marriage

Type of Restraint	Valid or Void	Example of Restraint
Total direct restraint on marriage	Void	O conveys Blackacre to A (unmarried) in fee simple, but if A marries said conveyance shall be null and void
Total direct restraint on marriage (but grantor's intent is to support an unmarried person until married)	Valid	O conveys Blackacre (which is income generating commercial property) to A (unmarried) in fee simple for the purpose of supporting A, a single woman, until such time as she marries, and upon her marriage Blackacre shall automatically revert to O
Partial direct restraint on marriage	Valid if restraint is reasonable	O conveys Blackacre to A (unmarried) in fee simple, but Blackacre shall automatically revert to O if A marries an attorney

Chapter Fourteen

Limitations on Future Interests: Doctrine of Destructibility of Contingent Remainders

The existence of future interests can limit the ability to transfer land. For example, if a future interest holder does not exist at the time of an original conveyance, a third party cannot buy that future interest because no one exists to sell it. Additionally, it is often unknown when or if a condition precedent will be satisfied. This creates uncertainty since ultimate ownership of property may be unsettled until a condition precedent is satisfied or it becomes impossible for a condition to ever be satisfied if one exists; thus restricting marketability of land. The common law disfavors anything that restricts the marketability of land. This chapter will discuss the *doctrine of destructibility of contingent remainders* which was developed by the law to enhance marketability by destroying contingent remainders under certain circumstances. Chapters fifteen to seventeen will discuss other doctrines developed for this same purpose.

The doctrine of destructibility of contingent remainders has been abolished, either by statute or case law, in most states today. However, it may still be law in a limited number of jurisdictions.

Where the doctrine is still in force, it applies only to contingent remainders that follow freehold estates.

The doctrine provides that a contingent remainder can be destroyed for two reasons: due to *failure to vest* or due to *merger*.

Failure to Vest

A contingent remainder is destroyed under the "doctrine of destructibility of contingent remainders" if it fails to vest by the end of the prior possessory estate

---

The following examples will examine what happens when a contingent remainder has not vested by the time the prior possessory estate has ended. Each example discusses the result if the doctrine of destructibility of contingent remainders is the law and if it has been abolished.

Explanatory Examples

(1) **O conveys Blackacre to A for life, then to B provided B is nineteen years old. Assume B is eighteen years old at the time of the original conveyance.** O's original conveyance creates a present life estate in A and a remainder in B. B's interest is a contingent remainder because a condition precedent exists (B must be nineteen). If A dies before B turns nineteen, B is unable to take the future interest upon A's death because his interest has not vested. As a result, under the doctrine of destructibility of contingent remainders B's interest would be destroyed upon A's death. O would then have a reversion which would give O a present possessory fee simple absolute interest in Blackacre. If the doctrine is abolished, B's contingent remainder would not be destroyed in the event A dies before B reaches nineteen. Instead, if B has not reached nineteen O's reversion would become a present possessory estate in fee simple subject to a springing executory interest in B. If B dies before he reaches nineteen O will have a fee simple absolute interest in Blackacre. Prior to reaching nineteen, B has a springing executory interest. B's contingent remainder is converted into a springing executory interest if it has not vested at the end of the prior possessory estate, thus allowing B time to satisfy the condition precedent. If B dies after A dies but before reaching nineteen, B's future interest is destroyed because he will never be able to satisfy the necessary condition to convert his future interest into a present possessory estate. As a result, O would end up with a fee simple absolute interest in Blackacre.

(2) **O conveys Blackacre to A for life, then to B provided B is nineteen years old. Assume B turns nineteen after the original conveyance but before A dies.** O's original conveyance creates a present life estate in A and a remainder in B. At the time of the original conveyance by O, B has a contingent remainder because a condition precedent exists (B must be nineteen). B's interest subsequently vests when he turns nineteen. Since his interest is vested before A dies, the doctrine of destructibility of contingent remainders does not apply and B owns Blackacre in fee simple absolute upon A's death. Once B reaches nineteen he has an indefeasibly vested remainder in Blackacre in fee simple absolute.

(3) **O devises Blackacre to A for life, then to A's children, and all other property to Z. Assume A subsequently dies without ever having any children.** O's

will creates a present life estate in A and a remainder in A's children. A's children, as a class, have a contingent remainder because at the time of the devise no children of A exist but the possibility that A could still have children remains. When A dies without ever having children there is no one in the class to take Blackacre. If the doctrine of destructibility of contingent remainders is in force the contingent remainder in A's children is destroyed upon A's death because it has not vested by the end of the prior possessory estate (at A's death). If the doctrine has been abolished the result is the same since the contingent remainder can never vest once A is dead because A cannot have children after her death. O retained a reversion in Blackacre which passes via her will to Z. Z has a present possessory fee simple absolute estate in Blackacre upon A's death.

(4) **O devises Blackacre to A for life, then to A's children. Assume A has no children at O's death. Subsequently, A dies after having given birth to two children, C1 and C2, who are alive at A's death.** O's devise creates a present life estate in A followed by a class gift in A's children. No children exist at O's death so the children have a contingent remainder at the time of the original conveyance. When C1 and C2 are born during A's lifetime the contingent remainder becomes a vested remainder subject to open. Upon being born, C1 and C2 are vested. At A's death the class closes and C1 and C2 get present possession of Blackacre. It is irrelevant in this example whether the doctrine of destructibility of contingent remainders is or is not in force because the contingent remainder vested before the end of the prior estate.

(5) **O wills Blackacre to A for life, then to A's children. Assume A has only one child, C1, born after O's death. A has no other children and C1 predeceases A. C1 dies intestate.** O's will creates a present life estate in A and a contingent remainder in A's children since no children existed at O's death. At C1's birth the contingent remainder becomes a vested remainder subject to open. The class of children cannot gain new members after A's death so the class closes upon A's death. Although she died intestate, C1 is vested, therefore at her death her heirs inherit her future interest. C1's heirs obtain a present possessory estate in fee simple absolute in Blackacre. It is irrelevant in this example if the doctrine of destructibility of contingent remainders is or is not in force because the contingent remainder vested before the end of the prior estate.

(6) **O conveys Blackacre to A for life, then to B's children who survive B. Assume B never has any children.** O's conveyance creates a present life estate in A and a contingent remainder in B's children. The remainder is contingent because no children of B exist at O's death. Additionally, the condition (B's children must survive B) is a condition precedent because it must be satisfied before any interest in B's children can vest. Upon A's death the contingent remainder is destroyed under the doctrine of destructibility of contingent re-

mainders because the contingent remainder has not yet vested. It is possible, however, that B could have children after A's death. If the doctrine is abolished, the interest in B's unborn children would become an executory interest upon A's death. O would have a reversion in Blackacre which would give O a fee simple subject to a springing executory interest in favor of B's children who are alive at B's death. If B subsequently dies without any surviving children the springing executory interest will be destroyed upon B's death. O would end up with a present possessory fee simple absolute interest in Blackacre whether the doctrine is or is not in force. If the doctrine is in force, O has a fee simple absolute interest at A's death; if the doctrine is abolished, O does not obtain a fee simple absolute interest until B's death.

(7) **O devises Blackacre to A for life, then to B's children who survive B. Assume B has one child, C1, who is alive at O's death and at B's death.** At O's death A has a present life estate and C1 has a contingent remainder because she cannot satisfy the condition precedent (surviving B) until B dies. C1's interest subsequently satisfies the condition precedent at B's death. However, what happens to C1's interest depends upon whether B dies before or after A's death. If B dies before A, C1's interest becomes a vested interest upon B's death. C1's interest will not be destroyed whether the doctrine of destructibility of contingent remainders is or is not in force. In contrast, if the doctrine is in force it will be determinative if A dies before B. If the doctrine is in force and B is alive at A's death, C1's interest will be destroyed because it cannot vest at A's death since the condition precedent cannot be satisfied until B dies. In this event, O would have a reversion in fee simple absolute. Conversely, if the doctrine has been abolished, C1's remainder would be converted into an executory interest upon A's death. O would have a reversion is fee simple subject to a springing executory interest in C1. If C1 survives B, C1 would own a present possessory interest in Blackacre in fee simple absolute. If C1 predeceases B, the executory interest would be destroyed and O would have a present possessory fee simple absolute estate in Blackacre.

Originally, at common law only the following interests could merge:

Fee simple
Life estate
Vested remainder
Reversion
Possibility of reverter
Right of entry

Executory interests, contingent remainders and leasehold estates could not merge.

> **Merger**
>
> (1) When one person becomes the owner of several *successive* interests the estates are typically merged together into the largest estate
>
> (2) A merger destroys a contingent remainder under the doctrine of destructibility of contingent remainders if subsequent to the original conveyance but prior to vesting of a contingent remainder all successive interests in the estate (other than a contingent remainder or an executory interest) are acquired and owned by one person
>
> (3) A merger will not automatically occur with regard to interests created in the same person if an intervening contingent remainder is created in another person, provided all of these interests are created simultaneously by the original transferor

Under modern law, most jurisdictions allow merger of all successive interests including contingent remainders, executory interests and leasehold estates. The one exception is that fee tail estates cannot merge with fee simple estates.

Explanatory Examples

The following examples will examine what happens when a merger occurs. Each example discusses the result if the doctrine of destructibility of contingent remainders is the law and if it has been abolished.

(1) **O conveys Blackacre to A for life, remainder to B provided B never sells alcohol on Blackacre during C's lifetime, and if alcohol is sold on Blackacre by B during C's lifetime then to C. Assume subsequent to O's conveyance, A conveys her life estate to B.** O's original conveyance creates a present life estate in A, a vested remainder subject to complete defeasance in a fee simple subject to an executory limitation in B, and a shifting executory interest in fee simple absolute in C. A's conveyance gives B ownership of two successive interests which merge into a single interest—a present fee simple subject to an executory limitation estate. C still has a shifting executory interest. The doctrine of destructibility of contingent remainders is irrelevant here because O's original conveyance did not create any contingent remainders.

(2) **O conveys Blackacre to A for life, remainder to B provided B never sells alcohol on Blackacre during C's lifetime, and if alcohol is sold on Blackacre by B during C's lifetime then to C. Assume subsequent to O's conveyance, C conveys her executory interest to B.** This is similar to the previous example except that C's subsequent conveyance gives B ownership of a vested remainder subject to complete defeasance in a fee simple subject to an executory limitation and a successive shifting executory limitation in Blackacre. The two successive interests owned by B merge into an indefeasibly vested remainder in a fee simple absolute in Blackacre. The doctrine of destructibility of contingent remainders is irrelevant here as well because O's conveyance did not create any contingent remainders.

(3) **O conveys Blackacre to A for life, then to B for life if B becomes a doctor, then to A. Assume B is not a doctor when O makes the conveyance.** O's conveyance creates a present life estate in A, followed by a contingent remainder in a life estate in B (becoming a doctor is a condition precedent), and followed by an indefeasibly vested remainder in fee simple absolute in A. A's present life estate and remainder interest will not merge because they were created simultaneously with B's intervening contingent remainder. The doctrine of destructibility of contingent remainders is irrelevant.

(4) **O conveys Blackacre to A for life, then to B for life if B becomes a doctor, then to A. Assume subsequent to the conveyance that A conveys all of her interests to X.** This is similar to the previous example except for the subsequent conveyance by A. Once X owns both of A's interests they merge into a fee simple absolute. If the doctrine of destructibility of contingent remainders is in force, B's contingent remainder will be destroyed. If the doctrine is abolished, B's interest is not destroyed by the merger.

(5) **O devises Blackacre to A for life, then to B for life if B becomes a doctor. O's will does not contain a residuary clause nor does it mention O's reversion. At O's death, A is her only heir.** O's devise gives A a present life estate followed by a contingent remainder in a life estate in B (condition precedent is he must become a doctor). O dies partially intestate because her will does not dispose of her reversion. The reversion goes to A via intestate succession because A is O's only heir. A owns a present possessory life estate and a reversion in fee simple absolute. A's present life estate and her reversion will not merge because they were created simultaneously with B's intervening contingent remainder. The doctrine of destructibility of contingent remainders is irrelevant.

(6) **O makes an inter vivos gift of Blackacre to A for life, then to B if B survives A. A subsequently conveys her life estate to O.** O's gift creates a present life estate in A followed by a contingent remainder in B (a condition precedent is that B must survive A). A's subsequent conveyance gives O a present life estate

measured by A's life. O also owns a reversion (created by operation of law) in fee simple because in the event that B's contingent remainder never vests, Blackacre will revert to O. Therefore, O owns all the interests in Blackacre except B's contingent remainder. If the doctrine of destructibility of contingent remainders is in force, A's interests merge and B's contingent remainder is destroyed, giving O a present possessory fee simple absolute in Blackacre. If the doctrine does not apply, B's contingent remainder is not destroyed, giving O a present possessory fee simple estate in Blackacre subject to a springing executory interest in a fee simple absolute in B. If B subsequently meets the condition (surviving A), B will take a present possessory estate in Blackacre in fee simple absolute. If B does not survive A, O will end up with a present possessory fee simple absolute estate in Blackacre. As a result, if the doctrine is not in force, O must wait until both A and B die before finding out what her interest in Blackacre will be.

(7) **O conveys Blackacre to A for life, then to B and his heirs if B becomes a veterinarian. Before B becomes a veterinarian, O conveys her reversion to A.** O's original conveyance creates a present life estate in A followed by a contingent remainder in B (B must satisfy a condition precedent—become a veterinarian). Subsequently, when A becomes the owner of O's reversion, A owns the entire interest in Blackacre except for B's contingent remainder. A merger of A's interests occurs which destroys B's contingent remainder if the doctrine of destructibility of contingent remainders is in force. A has a fee simple absolute estate in Blackacre. If the doctrine has been abolished, the interests acquired by A will merge but B's contingent interest will not be destroyed by the merger. A will have a fee simple subject to an executory limitation because B's interest will only divest or cut off A's interest if B becomes a veterinarian. A will not know what interest she will ultimately get until B becomes a veterinarian or B dies prior to becoming a veterinarian.

(8) **O conveys Blackacre to A for life, then one week after A's death, to B and her heirs if B becomes a veterinarian. Before B becomes a veterinarian and before A dies, X buys A's life estate and O's reversion.** O's conveyance creates a present life estate in A and an executory interest in B. B's interest is an executory interest (rather than a remainder) due to the one week time gap between the end of A's life estate and the time B's interest can become a present possessory estate. O retained a reversion in Blackacre because she only conveyed a life estate to A and an executory interest to B. After purchasing A's life estate and O's reversion, X owns the entire estate in Blackacre except for the original executory interest conveyed to B. The reversion and the life estate merge but B's executory interest is not destroyed because the doctrine of destructibility of contingent remainders does not apply to executory interests. X owns a fee simple subject to a springing executory interest in B.

(9) **O conveys Blackacre to A for life, then to B for life, then to C for life, then to D. Subsequent to O's original conveyance, A, B and D convey their interests to O.** O's conveyance creates a present life estate in A, a vested remainder subject to complete defeasance in a life estate in B, a vested remainder subject to complete defeasance in a life estate in C, and an indefeasibly vested remainder in fee simple absolute in D. After the conveyances by A, B and D, O owns all of the interests in Blackacre except for C's interest. C's interest is a vested remainder so it cannot be destroyed due to a merger under the doctrine of destructibility of contingent remainders.

Review Questions

(1) What is the underlying rationale for the doctrine of destructibility of contingent remainders?

(2) Do most states still follow the doctrine of destructibility of contingent remainders?

(3) Where the doctrine is still in force, does it apply to all contingent remainders?

(4) What does "failure to vest" mean under the doctrine of destructibility of contingent remainders?

(5) What is a merger?

(6) When does a merger of successive interests not occur?

(7) When does a merger destroy a contingent remainder under the doctrine of destructibility of contingent remainders?

(8) O conveys a ten year lease in Blackacre to A, then to B if B marries. Assume B has not married by the time A's lease ends. Is it relevant whether the doctrine of destructibility of contingent remainders is in force?

Review Questions: Answers

(1) To enhance marketability of land by destroying contingent reminders under certain circumstances.

(2) No. The doctrine has been abolished, either by statute or case law, in most states today. However, it may still be good law in a limited number of jurisdictions.

(3) No. It only applies to contingent remainders that follow freehold estates. If the prior estate is a non-freehold estate (leasehold), it does not apply.

(4) A contingent remainder is destroyed under the doctrine of destructibility of contingent remainders if it fails to vest by the end of the prior possessory estate.

(5) When one person becomes the owner of several successive interests the interests are typically merged together into the largest estate.

(6) A merger will not automatically occur with regard to interests created in the same person if an intervening contingent remainder is created in another person, provided all of these interests are created simultaneously by the original transferor.

(7) When subsequent to the original conveyance but prior to the vesting of a contingent remainder all successive interests in the estate (other than a contingent remainder or an executory interest) are acquired and owned by one person, the outstanding contingent remainder is destroyed by the doctrine of destructibility of contingent remainders.

(8) No. The doctrine does not apply to contingent remainders that follow a non-freehold estate. A lease is a non-freehold estate. B's contingent remainder is not affected by the doctrine. At A's death, O will get present possession of Blackacre via a reversion. O's estate is subject to a springing executory interest in B.

Summary of Main Points

A. Doctrine of destructibility of contingent remainders
1. The doctrine applies to a contingent remainder that immediately follows a freehold estate
2. The doctrine may destroy a contingent remainder
3. The doctrine is applicable in two situations
    a. Failure to vest—A contingent remainder is destroyed if it fails to vest by the end of the prior possessory estate
    b. Merger—When one person becomes the owner of several successive interests, the interests are typically merged together into the largest estate and any outstanding contingent remainder owned by a third party is destroyed
        i.   A merger will not automatically occur with regard to interests created in the same person if an intervening contingent remainder is created in another person, provided all of these interests are created simultaneously by the original transferor
        ii. Originally, at common law only the following interests could merge: fee simple; life estate; vested remainder; reversion; possibility of reverter and right of entry
        iii. Generally, under modern law, all interests (except a fee tail) can merge
B. Modern status of the doctrine of destructibility of contingent remainders
1. Most states have abolished the doctrine
2. Effects of doctrine being abolished
    a. Failure to vest
        i.   If a contingent remainder fails to vest at the end of the prior possessory estate it is automatically converted into a springing executory interest;
        ii. The transferor then becomes the present possessory owner via reversion; and
        iii. The transferor's interest is subject to the springing executory interest
    b. Merger
        i.   Merger rules still apply inasmuch as successive interests merge
        ii. A merger does not destroy an existing contingent remainder

Doctrine of Destructibility of Contingent Remainders

Doctrine applicable to	Contingent remainder that directly follows a freehold estate
Effect if doctrine applicable	Destroys contingent remainder
When doctrine is applicable	Applicable in two situations: (1) Failure to vest—contingent remainder is destroyed if it fails to vest by the time the prior possessory estate ends (2) Merger—merger of interests subsequent to the original conveyance destroys a contingent remainder if one person owns all interests except for the contingent remainder *Exception*: A merger will not automatically occur with regard to interests created in the same person if an intervening contingent remainder is created in another person, provided all of these interests are created simultaneously by the original transferor
Modern status of doctrine	Abolished in most states

Consequences of Doctrine of Destructibility of Contingent Remainders Being Abolished

Failure to vest	If a contingent remainder has not vested by the end of the prior possessory estate the following happens: (1) Contingent remainder is automatically converted into a springing executory interest; (2) Transferor becomes the present possessory owner of the estate; and (3) Transferor's ownership is subject to a springing executory interest
Merger	(1) Merger rules still apply inasmuch as successive interests merge (2) Such merger does not destroy any contingent remainders

Chapter Fifteen

Limitations on Future Interests: The Rule in Shelley's Case

This chapter will examine the *Rule in Shelley's Case* which bars the creation of certain remainders as a matter of law.

> **Rule in Shelley's Case**
>
> If a transferor (via conveyance or will) simultaneously creates a freehold estate in a transferee and a remainder interest in the transferee's heirs, the remainder, as a matter of law, is automatically converted into a remainder in the transferee

This Rule applies at the time of an initial conveyance. It can also be applied at a later time if subsequent circumstances convert an interest not subject to the rule to an interest that is subject to it. For example, if an executory interest is initially created, it is not subject to the Rule because the Rule only applies to remainders. If the executory interest is later converted into a contingent remainder, it then becomes subject to the Rule.

The merger doctrine (see Chapter Fourteen) may apply in the event that the Rule in Shelley's Case alters the original transfer.

Most states have abolished the Rule in Shelley's Case. A limited number of states continue to apply the Rule as a matter of law to conveyances of land.

Explanatory Examples

The following explanatory examples illustrate what happens both when the Rule in Shelley's Case is in force and when it has been abolished.

(1) **O conveys Blackacre to A for life, remainder to the heirs of A.** If the Rule is abolished, O's conveyance gives A a present life estate which is followed by a remainder in A's heirs. A cannot have heirs until she is dead, so the remainder in A's heirs is a contingent remainder. If the Rule is in force, the grantor's intent to give a contingent remainder to A's heirs is ignored. The Rule converts the remainder in A's heirs to a remainder in A. Under the Rule, O's original conveyance creates a present life estate in A in Blackacre followed by an indefeasibly vested remainder in A in fee simple absolute. Under the merger doctrine (discussed in Chapter Fourteen), A's successive interests merge into a present fee simple absolute in Blackacre.

(2) **O conveys Blackacre to A for life, remainder to B for life, remainder to the heirs of B.** If the Rule is abolished, O's conveyance creates a present life estate in A, a vested remainder subject to complete defeasance in B in a life estate and a contingent remainder in fee simple absolute in B's heirs. B's future interest is a contingent remainder because he cannot have heirs during his life. If the Rule is in force, the contingent remainder in B's heirs is converted into an indefeasibly vested remainder in B in fee simple absolute. Application of the merger doctrine would merge B's two interests into an indefeasibly vested remainder in fee simple absolute, giving A a present life estate followed by an indefeasibly vested remainder in fee simple absolute in B.

(3) **O conveys Blackacre to A for life, remainder to B for life, remainder to the heirs of A.** If the Rule is abolished, O's conveyance creates a present life estate in A, a vested remainder subject to complete defeasance in a life estate in B and a contingent remainder in fee simple absolute in A's heirs. The interest is contingent because A cannot have heirs until he is dead. If the Rule is in force, the contingent remainder in A's heirs is converted into an indefeasibly vested remainder in A in fee simple absolute. Unlike the prior examples, the merger doctrine would not apply here because A's two interests are not successive. They are separated by B's vested remainder in Blackacre in a life estate. Therefore, if the Rule is in force, A has a present life estate and an indefeasibly vested remainder in fee simple absolute which will become a present possessory interest upon B's death.

(4) **O grants a fifteen year lease in Blackacre to A, and a remainder to the heirs of A.** The Rule does not apply to this grant because O's conveyance creates a non-freehold estate (leasehold) followed by a remainder. The Rule only applies to freehold estates. A has a present possessory fifteen year leasehold interest in Blackacre. A's heirs have a contingent remainder in fee simple absolute in Blackacre.

(5) **O conveys Blackacre to A, but if B becomes an attorney, then to A's heirs. Assume B is not an attorney at the time of the original conveyance.** O's

original conveyance is not subject to the Rule because O does not create any remainders. The future interest in A's heirs is an executory interest because it will only become a present possessory interest by cutting off or prematurely divesting the prior estate. A has a present fee simple subject to an executory limitation in A's heirs. Executory interests are not subject to the Rule.

(6) **O conveys Blackacre to A, but if B becomes an attorney, then to A's heirs. Assume B is not an attorney at the time of the original conveyance by O but B becomes an attorney two weeks after the conveyance.** As discussed in the prior example, the Rule is not applicable at the time of O's original conveyance because it does not create any remainders. Once B becomes an attorney, A's fee simple defeasible interest is destroyed (divested). However, if A is still alive, her heirs are unknown so the executory interest in A's heirs cannot become a present possessory interest when A is divested of her present fee simple estate. Blackacre would go to O via a reversion which is subject to a springing executory interest in A's heirs. The Rule still does not apply in this example because none of the future interests become contingent remainders after the original conveyance by O.

(7) **O conveys Blackacre to A for life, and if B becomes an attorney to A's heirs upon A's death. Assume B is not an attorney at the time of the conveyance.** If the Rule is abolished, O's original conveyance creates a present life estate in A followed by a contingent remainder in fee simple absolute in A's heirs. If the Rule is in force, the contingent remainder in A's heirs is converted (by operation of law) into a remainder in A. A would own a present life estate and a contingent remainder in fee simple absolute in Blackacre. The remainder is contingent due to the condition precedent (B must become an attorney). If B dies without ever becoming an attorney the contingent remainder would be destroyed and Blackacre, upon A's death, would vest in O, because she retained a reversion at the time of the original grant.

(8) **O conveys Blackacre to A for life, and if B becomes an attorney to A's heirs upon A's death. Assume B is not an attorney at the time of the conveyance but B becomes an attorney two weeks later.** If the Rule is abolished, as discussed in the prior example, O's original conveyance creates a present life estate in A followed by a contingent remainder in fee simple absolute in A's heirs. Nothing changes once B becomes an attorney. If the Rule is in force, the contingent remainder in A's heirs is converted into a contingent remainder in A. When B becomes an attorney the contingent remainder is converted into a vested remainder because A is known and ascertained and no condition precedent exists. At this point, A has a present life estate and a vested remainder in fee simple absolute. Under the merger doctrine, A's two interests merge, giving A a present fee simple absolute in Blackacre when B becomes an attorney.

(9) **O writes a will which devises Blackacre to A for life, and if B becomes an attorney to C, but if B does not become an attorney to D for life and then to D's heirs. Assume a week after O writes his will and a year before O dies, B is killed in a car accident. B never became an attorney.** The transfer must be analyzed at O's death because a will has no legal effect until the testator's death. O's will purportedly gives C and D alternative contingent remainders. However, B predeceased O without ever becoming an attorney which destroys C's contingent remainder and converts D's contingent remainder into a vested remainder. At O's death, if the Rule is abolished, A has a present life estate, D has a vested remainder subject to complete defeasance in a life estate and D's heirs have a contingent remainder in fee simple absolute (D's heirs are unknown prior to D's death so the remainder must be contingent). If the Rule is in force, the contingent remainder in D's heirs will be converted into a vested remainder in D. D's life estate and D's remainder in fee simple absolute will merge into an indefeasibly vested remainder in Blackacre in fee simple absolute.

(10) **O conveys Blackacre to A for life, and if B becomes an attorney to C, but if B does not become an attorney to D for life and then to D's heirs. Assume a week after the conveyance B is killed in a car accident. B never became an attorney.** If the Rule is abolished, O's original conveyance creates a present life estate in A, alternative contingent remainders in C and D (only one of the remainders can vest depending upon whether B becomes an attorney) and a contingent remainder in D's heirs (D's heirs are unknown while D is alive and a condition precedent applies). Upon B's death, C's contingent remainder is destroyed because B cannot become an attorney after he is dead. D's interest is converted into a vested remainder subject to complete defeasance in a life estate in Blackacre. The contingent interest in D's heirs remains because D's heirs are unknown as long as D is alive. If the Rule is in force, the contingent remainder in D's heirs is converted into a remainder in D because the original conveyance creates a life estate in D and a remainder in D's heirs. These two interests will then merge into a contingent remainder in D in fee simple absolute. This merger occurs because both the contingent remainder in D in a life estate and the contingent remainder in D in a fee simple absolute are subject to the same condition precedent (B must not become an attorney). Therefore, if the Rule is in force, at the time of O's original conveyance A has a present life estate and C and D have alternative contingent remainders in Blackacre in fee simple absolute. At B's death, A has a present life estate and D has an indefeasibly vested remainder in Blackacre in fee simple absolute.

Review Questions

(1) Do most states apply the Rule in Shelley's Case today?

(2) Is the Rule in Shelley's Case a rule of law that applies regardless of the transferor's intent?

(3) Which transfers does the Rule in Shelley's Case apply to?

(4) If the Rule in Shelley's case is applicable, what does it do?

(5) Can application of the Rule in Shelley's Case trigger the merger doctrine?

Review Questions: Answers

(1) No. Most states have abolished the Rule in Shelley's Case. However, a limited number of states still apply the rule as a matter of law to conveyances of land.

(2) Yes.

(3) The Rule in Shelley's Case applies to transfers (via conveyance or will) of a freehold estate to a transferee where in the same transfer the transferor gives a remainder to the transferee's heirs.

(4) It converts (by operation of law) a remainder in the heirs of a transferee into a remainder in the transferee.

(5) Yes. Once the Rule in Shelley's Case is applied, successive interests in the same person may exist. Those interests may merge.

Summary of Main Points

A. Rule in Shelley's Case
   1. Rule applies when a transferor
      a. Transfers (via conveyance or will) a freehold estate to a transferee; and
      b. In the same conveyance or devise gives a remainder to the transferee's heirs
   2. Effect of the Rule
      a. Converts a remainder in the heirs of a transferee into a remainder in the transferee
   3. The Rule is applicable at the time of the original transfer
      a. The Rule also applies subsequent to the original transfer if an interest not subject to the Rule becomes subject to the rule due to subsequent occurrences
         i. For example, an executory interest is not subject to the Rule but it can become subject to the Rule if it is subsequently converted into a contingent remainder
   4. The Rule only applies to the transfer of land
B. Modern status of the Rule in Shelley's Case
   1. Most states have abolished the Rule in Shelley's Case
   2. A limited number of states still apply the Rule as a matter of law to conveyances of land

Summary of the Rule in Shelley's Case

Rule applicable to	Rule applies when transferor: (a) Transfers (via conveyance or will) a freehold estate in land to a transferee; and (b) In the same transfer or devise gives a remainder to the heirs of the transferee Examples: (1) O conveys Blackacre to A for life, then to A's heirs (if the Rule does not apply this creates a present life estate in A followed by a contingent remainder in A's heirs) (2) O conveys Blackacre to A for life, then to A's heirs if Blackacre is a farm at A's death (if the Rule does not apply this creates a present life estate in A and a contingent remainder in A's heirs)
Effect of Rule on above examples	The above conveyances, under the Rule, become: (1) O conveys Blackacre to A for life, then to A (A now has a present life estate followed by a vested remainder in fee simple absolute—additionally, under the merger doctrine A would have a present fee simple absolute estate) (2) O conveys Blackacre to A for life, then to A if Blackacre is a farm at A's death (A has a present life estate followed by a contingent remainder—so A essentially has a fee simple determinable estate)
Modern status of Rule	Abolished in most states but applicable to real property conveyances in a few states

Chapter Sixteen

Limitations on Future Interests: The Doctrine of Worthier Title

This chapter will examine the doctrine of worthier title which voids certain future interests given to a transferor's heirs.

> ### Doctrine of Worthier Title
> Future interests given to a transferor's heirs are void if:
> (1) A transferor makes an inter vivos transfer of a freehold or non-freehold estate to a transferee; and
> (2) The transferor, in the same conveyance, gives a future interest to the transferor's heirs

The doctrine of worthier title applies at the time of an initial inter vivos transfer. Typically, a transferor retains a reversion or other reversionary interest as a consequence of the future interest in a transferor's heirs being void.

The doctrine has gone through a substantial progression. Originally, it was a rule of law only applicable to real property. Later, it was applied to both inter vivos and testamentary transfers, before evolving into the current doctrine which applies only to inter vivos transfers of real property and inter vivos transfers of personal property.

Like the Rule in Shelley's Case (See Chapter 15), most jurisdictions have abolished the doctrine of worthier title. The states that continue to recognize this doctrine generally view it as a rule of construction, rather than a rule of law.

Explanatory Examples

The following explanatory examples illustrate what happens both when the doctrine of worthier title is in force and when it has been abolished.

(1) **O devises Blackacre to A for life, remainder to the heirs of O.** Today, the doctrine of worthier title is typically not applicable to testamentary transfers so it would not be applicable here. A has a present life estate and O's heirs have a remainder in Blackacre in fee simple absolute. The remainder in O's heirs is a vested remainder due to the fact that O's heirs would be immediately ascertainable at O's death because Blackacre is transferred by O's will.

(2) **O conveys Blackacre to A for life, remainder to B for life, remainder to the heirs of O.** If the doctrine of worthier title is abolished, A has a present life estate, B has a vested remainder subject to complete defeasance in a life estate, O's heirs have a contingent remainder in fee simple absolute and O has a reversion. The remainder is contingent because O does not have heirs prior to her death. If the doctrine is in force, the contingent remainder in O's heirs is void and O has a reversion in fee simple absolute. O would own Blackacre in fee simple absolute once both A and B die.

(3) **O conveys to A a fifteen year lease in Blackacre, remainder to the heirs of O.** If the doctrine has been abolished, A has a fifteen year leasehold (non-freehold estate) followed by a remainder in O's heirs. The remainder is contingent because O's heirs are unknown until O dies. O retains a reversion in fee simple absolute because it is possible that O could have no heirs. In contrast, if the doctrine is in force, the remainder in O's heirs is void and A has a present possessory fifteen year leasehold followed by a reversion in Blackacre in O in fee simple absolute.

(4) **O conveys Blackacre to A, but if B becomes an attorney, then to O's heirs. Assume B is not an attorney at the time of the original conveyance by O.** If the doctrine has been abolished, O's original conveyance creates a fee simple subject to an executory limitation interest in A, a shifting executory interest in O's heirs and a reversion in O in fee simple. If the doctrine is in force, however, the executory interest in O's heirs is void and O would have a possibility of reverter in fee simple absolute. A would continue to have a fee simple defeasible interest but it would be in the form of a fee simple determinable as opposed to a fee simple subject to an executory limitation.

(5) **O conveys Blackacre to A, but if B becomes an attorney, then to O's heirs. Assume B is not an attorney at the time of the original conveyance by O but B becomes an attorney two weeks after the conveyance.** If the doctrine is in force, the original conveyance to O's heirs is void, and, as discussed in the previous example, the original conveyance would give O a possibility of reverter. When B subsequently becomes an attorney, O's possibility of reverter changes from a future interest to a present fee simple absolute in Blackacre. In contrast, if the doctrine is abolished, the shifting executory interest in O's heirs cannot become vested upon B's becoming an attorney because O's heirs can-

not be ascertained at that time inasmuch as O is still alive. When B becomes an attorney several things happen: A is divested of her estate in Blackacre; O will acquire a fee simple interest in Blackacre subject to a springing executory interest in O's heirs; and if O dies with heirs, the heirs obtain a fee simple absolute interest in Blackacre. Moreover, if O dies without heirs the executory interest in O's heirs is destroyed because it can never vest. As a result, a fee simple absolute interest will go to a beneficiary under O's will, if she leaves an applicable will. In the absence of disposition via will, it will go to the state via escheat.

(6) **O writes a will which devises Blackacre to A for life, and if B becomes an attorney to C, but if B does not become an attorney to D for life, and then to O's heirs. Assume a week after O writes his will and a year before O dies, B is killed in a car accident. B never became an attorney.** The original conveyance must be analyzed at O's death because a will has no legal effect while the testator is alive. Typically, the doctrine would not apply today because a testamentary transfer rather than an inter vivos transfer is involved. At O's death A has a present life estate in Blackacre and D has a vested remainder for life, followed by a vested remainder in O's heirs in fee simple absolute (O's heirs are known at O's death). B never became an attorney so C's contingent remainder is destroyed at B's death because the condition precedent (B becoming an attorney) can no longer be satisfied.

(7) **O conveys Blackacre to A for life, then ninety days after A's death to O's heirs.** If the doctrine is abolished, the original conveyance creates a present life estate in A followed by an executory interest in O's heirs. It is an executory interest because O's heirs cannot gain possession of Blackacre at the end of the prior possessory estate (when A dies) due to the ninety day time gap. Upon A's death Blackacre reverts to O who has a fee simple interest subject to a springing executory interest in favor of O's heirs. O's heirs do not get possession of Blackacre until O is dead and A has been dead for ninety days. If the doctrine is in force, the future interest in O's heirs is void, giving A a present life estate followed by a reversion in O in fee simple absolute.

Review Questions

(1) Do most states apply the doctrine of worthier title today?

(2) Is the doctrine of worthier title a rule of law?

(3) What transfers does the doctrine of worthier title apply to?

(4) Where or when the doctrine of worthier title is applicable, what does it do?

Review Questions: Answers

(1) No. Most states have abolished the doctrine.

(2) No. It is viewed as a rule of construction in most of the states that still recognize it today.

(3) The doctrine of worthier title applies to inter vivos transfers of freehold or non-freehold estates in real or personal property to a transferee where in the same transfer the transferor gives a future interest to the transferor's heirs.

(4) It voids a future interest in the transferor's heirs. Typically, the transferor retains a reversion or other reversionary interest once the interest in the transferor's heirs is void.

Summary of Main Points

A. Doctrine of worthier title
   1. Doctrine applies when a transferor:
      a. Transfers (via inter vivos conveyance) a freehold or non-freehold estate to a transferee; and
      b. In the same conveyance gives a future interest to the transferor's heirs
   2. Effect of the doctrine:
      a. It voids a future interest in the transferor's heirs
      b. The transferor typically retains a reversion or other reversionary interest once the interest in the transferor's heirs is void
   3. The doctrine is applicable at the time of the original transfer
   4. The doctrine applies to both real property transfers and personal property transfers
B. Modern status of the doctrine of worthier title
   1. Most states have abolished the doctrine of worthier title
   2. States that still recognize the doctrine view it as a rule of construction not a rule of law

Summary of the Doctrine of Worthier Title

Doctrine applicable to	Doctrine applies to: Inter vivos transfers of freehold or non-freehold estates in real or personal property to a transferee where in the same transfer a future interest is given to the transferor's heirs Examples: (1) A conveys Blackacre to B for life, then to the heirs of A (If the doctrine does not apply, a present life estate in B followed by a contingent remainder in A's heirs is created) (2) A conveys a fifteen year leasehold in Blackacre to B, remainder to the heirs of A (If the doctrine does not apply, a fifteen year estate for years leasehold estate in B followed by a contingent remainder in A's heirs is created)
Effect of doctrine on above examples	Above transfers, under the doctrine, become: (1) A conveys Blackacre to B for life (B has a present life estate followed by a reversion in A in fee simple absolute) (2) A conveys a fifteen year leasehold in Blackacre to B (B now has a present fifteen year estate for years leasehold followed by a reversion in A in fee simple absolute)
Modern status of doctrine	Abolished in most states but applicable (as rule of construction) to inter vivos transfers of real and personal property in a few states

Comparison of the Rule in Shelley's Case (See Chapter Fifteen) and the Doctrine of Worthier Title

Rule in Shelley's Case	Doctrine of Worthier Title
O conveys to A for life, then to A's heirs *Interest in A's heirs subject to rule if it is in force*	O conveys to A for life, then to O's heirs *Interest in O's heirs subject to doctrine if it is in force*
Abolished in most states	Abolished in most states
Rule of law which ignores grantor's intent	Rule of construction (which can be rebutted by grantor) which ignores grantor's intent
Applicable to real property	Applicable to real or personal property
Applies to remainders	Applies to remainders and executory interests
Applies to transfers via conveyance or will	Applies to inter vivos transfers

Chapter Seventeen

Limitations on Future Interests: The Rule Against Perpetuities

This chapter will examine the Rule Against Perpetuities (RAP) which voids certain nonreversionary contingent future interests without regard to the transferor's intent. If an interest violates the RAP it is void by operation of law.

As discussed in Chapter Thirteen, a condition directly barring the transfer of an estate is a void total direct restraint on alienation. The RAP is a public policy based rule originally developed to prevent the use of indirect means to restrict the transferability of property by attaching contingent future interests to estates. The RAP is still in effect today and it serves to prevent long-term dead hand control of real property which can negatively affect its marketability.

The common law RAP is generally stated as follows:

> No interest is good unless it must vest, if at all, not later than twenty-one years after some life in being at the creation of the interest.

Interests Subject to the RAP
(1) Contingent remainder
(2) Vested remainder subject to open
(3) Executory interest + *options*

RAP only applies to [handwritten]

Although executory interests are subject to the RAP, one exception exists. Some executory interests are actually vested interests rather than contingent interests. Such vested executory interests are not subject to the RAP. Typically, this situation, which is unusual, arises only when a third party future interest is a springing executory interest due solely to a gap existing between the end of the prior possessory estate and the time when the executory interest becomes a possessory interest.

Explanatory Examples

(1) **O conveys Blackacre to A for life, then ten days after A's death to B.**
O's conveyance creates a present possessory life estate in Blackacre in A followed by a future interest in B. B's interest will definitely become a present possessory interest ten days after A's death. B's interest is not a remainder because it cannot become a present possessory interest immediately at the end of the prior possessory estate (at A's death). At A's death Blackacre goes to O (via a reversion) who has possession of Blackacre subject to a springing executory interest in B. Ten days after A's death possession of Blackacre goes from O to B. B's springing executory interest is vested and therefore it is not subject to the RAP.

(2) **O wills Blackacre to A but the transfer will not take place until twelve years after O's death.** O's will creates a future interest in Blackacre in A in fee simple absolute. A will definitely get possession of Blackacre twelve years after O's death. If A dies prior to the end of the twelve year period, A's interest will go to her will beneficiary or, if she dies intestate, to her heirs via intestate succession. A's interest both looks like and behaves like a vested remainder. However, it is not a remainder due to the time gap between O's death and the time when A takes possession of Blackacre. A's interest, due to the time gap, is a springing executory interest. This executory interest is not subject to the RAP because, unlike most executory interests, it is not a contingent interest.

The RAP is *not* applicable to the following interests even though some of these interests are subject to contingencies:

Indefeasibly vested remainder
Vested remainder subject to complete defeasance
Possibility of reverter
Right of entry
Reversion
Present estate
Fee tail (the future interests in lineal descendants who take under the fee tail)

Typically, at common law neither a state nor its political subdivisions (cities, counties and townships) are subject to the RAP if they receive a property interest. Additionally, the RAP usually does not apply to an interest given to a charity which is followed by an interest in another charity. Some states have statutory provisions which regulate this charitable exception. Moreover, some states have enacted statutes that terminate some reversionary contingent future interests retained by a transferor (right of entry, possibility of reverter or reversion) that are not subject to the RAP. These statutes will typically terminate such interests after a certain period of time or under certain conditions.

Explanatory Examples

(1) **O conveys Blackacre to Charity A, but if Charity A ceases operating a charitable enterprise on Blackacre then Blackacre shall immediately go to Charity B.** O's conveyance creates a present fee simple subject to an executory limitation in Charity A. Charity B has a shifting executory interest in Blackacre which will only become a present possessory interest if Charity A violates the stated condition (cease operating a charitable enterprise on Blackacre). Generally, an executory interest is subject to the RAP. However, O's grant gives a present possessory interest to a charitable organization which is followed by another grant to a charitable organization. Under the above exception, the RAP does not apply to this executory interest.

(2) **O conveys Blackacre to A, but if A ceases operating a business enterprise on Blackacre then Blackacre shall immediately go to B.** O's conveyance is identical to the grant in the prior example. However, the interests created are not given to charitable organizations. A has a present fee simple subject to an executory limitation. A's interest is not subject to the RAP because it does not apply to present possessory interests. However, the RAP applies to B's shifting executory interest so it must be analyzed to determine if it violates the RAP.

In addition to the above future interests that are subject to the RAP, *in gross options to purchase land* are also subject to the RAP. In fact, such options have been the source of modern litigation with regard to applicability of the RAP. An option to purchase land is essentially a contract right which gives an option owner the right (but not the obligation) to purchase land. An option included in or appended to an estate is not an in gross option and therefore it is not subject to the RAP. However, if an option is not included in or appended to an estate it is an in gross option subject to the RAP.

Explanatory Examples

(1) **O leases Blackacre to A for ten years subject to A's option to purchase Blackacre for the sum of $85,000 at anytime during the lease term.** O's transfer creates a present ten year estate for years leasehold in A. Such a present interest is not subject to the RAP. O retains a reversion in Blackacre which becomes a present possessory interest if the lease term ends without A purchasing Black-

acre. Although it is unclear if O's reversion will or will not become a present possessory interest in the future, reversions are not subject to the RAP. Finally, the transfer creates an option which gives A the right to purchase Blackacre during the lease term. This option is a part of the lease (or is appended to the lease) so it is not an in gross option subject to the RAP.

(2) O leases Blackacre to A for ten years subject to an option that gives B the right to purchase Blackacre for the sum of $85,000 at anytime during the term of A's lease. O essentially creates the same interests as in the prior example except that a third party, B, is given the option to purchase Blackacre. B has no other interest in Blackacre other than the option, so B owns an in gross option on Blackacre which is subject to the RAP.

(3) O sells Blackacre to A subject to an option that allows O to repurchase Blackacre at the current market price. O's transfer creates a present fee simple estate in Blackacre in A. A's interest is not subject to the RAP because present estates are not subject to the RAP. However, O has an option to repurchase Blackacre. O's option is an in gross option since O transferred the entire interest in Blackacre to A. O's option is subject to the RAP.

The meaning of *vest* under the RAP is defined as follows:

(a) A contingent remainder vests when it becomes a vested remainder. A contingent remainder becomes a vested remainder when the owner of the interest exists (is known and ascertained) and no condition precedent exists which must be satisfied by the owner. It is possible for a contingent remainder to vest before it becomes a present possessory estate.

(b) An executory interest typically vests when it becomes a present possessory interest or when it is transformed or converted into a vested remainder.

(c) A vested remainder subject to open vests when all potential class members are vested. If every potential member of the class exists (is known and ascertained) and no member is subject to a condition precedent the remainder is vested.

> **Life in Being** (also called *Measuring Life*)
> To apply the RAP you must first identify a measuring life who is a natural person who must be:
> (1) A person that actually existed at the time the interest subject to the RAP was created, or
> (2) A person conceived (but not yet born) at the time the interest subject to the RAP was created provided he or she is subsequently born alive

A measuring life must be an actual person (human) so a corporation or other legal person cannot be used for the measuring life.

> ## The Perpetuities Period
> The perpetuities period is the time period during which you must determine with *absolute certainty* what will happen to the interest subject to the RAP. The perpetuities period is the measuring life plus twenty-one years. However, there is one exception—the perpetuities period is extended to include periods of actual gestation which is the time between conception and birth if a conceived but unborn child is used as the measuring life. The twenty-one year period will begin when the child is actually born

> If an interest subject to the RAP violates the RAP, it is void

In practical terms this means that the contingent interest that violates the RAP is eliminated from the original transfer. The remainder of the transfer is generally left intact and the transfer is treated as if the void interest never existed. This is sometimes referred to as the *doctrine of separability* because it allows valid interests to be separated from interests that are void under the RAP.

Sometimes when an interest is void under the RAP and it is subsequently eliminated, other interests can be affected. The result may be to alter the remaining interests or to create new interests. For example, a fee simple subject to an executory limitation may become a fee simple determinable or a fee simple absolute if the executory interest is void under the RAP. If a fee simple determinable is created a possibility of reverter will also be created.

Ultimately, the consequences that arise from elimination of a void interest can only be ascertained by examination of the remaining transfer after the void interest is crossed out.

The elimination of an interest by the RAP may also result in the application of the merger doctrine. (See Chapter Fourteen). If an inter vivos grant includes a life estate or a fee tail interest that is followed by a future interest that is void under the RAP, an implied in law reversion in the original transferor is created.

If a testamentary transfer includes a life estate or a fee tail interest that is followed by a future interest that is void under the RAP, typically the residuary clause in the will controls who gets the implied in law reversion. If no residuary clause exists the implied in law reversion is transferred by intestate succession.

Sometimes when an interest is eliminated because it is invalid under the RAP, it leaves a remaining transfer that is inconsistent with the transferor's intent. If a court determines that the invalid interest is essential to the grantor's intended plan, such that its elimination totally frustrates the grantor's intent, a court may strike the entire grant under the *doctrine of infectious invalidity*.

When Does the RAP Apply?
(1) Inter vivos transfer—at the time of the transfer
(2) Gift—at the time the gift is effective
(3) Will—at the time of decedent's death

General Rules for Applying the RAP
(1) An interest subject to the RAP is valid under the RAP if at the time the interest is created (or at decedent's death for a testamentary transfer) a natural person (human) exists about whom we can say we know with absolute certainty that during that person's life the interest will:
  (a) Vest;
  (b) Fail; or
  (c) Either vest or fail
(2) An interest subject to the RAP is valid under the RAP if at the time the interest is created (or at decedent's death for a testamentary transfer) a natural person (human) exists about whom we can say we know with absolute certainty that within twenty-one years of that person's death the interest will:
  (a) Vest;
  (b) Fail; or
  (c) Either vest or fail

To apply the RAP, try each measuring life to see if the interest is valid in light of the above *General Rules for Applying the RAP*. If the interest is valid based on *any* measuring life the interest is valid under the RAP. The measuring life that renders the interest valid is called the *validating life.*

Each interest subject to the RAP is evaluated separately. The same or a different measuring life and/or validating life can be used to evaluate each interest subject to the RAP.

It is best to systematically try every possible measuring life one at a time. Typically, the measuring lives may include the transferor, one or more transferees and any other person mentioned or referred to in the transfer. You can also try any person who is closely associated with the transfer whose actions or death may affect whether the interest subject to the RAP will vest. For example, if grandparents convey property to their grandchildren, the grandchildren's parents can be used as measuring lives even if they are not mentioned in the conveyance. The parent's death can affect vesting because upon their death the class of grandchildren can no longer be enlarged since you cannot have children after you are dead.

Things to keep in mind when applying the RAP:

- Each interest subject to the RAP is evaluated separately
- Each interest is evaluated under the facts that existed at the time the interest was created
- Testamentary interests are created at the time the testator dies, not when the will is drafted or executed
- You cannot get married after you are dead
- You cannot have children after you are dead
- Additional children cannot become members of a class of children after the parents are deceased because no more children can be born after the parents are dead
- Any living person is presumed fertile for purposes of having children regardless of age or health concerns
- The RAP is not evaluated based on probabilities. It is based on knowing to an *absolute certainty* whether an interest will vest, fail or either vest or fail during the perpetuities period
- A measuring life must be a natural person who is alive at the time of the original transfer (or at least conceived at the time of the original transfer provided he or she is subsequently born alive)
- Anyone who is born after the original transfer cannot be used as a measuring life (unless he or she was conceived at the time of the original transfer)
- Generally, any shifting executory interest which follows a fee simple defeasible is void under the RAP unless the executory interest is in a life estate
- If an interest is void under the RAP it is eliminated and the remaining conveyance or transfer is treated as if the void interest never existed. After elimination of the interest the remaining conveyance or transfer may be subject to the merger doctrine
- Whether the doctrine of destructibility of contingent remainders is or is not applicable can effect whether an interest is void or valid under the RAP

✓· The rule of convenience can affect whether a class gift is void or valid under
the RAP (See Chapter Seven for discussion of the rule of convenience)

Explanatory Examples

(1) **O conveys Blackacre to A for life, then to B provided B graduates from
law school. Assume B has not graduated from law school at the time of O's conveyance.** The first step is to determine if any interests exist that are subject to
the RAP. O's original conveyance creates a present life estate in A which is not
subject to the RAP. O also creates a contingent remainder in B (B must graduate from law school which is a condition precedent) which is subject to the
RAP. Finally, O has retained a reversion in Blackacre which is not subject to the
RAP. The next step is to determine if B's contingent remainder is valid under
the RAP. First, try O as a measuring life. O could die the next day and thirty
years later B could graduate from law school, so O cannot be the validating
life. Next, try A as the measuring life. A could die the next day and thirty years
later B could graduate from law school, so A cannot be the validating life. Finally, try B as the measuring life. B cannot graduate from law school once he
is dead so it can be stated with absolute certainty that B's interest will have either vested at his death (if he graduated from law school), or it will have failed
if he dies without having graduated from law school. Therefore, B's interest
cannot vest beyond the perpetuities period (B's life plus twenty-one years). B
is a validating life and B's interest is valid under the RAP.

(2) **O conveys Blackacre to A for life, then to B in fee simple, but if Blackacre is ever used for commercial purposes it shall go to C in fee simple absolute.** O's conveyance creates a present life estate in A followed by a vested
remainder subject to complete defeasance in B. C has a shifting executory interest which can only become a vested interest if the commercial use restriction is violated. Neither A's interest nor B's interest is subject to the RAP.
However, C's interest is subject to the RAP. First, try O as the measuring life.
A could die the day after O's conveyance and the next day B could violate the
condition. Under this situation C would take possession of Blackacre. However, O and A could die, and the condition might not be violated until eighty-
five years later. Finally, O, A and B could die leaving X to inherit Blackacre via
intestate succession. X could then violate the condition seventy-five years later.
Alternatively, the condition might never be violated. In light of this, it cannot
be said with absolute certainty if the condition will or will not be violated. Nor
can it be stated with absolute certainty when the condition will be violated in
the event it is violated. If you try A, B, C or anyone else as a measuring life, you

get the same result. C's interest is void under the RAP. C's interest is therefore stricken and the grant states: "O conveys Blackacre to A for life, then to B in fee simple." The RAP alters O's intent. O attempted to give B a vested remainder subject to complete defeasance but application of the RAP automatically converts B's interest intro an indefeasibly vested remainder in fee simple absolute. This example illustrates the general rule that any third party interest (other than a life estate) that follows a fee simple defeasible estate is usually void under the RAP.

(3) **O conveys Blackacre to A for life, then to B in fee simple, but if Blackacre is ever used for commercial purposes it shall go to C for life.** This conveyance is the same as the prior example except that C has a shifting executory interest in a life estate rather than in a fee simple absolute. C's future interest must vest prior to her death because a life estate naturally ends at death. Therefore, her interest cannot vest once she is dead. We do not know if C's interest will ever vest because we do not know if the condition will ever be violated. However, we can say with absolute certainty that at C's death her interest will have either vested or it will have failed to vest, so her interest is valid under the RAP based on using C as the validating life. Neither O, A nor B will work as a validating life. The day after O makes the original conveyance, O, A and B could all die. X could then inherit Blackacre and seventy-five years later X could violate the condition at a time when C is still alive. However, we cannot say with absolute certainty that this will or will not happen. It is also possible that one day after O's conveyance A could die and ten days later B could violate the condition while both O and C are still alive. Consequently, O, A or B cannot be validating lives since it is impossible to say with absolute certainty what will happen during their lives and within twenty-one years after their deaths.

(4) **O conveys Blackacre to A for life, then to B in fee simple so long as Blackacre is never used for commercial purposes, then to C in fee simple absolute.** O's conveyance is very similar to the conveyance in example (2). It creates a present life estate in A followed by a vested remainder subject to complete defeasance in B and a shifting executory interest in C. Neither A's interest nor B's interest is subject to the RAP. However, C's interest is a shifting executory interest because her interest can only become a vested interest if the commercial use condition is violated. Therefore, C's interest must be evaluated under the RAP. Under the same analysis used in example (2), C's interest is void under the RAP. If C's interest is stricken the resulting grant states: "O conveys Blackacre to A for life, then to B in fee simple so long as Blackacre is never used for commercial purposes." In contrast to example (2), B is still subject to the condition. However, the effect of the RAP is to eliminate C's interest so

that upon breach of the condition Blackacre will go back to O. In light of the wording used in the conveyance ("so long as") the resulting estate is a fee simple determinable which means O has a possibility of reverter (see Chapter Ten). Consequently, the RAP changes B's interest from a fee simple subject to an executory limitation to a fee simple determinable. In contrast, in example (2), the RAP changed B's interest from a fee simple subject to an executory interest to a fee simple absolute.

(5) O conveys Blackacre to A for life, then to B in fee simple, but if B ever uses Blackacre for commercial purposes it shall go to C in fee simple absolute. This conveyance is also the same as the conveyance in example (2), except that the divesting condition only applies to conduct by B. In example (2), the condition applied both to B and to anyone who acquired Blackacre from B. In example (2), if B willed Blackacre to X who then sold it to Z the condition would still apply to the land. If Z breached the condition C's executory interest would become vested. Therefore, it is impossible to say with absolute certainty if C's interest will ever vest, or if it vests, when it will vest. In this example, unlike in example (2), the divesting condition only applies to B, so B can be used as the measuring life. The condition cannot be violated by B after B is dead. The condition can only be violated during B's life. It can be said with absolute certainty that at B's death the condition will either have been violated or it will not have been violated. As a result, C's interest will vest during B's life if B violates the condition. Or, if B dies without violating the condition, C's interest will have failed to vest because the condition can never be violated after B's death. B's life is the validating life. C's interest is valid under the RAP.

(6) O conveys Blackacre to A for life, then to the first child of B to attain the age of twenty-one. Assume B has no children at the time of O's conveyance. O's conveyance creates a present possessory life estate in A followed by a remainder in one of B's children. The remainder is subject to a condition precedent (first child to reach twenty-one) so it is a contingent remainder in fee simple absolute. It cannot be stated with absolute certainty when B's first child will reach twenty-one. B might have no children. But it is absolutely certain that B cannot have children after she is dead. B is a validating life. It can be said with absolute certainty that the contingent remainder will vest or fail within twenty-one years after B's death. At B's death the contingent remainder will fail if B dies without children. Alternatively, if B dies with children it will be known with absolute certainty if any child reached twenty-one within twenty-one years after B's death. Therefore, it can be stated with absolute certainty that the contingent remainder will have vested or failed twenty-one years after B dies. The contingent remainder is therefore valid under the RAP.

(7) **O conveys Blackacre to A for life, then to the first child of B to attain the age of twenty-five. Assume B has no children at the time of O's conveyance.** This conveyance is the same as example (6), except the condition precedent requires the first child to attain the age of twenty-five. B might have a child, C, the day after the conveyance by O. That child could reach twenty-five while O, A and B are all alive. Alternatively, O, A and B could all die without B having any children. Additionally, the day after O's conveyance B could give birth to a child, and the next day O, A, B and any other potential measuring life could die. In this situation it is impossible for C to attain the age of twenty-five within twenty-one years of the death of everyone, so the contingent remainder is void under the RAP. As a result, A still has a present life estate but O now has a reversion in fee simple absolute which becomes a present possessory interest upon A's death.

(8) **O conveys Blackacre to A, but if Blackacre is ever used for the sale of alcohol then to O's wife, B, for life.** O's conveyance creates a present possessory fee simple subject to an executory limitation in A. This is a present estate not subject to the RAP. It also creates a shifting executory interest in a life estate in B which is subject to the RAP. At the time of O's original conveyance it is impossible to know when the condition (selling alcohol on Blackacre) will be violated, or if it will be violated at all. Therefore, neither O nor A can be the validating measuring life. However, what if B is used as the measuring life? B's interest is a life estate so it ends at her death. We know with absolute certainty at the time of O's original conveyance that B's executory interest will either become a present possessory interest (vest) or it will permanently fail at B's death. Consequently, B is a validating life and B's executory interest is valid under the RAP.

(9) **O conveys Blackacre to A, but if Blackacre is ever used for the sale of alcohol then to O's wife for life.** **Assume O is unmarried at the time of the conveyance but O marries B two days after the conveyance.** This conveyance is similar to example (8), except that the executory interest goes to O's wife rather than to a specific person. In the prior example, the exectuory interest went to O's wife who is specifically named (B). In this example, O is unmarried at the time of the conveyance so it is unknown at the time of O's conveyance who owns the executory interest. At the time of the conveyance it is unknown if O will ever marry, or if he does marry, who he will marry. Additionally, O could marry and get divorced and then remarry. First, try O or A as the measuring life. Both could die and one-hundred years after their deaths the condition could be violated. Alternatively, the condition could be violated while O and A are alive. O could divorce B, marry X and subsequently die. Ninety years later the owner of Blackacre could violate the condition at a time

when X is still alive. This would allow X's executory interest to potentially vest more than twenty-one years after all persons alive at the time of the original conveyance have died. Therefore, no measuring life exists at the time of the conveyance for which we can say with absolute certainty that within twenty-one years of that person's death the executory interest will definitely have vested or have failed. The executory interest is void under the RAP. As a result, A has a present fee simple absolute in Blackacre.

(10) **O conveys Blackacre to A for life then to A's widow. Assume A is married to B at the time of O's original conveyance.** O's conveyance creates a present life estate in A followed by a remainder in A's widow. At the time of the conveyance A is alive and married to B so no widow is known and ascertained at the time of the conveyance. Consequently, the interest in A's widow is a contingent remainder which is subject to the RAP. First, try O as a measuring life. At the time of O's original conveyance it is impossible to say with absolute certainty that the contingent remainder will vest or fail within twenty-one years of O's death. Therefore, O does not work as a validating life. Next try A as a measuring life. A and B could divorce so that at A's death B would not be A's widow. Alternatively, A and B could remain married until A's death so that B would be A's widow at his death. B could predecease A, and if A did not remarry there would be no widow at A's death. Finally, A and B could divorce and A could marry X. Then at A's death X would be his widow. Although it is unknown which scenario will occur at the time of the conveyance it will be known at A's death that either he leaves a widow or he does not leave a widow. In other words, the contingent remainder in A's widow will either vest at A's death or it will never vest. A is a validating life which makes the contingent remainder in A's widow valid under the RAP.

(11) **O conveys Blackacre to A, but if Blackacre is ever used for commercial purposes then to A's widow for life. Assume A is married to B at the time of O's original conveyance.** O's conveyance creates a present fee simple subject to an executory limitation in A which is not subject to the RAP. It also creates a shifting executory interest in a life estate in A's widow which is subject to the RAP. At the time of O's original conveyance it is unknown when the condition will be violated or if it will ever be violated. It could be violated the day after the conveyance, five-hundred years later or never. First, try O as a measuring life. At the time of O's original conveyance it is impossible to say with absolute certainty that the executory interest will vest or fail within twenty-one years of O's death, so O does not work as a validating life. Likewise, B can not be a validating life. A's widow cannot be used as a measuring life because we cannot say with absolute certainty who A's widow is until A's death. A could divorce B and remarry. Next, try A as a measuring life. A and B could divorce

so that at A's death B would not be A's widow. Alternatively, A and B could remain married until A's death so that B would be A's widow at his death. B could predecease A, and if A did not remarry there would be no widow at A's death. Finally, A and B could divorce and A could marry X. Then at A's death X would be his widow. It is possible the condition (commercial use) could be violated fifty years after A's death. Hence, A cannot be a validating life. The widow's executory interest is void under the RAP which means A has a present fee simple absolute estate in Blackacre.

(12) **O conveys Blackacre to A for life, then to B if B is alive at A's death.** O's conveyance creates a present possessory life estate in A which is not subject to the RAP. It also creates a contingent remainder in a fee simple absolute in B which is subject to a condition precedent (B must survive A) which is subject to the RAP. First, try O as a measuring life. It is impossible to know with absolute certainty when or if B will satisfy the condition precedent. Moreover, it is impossible to know if B's interest will vest during O's life or within twenty-one years of O's death, so O cannot be a validating life. Next, try A as a measuring life. At A's death it will be known with absolute certainty whether B is or is not alive. Therefore, we can say with absolute certainty that at A's death B's interest will have vested (if B is alive) or it will never vest (if B is deceased). Consequently, A can be a validating life which makes B's contingent remainder valid under the RAP. Could B also be used as a measuring life? At B's death his contingent remainder will have previously vested if A predeceased B or it will have permanently failed at B's death if B predeceases A. Therefore, either A or B can be used as a validating life which will render B's contingent remainder valid under the RAP.

The RAP and Class Gifts

Application of the RAP to class gifts can be confusing. First, it is useful to review the different types of class gifts that can be created (see Chapter Seven for a discussion of class gifts).

A transfer can be made to a group or class of individuals. If the group of individuals who make up the class can change (increase or decrease) subsequent to the original transfer it is a class gift.

Future interests that are class gifts subject to the RAP fall into one of the following categories:

Executory interest in a class
Contingent remainder in a class
Vested remainder subject to open

If a future interest in a class gift can become a present possessory estate at the natural end of the prior possessory estate it is a remainder. If all the class members are subject to a condition precedent it is a contingent remainder in a class gift. If at least one class member is known and ascertained and not subject to a condition precedent and additional persons can potentially enter the class, it is a vested remainder subject to open. Finally, if the future interest in the class can only become vested by prematurely terminating the prior possessory estate it is an executory interest in a class.

At common law the general rule is that the entire class gift is void under the RAP if the interest of any class member is void under the RAP. This **all or nothing rule** means that if it cannot be stated with absolute certainty that every class member's interest will vest or fail within the perpetuities period the entire class gift is void and stricken from the conveyance. This all or nothing rule applies equally to class gifts that are executory interests, contingent remainders or vested remainders subject to open.

It is important to know when a class gift closes in order to apply the RAP. A class gift closes when no additional class members can be added to the class. Additionally, a class can close due to application of the rule of convenience (see Chapter Seven for discussion of this rule). In some cases the rule of convenience can save a class gift that would otherwise violate the RAP. Keep in mind that it may not be known with absolute certainty whether the rule of convenience will apply. Therefore, the rule of convenience will not always save a class gift from violating the RAP.

A vested class member must be available to take the future interest at the end of the prior possessory estate for the rule of convenience to apply. If no vested class members exist at the time of the original conveyance it may be impossible to know with absolute certainty, at the time of the original conveyance, if a vested class member will or will not exist at the end of the prior possessory estate. If the prior possessory estate ends without any vested class member existing then the rule of convenience does not apply. In contrast, if a vested class member exists at the end of the prior possessory estate the rule of convenience will apply.

If a vested class member exists at the time of the original conveyance of the class gift, the rule of convenience will typically apply because it is known with absolute certainty at the time of the original conveyance that a vested class member will exist at the end of the prior possessory estate. If the vested class member survives the end of the prior possessory estate the surviving member will take the class gift under the rule of convenience. If the vested class member does not survive until the end of the prior possessory estate her descendants or will beneficiaries will inherit her interest.

Explanatory Examples

(1) **O conveys Blackacre to A for life, then to A's children in fee simple. Assume A has no children at the time of O's conveyance.** O's conveyance creates a present life estate in A which is not subject to the RAP, followed by a contingent remainder in a class gift in A's children which is subject to the RAP. The children have a contingent remainder because no children exist at the time of O's conveyance. A cannot have children after she is dead. Therefore, it can be said with absolute certainty that the interest in A's children will either vest at A's death (if A has any children) or it will fail at A's death (if A dies without ever having any children). The class must close at A's death since she cannot have children after her death. The interest in A's children is valid under the RAP based on the use of A as a validating life.

(2) **O conveys Blackacre to A for life, then to B's children in fee simple. Assume B has no children at the time of O's conveyance.** O's conveyance creates a present life estate in A which is not subject to the RAP, followed by a contingent remainder in a class gift in B's children which is subject to the RAP. The children have a contingent remainder because no children exist at the time of O's conveyance. B cannot have children after she is dead. Therefore, it can be said with absolute certainty that the interest in B's children will vest at B's death (if B has any children) or it will fail to vest at B's death (if B dies without ever having any children). The interest in B's children is valid under the RAP based on the use of B as a validating life. A will not work as a validating life in this example because B could die before A, with or without children, or B could die fifty years after A's death, with or without children.

(3) **O dies leaving a will which states that Blackacre shall go to my wife for life and then to my wife's children. Assume O is survived by his wife, A, who is ninety-five years old and who has never had any children.** O's will creates a present possessory life estate in A which is not subject to the RAP, followed by a future interest in a class gift in A's children. The children have a remainder because their interest can only become a possessory interest at the end of the prior possessory estate (at A's death). However, no children exist at O's death so the remainder is a contingent remainder which is subject to the RAP. A is alive at O's death so A can be used as a measuring life. A cannot have children after her death so it can be stated with absolute certainty that at A's death the contingent remainder will either have vested (if A had children) or failed (if A died without children). Consequently, the contingent remainder is valid under the RAP because A is a validating life. The fact that A is ninety-five years old is irrelevant for purposes of the RAP. The RAP deals in absolute certainty which

means that no matter how unlikely, all persons, regardless of age or health are considered capable of having children.

(4) **O dies leaving a will which states that Blackacre shall go to my wife for life and then to my wife's grandchildren. Assume O is survived by his wife, A, who is ninety-five years old and who has never had any children.** This conveyance is the same as example (4) except that A's grandchildren have a contingent remainder instead of her children. First, try A as a measuring life. A has no children at O's death but she could have children subsequent to O's death. A could then die leaving a living child. That child could then have a child (A's grandchild) thirty years after A's death. Alternatively, A could have a child and that child could give birth to a child (A's grandchild) during A's lifetime. Consequently, we cannot say with absolute certainty that the contingent remainder in A's grandchildren will definitely vest or fail within twenty-one years of A's death. If A has children they cannot be used as measuring lives because they were not in existence at O's death. In fact, no measuring life can be a validating life. The day after O dies A could give birth to a child and the next day everyone, except A and her husband, could die, and more than twenty-one years later A could give birth to a child. Hence, the contingent remainder in A's grandchildren is void under the RAP. As a result, the will gives A a present life estate and O retains a reversion in fee simple absolute. At A's death Blackacre goes to O's heirs or will beneficiaries, depending upon who owns the reversion in Blackacre. If the doctrine of destructibility of contingent remainders is in force would it save this class gift? The answer is no, because it is unknown at the time of the original conveyance whether the class gift will be a contingent remainder or a vested remainder subject to open at A's death. If no grandchildren are born by the time A dies the contingent remainder will be destroyed at A's death. However, it is possible for a grandchild to be born subsequent to O's original conveyance. Upon the birth of a grandchild the class gift changes from a contingent remainder to a vested remainder subject to open. A vested remainder subject to open is not subject to the doctrine of destructibility of contingent remainders. Therefore, the doctrine does not save the class gift from the RAP because at the time of O's original conveyance it cannot be stated with absolute certainty whether the doctrine will or will not apply at A's death. Likewise, the rule of convenience will not save the class gift from the RAP because it is unknown with absolute certainty if any class member will exist who can take Blackacre at A's death.

(5) **O conveys Blackacre to A for life, then to A's widow for life, then to A's children who are then living. Assume at the time of O's conveyance that A is married to B and they have one child, C.** O's conveyance creates a present possessory life estate in Blackacre in A which is not subject to the RAP. A's widow

A → LE

A's widow → cont. rem. in LE

A's Kids → cont. remainder ~~in both~~ subj to cond. prec.

has a remainder in Blackacre for life. A's widow is an unascertained person at the time of the conveyance because B could subsequently die and A could marry D, then A could die leaving D as the surviving widow at A's death. Therefore, A's widow has a contingent remainder. A's children have a contingent remainder in a class gift in Blackacre due to the existence of a condition precedent (children must survive A's widow). Both contingent remainders are subject to the RAP and each must be analyzed separately under the RAP. First, examine the contingent remainder in A's widow. If A is used as a measuring life the contingent remainder is valid under the RAP because it can be stated with absolute certainty that at A's death he will either be survived by a widow or he will not be survived by a widow. A is a validating life for this contingent remainder. Next, the contingent remainder in A's children must be analyzed under the RAP. The problem is that it cannot be stated with absolute certainty who A's widow is until A dies because B could die and A could remarry any number of times. A's widow cannot be definitively determined until A's death. For example, after O's original conveyance B and C could die the next day, A could subsequently marry X (who was born after O's conveyance) and A and X could give birth to Z. A and every other possible measuring life could die the next day leaving both X and Z alive. Z's interest will only vest if Z is alive at X's death. Z could predecease X or X could predecease Z. Alternatively, X could live twenty-five years after A and all other possible measuring lives die. Then, if X died leaving Z alive, Z's contingent remainder would have vested more than twenty-one years after the death of all possible measuring lives. Neither X nor Z can be used as measuring lives since they were both born after O's conveyance. Hence, it cannot be stated with absolute certainty when or if the contingent interest in A's children will vest, so the contingent remainder in A's children is void under the RAP. As a result, O's conveyance creates a present possessory life estate in Blackacre in A followed by a contingent remainder in Blackacre in A's widow. At the death of A's widow Blackacre goes back to O via a reversion. If the doctrine of destructibility of contingent remainders is in force will it save the class gift? The condition precedent rendering the class gift a contingent remainder is a survival condition. Only class members who are alive at the death of A's widow satisfy the condition precedent. Therefore, the contingent remainder in A's children will not become a different interest prior to the death of A's widow. Consequently, if the doctrine applies, we know with absolute certainty that the contingent remainder in A's children will either vest at the death of A's widow (if any of A's children are alive at that time), or the contingent remainder will be destroyed at the death of A's widow (if no surviving children are alive at that time). The problem is that A's widow is still unknown at the time of O's original conveyance, and it is unknown when A's widow will die. A's widow could die beyond the perpetuities period. As a result, the doctrine, if it is in force, does not save the class gift in A's children from the RAP. The rule of convenience also does not save the gift in A's children because it is unknown when A's widow will die. It is unknown at the time of the original conveyance if anyone will be vested such that they can take possession of Blackacre at the death of A's widow.

(6) **O conveys Blackacre to A for life, then to A's widow for life, then to A's children. Assume at the time of O's conveyance that A has never had any children.** This conveyance is essentially the same as the prior example except for the absence of the condition precedent (children must survive A's widow). Like the prior example, the contingent remainder in A's widow is valid under the RAP. A's children have a contingent remainder in a class gift because no children exist. First, try A as a measuring life. A cannot have children after she is dead. Therefore, it can be stated with absolute certainty that during A's lifetime she either will have children—whose interest would vest once they exist—or she will not have any children. Therefore, A is a validating life and the contingent remainder in A's children is valid under the RAP because it will either vest or fail during A's lifetime.

(7) **O drafts a will on January 1, 1950 which states that Blackacre shall go to A for life and then to A's lineal descendants provided they are alive on January 1, 2010. Assume O dies on June 1, 1960, while A is still alive and the will makes no mention of any other property nor does it contain a residuary clause.** O's will is effective at his death on June 1, 1960. The date the will was drafted is irrelevant. At O's death A has a present possessory life estate that is not subject to the RAP. A's lineal descendants have a contingent remainder in a class gift. It is unknown at the time of O's death what lineal descendants, if any, will be alive on January 1, 2010. First, try O as a measuring life. It is unknown whether the contingent remainder will vest or fail within twenty-one years of O's death. Likewise, A cannot be a validating life because A could die a week after O and then twenty-one years later we still would not know what lineal descendants would get Blackacre. Alternatively, A could live beyond January 1, 2010. Lineal descendants cannot be used as measuring lives unless they are alive at O's death. However, at the time of O's death we cannot say with absolute certainty whether any lineal descendant will or will not subsequently be alive on January 1, 2010. It is impossible to say with absolute certainty whether any lineal descendant will take Blackacre until January 1, 2010. The contingent remainder in A's lineal descendants is void under the RAP. Therefore, at A's death Blackacre goes to the owner of O's reversion. The will does not convey the reversion. Therefore, O is partially intestate, at least with regard to the reversion, so it passes to O's heirs via intestate succession.

(8) **O drafts a will on January 1, 1950 which states that Blackacre shall go to A for life and then to A's lineal descendants that are alive on January 1, 2010.** Assume O dies on June 1, 2000, while A is still alive and the will makes no mention of any other property nor does it contain a residuary clause. This example contains the same will as example (7). The only difference is the date O dies (June 1, 2000). At O's death, A has a present possessory life estate that is not subject to the RAP. A's lineal descendants have a contingent remainder in a class gift which will either vest or fail on January 1, 2010 because only lineal descendants who are alive on that date can become vested. First, try A as the measuring life. Even if A dies one second after O dies the interest in the lineal descendants will vest, if at all, on January 1, 2010. This date is less than twenty-one years after O's death so the contingent remainder in the lineal descendants will either vest or fail on that date. Therefore, it can be stated with absolute certainty that the lineal descendants' future interest will either vest or fail within the perpetuities period based on the use of A as a validating life. The contingent remainder is valid under the RAP.

(9) **O conveys Blackacre to A for life, then to O's heirs.** O's conveyance creates a present possessory life estate in A which is not subject to the RAP, followed by a contingent remainder in O's heirs which is subject to the RAP. O's heirs have a contingent remainder because O's heirs are unknown so long as O is alive. First, try O as a measuring life. It can be stated with absolute certainty at the time of the original conveyance that at O's death he will have heirs or he will not have heirs. The contingent remainder will either vest at O's death (if he has heirs alive at his death) or it will permanently fail (if he dies without any heirs), so A can be a validating life. This analysis is based on the premise that the doctrine of worthier title is abolished (see Chapter Sixteen). If the doctrine of worthier title is in force the analysis would change. Application of the doctrine would eliminate the contingent remainder in O's heirs. By operation of law the contingent remainder would become a reversion in the grantor (O) so no future interests subject to the RAP would exist.

(10) **O conveys Blackacre to A for life, then to A's heirs.** This example is like example (9) except the contingent remainder goes to A's heirs instead of to O's heirs. A is a validating life because it can be stated with absolute certainty at the time of O's original conveyance that at A's death he will have heirs or he will not have heirs. Therefore, the contingent remainder is valid under the RAP because it will either vest at A's death (if he has heirs alive at his death) or it will permanently fail (if he dies without any heirs). This analysis is based on the premise that the rule in Shelley's case is abolished (see Chapter Fifteen). If the Rule in Shelley's Case is in force the analysis would change. First, application of the Rule would eliminate the contingent remainder in A's heirs. By operation of

law it would become a remainder in A. Therefore, the conveyance would be altered to state, "O conveys Blackacre to A for life, then to A." A's future interest
is a vested remainder because A is known and ascertained and no condition precedent exists which must be satisfied before A's future interest can become vested.
Next, a merger would occur between the present life estate in A and the vested
remainder in A. Therefore, A would own Blackacre in fee simple and no future interest would exist. As a result, the RAP would not be applicable.

(11) **O conveys Blackacre to A for life, then to my heirs who are living at
the time of final distribution of my estate subsequent to my death. Assume the
doctrine of worthier title is not applicable.** O's conveyance creates a present life
estate in A which is not subject to the RAP, followed by a contingent remainder in O's heirs (class gift) which is subject to the RAP. The remainder is contingent because at the time of O's conveyance the heirs are not known and
ascertained (you cannot have heirs while you are alive), and a condition precedent exists (they must be alive at the final distribution of O's estate). At the
time of O's original conveyance it is not known with absolute certainty how long
it will take to complete the final distribution of O's estate. It could occur one
year after O's death or it could occur twenty-five years after O's death. Consequently, O cannot be a validating life. In fact, no measuring life will work as
a validating life. The day after O dies a lineal descendant of O could be born.
The next day every person alive at the time of O's original conveyance could
die. It could then take twenty-five years to complete the final distribution of
O's estate. Therefore, it cannot be stated with absolute certainty at the time of
O's original conveyance that the interest in O's heirs will vest or fail within
twenty-one years of the death of any measuring life. The interest in O's heirs
is void under the RAP. As a result, the conveyance is altered by operation of law
to provide a present life estate in A followed by a reversion in O.

(12) **O conveys Blackacre to A for life, then to the children of A. Assume that
at the time of O's conveyance A has one child, X.** O's conveyance creates a present possessory life estate in A which is not subject to the RAP. It also creates a class
gift in A's children. At the time of O's conveyance A has one child, X. X is not subject to any condition precedent so his interest is vested at the time of O's conveyance.
However, since A is still alive she could have more children after O's conveyance
so A's children have a vested remainder subject to open which is subject to the RAP.
Under the all or nothing rule the entire class gift is void under the RAP if the interest of any one class member is void under the RAP. If we use A as the measuring life we can state with absolute certainty that A will not have any children
after she dies. Therefore, any members of the class of A's children will have entered the class by A's death. No children can enter the class after A dies. Therefore, A is a validating life and the class gift in A's children is valid under the RAP.

(13) **O conveys Blackacre to A for life, then to my grandchildren who graduate from law school. Assume at the time of O's conveyance that O has one child, X, and X has a child, Z, who has graduated from law school.** O's conveyance creates a present life estate in A which is not subject to the RAP, and a remainder in O's grandchildren. The remainder is a class gift because the number of grandchildren can change. At the time of O's conveyance one grandchild, Z, is alive but additional grandchildren can enter the class subsequent to the conveyance. The class members are subject to a condition precedent (graduation from law school). However, Z already graduated from law school at the time of O's conveyance so Z's interest is vested. As already noted, other grandchildren can enter the class. These subsequent members of the class will all be subject to the condition precedent. The remainder in the grandchildren is a vested remainder subject to open which is subject to the RAP. In light of the all or nothing rule, if the interest of any one grandchild violates the RAP then the entire class gift is void. If we use X as a measuring life it can be stated with absolute certainty that X cannot have more children (who would be O's grandchildren) once X dies. However, the day after O's original conveyance a child, M, could be born to O. M could not be used as a measuring life because M was not alive at the time of O's conveyance. At some future date M could have a child who would be O's grandchild. It is impossible to know when M would have a child so we cannot say with absolute certainty whether the interests of all members of the class will vest or fail within twenty-one years of any measuring life. Moreover, in addition to being born, any child must satisfy the condition precedent (graduation from law school) before their interest can vest. It is impossible to know with absolute certainty when any future born grandchildren will graduate from law school. Based on these facts it would appear that the interest in the grandchildren is void under the RAP. But the interest will be saved if the rule of convenience (see Chapter Seven) applies because it provides for the class to close at the end of the prior possessory estate if any class member exists who can take present possession of Blackacre at that time. In this example, Z's interest is vested at the time of O's conveyance because he has already graduated from law school. Therefore, the rule of convenience will close the class at A's death. If Z is alive at A's death he will get Blackacre subject to sharing it with any other grandchildren who have graduated from law school prior to A's death. If Z predeceases A his heirs or will beneficiaries will take Z's interest in Blackacre. In light of the rule of convenience, A can be used as a validating life because it can be stated with absolute certainty that the class gift will vest at A's death.

(14) **O conveys Blackacre to A for life, then to my grandchildren who graduate from law school with the understanding that no grandchild shall take**

any interest in Blackacre until it is known whether all my grandchildren graduate from law school. Assume at the time of O's conveyance that O has one
child, X, and X has a child, Z, who has graduated from law school. This conveyance is essentially the same as example (13). However, the wording of this
grant expresses the grantor's intent that the class gift remain open until all
grandchildren have an opportunity to graduate from law school. Such intent
by the grantor eliminates application of the rule of convenience. That rule is
a default rule which applies generally unless the grant clearly expresses an intent that the class remain open until it is determined if all class members satisfy the condition precedent. Therefore, based on the analysis in the prior
example the class gift in O's grandchildren is void under the RAP. As a result,
at the end of A's life estate there is a reversion to O.

(15) O conveys Blackacre to A for life, then to O's children who become
doctors. Assume at the time of O's conveyance that O has two children, D and
E; and that D is a doctor and E is not a doctor. O's conveyance creates a present life estate in A which is not subject to the RAP followed by a remainder in
O's children. The remainder is subject to a condition precedent (must become
a doctor). This would make the remainder a contingent remainder if no children existed who were doctors at the time of O's original conveyance. However, D is a doctor at the time of the conveyance so O's children have a vested
remainder subject to open in a class gift. It cannot be stated with absolute certainty when or if D will become a doctor. Additionally, O could have more
children after her original conveyance. It is impossible to know when or if any
such later born children will become doctors. Like example (14), the class gift
would be void under the RAP but for the rule of convenience which preserves
the validity of the class gift. A can be used as a validating life because at A's
death the class will close pursuant to the rule of convenience. Indeed, at the time
of closing we can state with absolute certainty that a person exists to take Blackacre because D's interest was vested as of the date of O's original conveyance.

(16) O conveys Blackacre to A for life, then to O's children who become
doctors. Assume at the time of O's conveyance that O has two children, D and
E; and that neither of them are doctors. This example is the same as example
(15) except for one factual distinction. No class member has satisfied the condition precedent (become a doctor) at the time of O's original conveyance.
Therefore, in contrast to the prior example, here the class gift is a contingent
remainder rather than a vested remainder subject to open. At the time of O's
original conveyance it cannot be stated with absolute certainty whether any of
O's children (now existing or later born) will or will not become doctors. Additionally, no vested class member exists at the time of O's conveyance so it is
impossible to say with absolute certainty that the class will close under the rule

of convenience at the end of the prior possessory estate (at A's death). The rule of convenience only applies if a class member exists who can take a present possessory interest in Blackacre at A's death. At the time of O's conveyance it is unknown if a vested class member will exist at A's death. It is possible the interest of a class member could vest prior to A's death or within twenty-one years of A's death. However, it is equally possible that the first class member to complete medical school will do so more than twenty-one years after every possible measuring life dies. Consequently, unlike the prior example, the contingent remainder is void under the RAP, so at A's death Blackacre goes back to O via a reversion. If in force, will the doctrine of destructibility of contingent remainders (see Chapter Fourteen) save the contingent remainder in O's children from violating the RAP? The doctrine provides for destruction of the contingent remainder if no child has a vested interest at A's death. Additionally, if a child's interest does vest prior to A's death the rule of convenience will close the class at A's death. As a result, the remainder in O's children will either vest or be destroyed at A's death if the doctrine of destructibility of contingent remainders is in force. Therefore, A can be used as the validating life to render the contingent remainder valid under the RAP if both the rule of convenience and the doctrine of destructibility of contingent remainders are in force.

(17) **O conveys Blackacre to A for life and then to all members of O's 2003 property law class who take the Massachusetts Bar Exam. Assume at the time of O's conveyance forty-nine out of fifty people in the class have taken the Massachusetts Bar Exam.** O's conveyance creates a present life estate in A which is not subject to the RAP, followed by a remainder in the members of the 2003 property class. The remainder is subject to a condition precedent (taking the Massachusetts Bar Exam). Forty-nine class members have already vested (taken the exam) and one class member still has a contingent interest because she has not taken the Massachusetts Bar Exam. Therefore, the remainder is a vested remainder subject to open which is subject to the RAP. The class member who has not yet taken the Massachusetts Bar Exam can be used as a validating life. A person cannot take the exam after death. Therefore, at her death she will have either taken the Massachusetts Bar Exam or she will not have taken it. Hence, the vested remainder subject to open is valid under the RAP.

(18) **O conveys Blackacre to A for life and then to all members of O's 2003 property law class who pass the Massachusetts Bar Exam. Assume at the time of O's conveyance forty-nine out of fifty people in the class have passed the Massachusetts Bar Exam.** O's conveyance is the same as example (17) except for a change in the condition precedent. In the prior example, the condition precedent was taking the Massachusetts Bar Exam. In this example, the con-

dition precedent is passing the Massachusetts Bar Exam. Although unlikely, it is possible that the last class member could take the Massachusetts Bar Exam, she could die the next day and due to administrative delays the exam is not graded for twenty-three years. It will not be known if she passed the exam until it is graded. Consequently, it is possible for all potential measuring lives to die the day after she takes the bar exam and due to administrative delay it is not graded for twenty-three years. Then it will not be known until twenty-three years later if she passed or failed the exam. Hence, the class gift would appear to be void under the RAP. Nevertheless, this is a situation where the class gift is saved by the rule of convenience. Forty-nine class members are vested at the time of O's original conveyance. Therefore, at the end of the prior possessory estate (at A's death) the rule of convenience will close the class without regard to whether the remaining class member has passed the exam. A can be used as a validating life so the class gift is valid under the RAP.

(19) **O conveys Blackacre to A for life, then to her surviving children if they reach twenty-five years old. Assume at the time of O's conveyance that A does not have any children.** O's conveyance creates a present life estate in A which is not subject to the RAP, followed by a contingent remainder in her children which is subject the RAP. The children's interest is subject to two precedent conditions. The children must survive A and they must reach twenty-five years old. Additionally, at the time of O's original conveyance A does not have any children. First, try A as a measuring life. A could have a child, X, and then A and all possible measuring lives could die the next day. Under these facts, X's interest would not vest within twenty-one years of the death of all the measuring lives since A must reach twenty-five to satisfy the condition precedent. Alternatively, X could reach twenty-five during A's lifetime. Hence, it cannot be stated with absolute certainty that the children's future interest will either vest or fail within the perpetuities period. The analysis will be the same if O is used as a measuring life, so the contingent remainder is void under the RAP. The rule of convenience will not save the class gift in A's children because at the time of O's original conveyance no class member existed. It is possible A will not have any children who reach twenty-five at her death. If this happens the rule of convenience will not close the class at A's death because no vested class member exists. Upon invalidation of the class gift under the RAP the conveyance is altered so that A has a present life estate followed by a reversion in O. If the doctrine of destructibility of contingent remainders is in force will it save the class gift? Under the doctrine the contingent remainder in A's children will either vest at A's death (if a twenty-five year old child existed) or be destroyed (if no class members have reached twenty-five). If a class member was twenty-five at A's death the rule of convenience would close the class at that time. A

survival condition exists for A's children (must survive A) so during A's lifetime the contingent remainder in A's children cannot be converted into a vested remainder subject to open. Hence, if the doctrine of destructibility of contingent remainders is in force it can be stated with absolute certainty that the contingent remainder in A's children will vest or be destroyed at A's death. Therefore, the class gift would be valid under the RAP if A is used as a validating life and the doctrine of destructibility of contingent remainders is in force.

> **Modern Status of the RAP:**
> **The Cy Pres Doctrine**

Some states have modified the common law RAP to avoid the harsh nature of its application. One such modification is the application of an equitable doctrine which allows a transfer to be judicially modified so that it is valid under the RAP. Typically, such modification must remain consistent with the grantor's intent (or at least be as close as possible to the grantor's intent). This doctrine, referred to as *cy pres*, is currently utilized only in a minority of states.

Explanatory Example

O conveys Blackacre to A for life, then to the first child of B to attain the age of twenty-five years old. Assume B has no children at the time of O's conveyance. This is an explanatory example that was previously discussed above. Since B has no children at the time of the conveyance B's children have a contingent remainder. B might have a child, C, the day after the conveyance by O. That child could reach twenty-five while O, A and B are all alive. Alternatively, O, A and B could all die without B having any children. Additionally, the day after O's conveyance B could give birth to a child and the next day O, A, B and any other potential measuring life could die. In that situation it is impossible for C to attain the age of twenty-five within twenty-one years of the death of everyone. Hence, the contingent remainder is void under the RAP. In a jurisdiction which has adopted the cy pres doctrine the court could change the twenty-five year condition to a twenty-one year condition. This change makes the conveyance valid under the RAP while still being relatively consistent with the grantor's intent.

> **Modern Status of the RAP:**
> **The Wait and See Doctrine**

A second modification of the common law RAP is the *wait and see doctrine* which has been enacted, in one form or another, in a majority of states. In its most basic form the doctrine requires everyone to wait to see what actually happens after a transfer. This allows the focus to be on what actually happens rather than on what might hypothetically happen. The doctrine is applied as follows:

- Determine if an interest exists that is void under the common law RAP
- If such an interest exists, instead of allowing the RAP to destroy it, everyone would wait to see what actually happens to the interest
- If the interest ultimately vests within the perpetuities period it is valid
- If the interest ultimately does not vest within the perpetuities period it is void

Explanatory Example

O conveys Blackacre to A for life, then to the first child of B to attain the age of twenty-five years old. Assume B has no children at the time of O's conveyance. This is the same explanatory example used previously under the section on the cy pres doctrine. The children of B have a contingent remainder which is void under the common law RAP. However, if the wait and see doctrine is used the grantees must wait to see whether the contingent remainder does or does not vest within the perpetuities period. For example, if B has an only child, X, who reaches twenty-five during A's lifetime X's interest has vested within the perpetuities period if A is used as the measuring life (the RAP would not invalidate X's interest if the wait and see doctrine applied). But what if B never has a child or B has a child but she does not reach twenty-five within twenty-one years after the death of any potential measuring life? In both of these situations the contingent remainder is void under the RAP and it would not be saved by the wait and see doctrine because it did not in fact vest within the perpetuities period. Ultimately, the wait and see doctrine requires everyone to wait to see what happens. In contrast, the common law RAP requires an immediate determination to be made at the time of the original conveyance with regard to whether an interest is valid or void.

> **Modern Status of the RAP:**
> **A Combined Approach**
> **under the Uniform**
> **Statutory RAP (USRAP)**

Some states have replaced the common law RAP with a uniform statutory rule called the Uniform Statutory Rule Against Perpetuities (USRAP). The USRAP is a combination of the common law RAP, the cy pres doctrine and the wait and see doctrine.

The USRAP can be summarized as follows:

(1) If a future interest is valid under the common law RAP it is valid under the USRAP

(2) If a future interest is void under the common law RAP then a ninety year wait and see period applies:

    (a) The ninety year period starts to run at the time of the original transfer

    (b) Everyone must wait to see if the interest actually vests or terminates within the ninety year waiting period

(3) If an interest is not valid under either the common law RAP or the ninety year wait and see period, it can be reformed by a court, consistent with the transferor's intent, to make it valid

Explanatory Examples

(1) **O wills Blackacre to A for life, remainder to A's children who attain the age of twenty-one years old. Assume A has no children at O's death.** The remainder in A's children is a contingent remainder subject to the RAP. It is a contingent remainder because no children exist at O's death and a condition precedent applies (A's children must reach twenty-one). Try A as a measuring life. A cannot have any children after she is dead. Therefore, it can be stated with absolute certainty that twenty-one years after A's death any children will have either reached twenty-one years old or they will never reach that age because they are deceased. It is impossible for any child of A to attain the age of twenty-one more than twenty-one years after A's death. Therefore, the contingent remainder in A's children is valid under the common law RAP. The USRAP does not change this result. Consequently, the interest is also valid under the USRAP.

(2) **O conveys Blackacre to A for life, then to the first child of B to attain the age of twenty-five years old. Assume B has no children at the time of O's conveyance.** This is an explanatory example that was previously discussed above. Since B has no children at the time of the conveyance and a condition precedent applies (must attain twenty-five) B's children have a contingent remainder. B might have a child, C, the day after the conveyance by O. That

child could reach twenty-five while O, A and B are all alive. Alternatively, O, A and B could all die without B having any children. Additionally, the day after O's conveyance B could give birth to a child and the next day O, A, B and any other potential measuring life could die. In this situation it is impossible for C to attain the age of twenty-five within twenty-one years of the death of everyone. Hence, the contingent remainder is void under the common law RAP. If the USRAP applies, the parties would have to wait for up to ninety years to see if B has any children who reach twenty-five. If B has a child that reaches twenty-five within the ninety year period the child's interest will immediately vest upon reaching twenty-five. In most situations the parties will not have to actually wait the full ninety years. For example, if B dies without children ten years after O's original conveyance the interest in B's children has permanently failed at that point because B cannot have any children after her death. Alternatively, assume at B's death she has a five year old child, Y, and a ten year old child, Z. Z will either reach twenty-five in fifteen years or he will not. If Z dies before reaching twenty-five then the parties must wait five more years to see if Y reaches twenty-five or dies before that age. In either situation the waiting period will be less than ninety years.

(3) **O conveys Blackacre to A for life, then to my heirs who are living at the time of final distribution of my estate subsequent to my death. Assume the doctrine of worthier title is not applicable.** O's conveyance creates a present life estate in A followed by a contingent remainder in O's heirs (class gift) which is subject to the RAP. The remainder is contingent because at the time of O's conveyance the heirs are not known and ascertained (you cannot have heirs while you are alive), and a condition precedent exists (heirs must be alive at the final distribution of O's estate). At the time of O's original conveyance it is not known with absolute certainty how long it will take to complete the final distribution of O's estate. It could occur within a year after O's death, or it could occur twenty-five years after O's death. Consequently, O cannot be used as the validating life nor will any other measuring life work. The day after O dies a lineal descendant of O could be born. The next day every person alive at the time of O's original conveyance could die. It could then take twenty-five years to complete the final distribution of O's estate. Therefore, it cannot be stated with absolute certainty at the time of O's original conveyance that the interest in O's heirs will vest or fail within twenty-one years of the death of any measuring life. The contingent remainder in O's heirs is therefore void under the common law RAP. If the USRAP applies the parties would have to wait for up to ninety years to see when the final distribution of the estate takes place. It is highly unlikely that it would take ninety years to finalize the estate. Therefore, the contingent remainder in the heirs will most likely vest or fail in a period

of time substantially shorter than the ninety year wait and see period under the USRAP.

(4) **O wills Blackacre to A for life, then one hundred years after A's death to A's then living lineal descendants.** The interest in A's lineal descendants is subject to a contingency. They must be alive one hundred years after A's death. It is impossible to know with absolute certainty at O's death what, if any, lineal descendants will be alive one-hundred years after A's death. A's lineal descendants have an executory interest that is void under the common law RAP. If the USRAP applies the parties will have to wait ninety years from O's death to see if the interest in A's lineal descendants vests. However, we know the interest will not vest within the ninety year wait and see period because the conveyance requires waiting one-hundred years after A's death. In this situation, under the USRAP, a court may modify the conveyance so that it is valid. In this example, a court may modify the contingency from one-hundred years after A's death to ninety years after O's death. The interest would now come within the wait and see period under the USRAP.

Review Questions

(1) Is the RAP a rule of law that makes the transferor's intent irrelevant?

(2) What future interests are subject to the RAP?

(3) What interests are not subject to the RAP?

(4) What happens to a future interest that violates the RAP?

(5) When is a transfer analyzed under the RAP?

(6) What is a "life in being" or a "measuring life"?

(7) Can a legal person such as a corporation be a measuring life?

(8) What is a "validating life"?

(9) What is the "perpetuities period"?

(10) What is the minimum number of measuring lives that must be validating lives for an interest to be valid under the RAP?

(11) Must each interest in a transfer or conveyance subject to the RAP be evaluated separately under the RAP?

(12) Can a different validating life be used for different interests in the same transfer that are each subject to the RAP?

(13) Can the same validating life be used for different interests in the same transfer that are each subject to the RAP?

(14) Is application of the RAP based on the likelihood or the absolute certainty that an interest subject to the RAP will vest, fail, or either vest or fail during the perpetuities period?

(15) What is the "all or nothing rule" under the RAP?

(16) What is the "cy pres" doctrine?

(17) What is the "wait and see" doctrine"?

(18) What is the USRAP?

(19) O conveys Blackacre to A, but if Blackacre is ever used for commercial purposes it shall automatically go to B. Does the common law RAP affect this conveyance?

(20) O conveys Blackacre to A, but if Blackacre is ever used for commercial purposes it shall automatically go to B for life. Does the common law RAP affect this conveyance?

(21) O conveys Blackacre to A, but if Blackacre is ever used for commercial purposes it shall automatically go to A's children. Does the common law RAP affect this conveyance?

Review Questions: Answers

(1) Yes.

(2) Contingent remainder; vested remainder subject to open; and executory interest.

(3) Indefeasibly vested remainder; vested remainder subject to complete defeasance; possibility of reverter; right of entry; reversion; present estate; fee tail (the future interests in lineal descendants who take under the fee tail).

(4) Typically it is void so the transfer is read as if the void interest never existed.

(5) At the time of the original conveyance. For inter vivos transfers this is at the time of the transfer. For a gift this is at the time the gift is effective. For a will this is at the decedent's death.

(6) A "life in being" (also called "measuring life") is any natural person who actually existed at the time the interest subject to the RAP was created, or a person conceived (but not yet born) at the time the interest subject to the RAP was created provided he or she is subsequently born alive.

(7) No. Only a natural person (a human) can be a measuring life.

(8) A "measuring life" that renders an interest subject to the RAP valid is called a "validating life."

(9) The "perpetuities period" is the time period during which you must determine with absolute certainty what will happen to an interest subject to the RAP. The perpetuities period is the measuring life plus twenty-one years. However, there is one exception—the perpetuities period is extended to include periods of actual gestation which is the time between conception and birth if a conceived but unborn child is used as the measuring life. The twenty-one year period starts to run when the child is actually born.

(10) One.

(11) Yes.

(12) Yes.

(13) Yes.

(14) Absolute certainty.

(15) At common law the "all or nothing rule" states that an entire class gift is void under the RAP if the interest of any class member is void under the RAP. This all or nothing rule means that if it cannot be stated with absolute certainty that every class member's interest will vest or fail within the perpetuities period the entire class gift is void and stricken from the conveyance. This all or nothing rule applies equally to class gifts that are executory interests, contingent remainders or vested remainders subject to open.

(16) The "cy pres" doctrine is an equitable doctrine that allows a court to limit the harshness of the RAP. The doctrine allows a court to modify an interest that is invalid under the RAP so that it is valid under the RAP. Typically, such modification must remain consistent with the transferor's intent (or at least be as close as possible to the transferor's intent).

(17) The "wait and see" doctrine is a doctrine that allows a court to minimize the harshness of the RAP. It requires waiting to see what actually happens during the perpetuities period. This allows the focus to be on what actually happens rather than on what might hypothetically happen. If an interest that is void under the RAP actually vests during the perpetuities period, it is valid under the wait and see doctrine.

(18) Some states have replaced the common law RAP with a uniform statutory rule called the Uniform Statutory Rule Against Perpetuities (USRAP). The USRAP is a combination of the common law RAP, the cy pres doctrine and the wait and see doctrine. If a future interest is valid under the common law RAP it is valid under the USRAP. If a future interest is void under the common law RAP then a ninety year wait and see period applies. Additionally, if an interest is invalid under either the common law RAP or the ninety year wait and see period, it can be reformed by a court, consistent with the transferor's intent, to make it valid.

(19) Yes. A has a present fee simple subject to an executory interest estate in Blackacre. The RAP does not apply to this estate because it is a present estate. B has a shifting executory interest in a fee simple absolute estate in Blackacre. Executory interests are subject to the RAP. At the time of O's original conveyance it cannot be stated with absolute certainty if or when the commercial use condition will be violated. It could be violated by A, it could be violated after A is dead, it could be violated thirty years after all possible measuring lives are dead, or it could never be violated. Therefore, B's executory interest is void under the RAP so the original conveyance becomes a present fee simple absolute estate in A.

(20) No. This is the same conveyance as the prior problem except that B has a shifting executory interest in a life estate instead of in a fee simple absolute. B can be used as a validating life because the commercial use condition will or will not be violated by B's death. If it is violated during B's lifetime Blackacre will immediately go to B for his remaining lifetime. If the commercial use condition is not violated during B's lifetime, B's executory interest will fail because it can never become a present possessory estate once B is dead. The RAP does not affect this conveyance.

(21) No. This is the same conveyance as problem (19) above, except the shifting executory interest is a class gift in A's children. A can be used as a val-

idating life. It can be stated with absolute certainty that A will either have children or she will never have had children at her death. The interest in A's children will either vest at A's death (if A has any children) or it will fail at A's death (if she never had any children). The interest in A's children cannot vest subsequent to A's death. The RAP does not affect this conveyance.

Summary of Main Points

A. Rule Against Perpetuities (RAP)—background
1. The RAP is a rule of law and, therefore, the intent of the transferor is generally irrelevant
2. The RAP eliminates certain contingent future interests by operation of law
3. The effect of the RAP is to minimize long-term dead hand control of property which can adversely affect marketability of the property

B. What property interests are subject to the RAP
1. The following interests are subject to the RAP
    a. Contingent remainder
    b. Vested remainder subject to open
    c. Executory interest
    d. In gross option to purchase land
2. Transferees not subject to the RAP
    a. A future interest owned by a governmental entity is generally not subject to the RAP
    b. A future interest given to a charitable organization is typically not subject to the RAP provided the interest is followed by an interest in another charitable organization
3. Interests not subject to the RAP
    a. Indefeasibly vested remainder
    b. Vested remainder subject to complete defeasance
    c. Possibility of reverter
    d. Right of entry
    e. Reversion
    f. Present estate
    g. Fee tail (future interest in the lineal descendants who take under a fee tail)

C. Statement of the common law RAP
1. No interest is good unless it must vest, if at all, not later than twenty-one years after some life in being at the creation of the interest

D. Definition of terms in the common law RAP
1. "Vest"
    a. A contingent remainder will vest when the transferee of the remainder is both known and ascertained, and no condition precedent must be satisfied before the transferee can take the interest
        i. A contingent remainder can vest before the transferee takes possession such as when events subsequent to the original

        transfer convert the contingent remainder into a vested remainder before it becomes a present possessory interest

    b. A vested remainder subject to open vests when all potential class members are vested

        i. This happens when all class members are known and ascertained, and no condition precedent exists which must be satisfied by any class member

    c. An executory interest generally will vest either when

        i. It becomes a present possessory interest; or

        ii. It is converted into a vested remainder

  2. "Life in being" (also called a measuring life)

    a. Any natural person (human) who is alive at the time the interest subject to the RAP is created can potentially be used as a measuring life

    b. A natural person who is conceived (but not yet born) at the time the interest subject to the RAP is created can potentially be used as a measuring life provided they are subsequently born alive

    c. A corporation or other legal person cannot be used as a measuring life

    d. A measuring life that renders an interest valid under the RAP is called a validating life

  3. "Not later than twenty-one years after some life in being at the creation of the interest" (called the perpetuities period)

    a. The perpetuities period is the time period during which you must determine with absolute certainty what will happen to the interest subject to the RAP

    b. The perpetuities period is a measuring life plus twenty-one years

        i. The perpetuities period can be extended to include periods of actual gestation which is the time between conception and birth if a conceived but unborn child is used as the measuring life; the twenty-one year period will start to run when the child is actually born

E. Applying the common law RAP

  1. An interest subject to the RAP will violate the RAP if it cannot be stated with absolute certainty that during the perpetuities period the interest will

    a. Vest;

    b. Fail; or

    c. Either vest or fail

F. Guidelines for applying the RAP

1. The RAP analysis is performed at the time the interest subject to the RAP is originally created
    a. For an inter vivos transfer it is at the time of the transfer
    b. For a gift it is at the time the gift is effective
    c. For a will it is at the decedent's death
2. An interest subject to the RAP is valid under the RAP if any of the following is true
    a. At the time the interest was created a natural person existed about whom we could say we know with absolute certainty that during that person's life the interest will vest
    b. At the time the interest was created a natural person existed about whom we could say we know with absolute certainty that during that person's life the interest will fail
    c. At the time the interest was created a natural person existed about whom we could say
        i.   We do not know with absolute certainty that during that person's life the interest will vest;
        ii. We do not know with absolute certainty that during that person's life the interest will fail; but
        iii. We can say with absolute certainty that it will either vest or fail during that person's life
    d. At the time the interest was created a natural person existed about whom we could say we know with absolute certainty that the interest will vest within twenty-one years of that person's death
    e. At the time the interest was created a natural person existed about whom we could say we know with absolute certainty that the interest will fail within twenty-one years of that person's death
    f. At the time the interest was created a natural person existed about whom we could say we know with absolute certainty that the interest will vest during that person's life or within twenty-one years after that person's death
    g. At the time the interest was created a natural person existed about whom we could say we know with absolute certainty that the interest will fail during that person's life or within twenty-one years after that person's death
    h. At the time the interest was created a natural person existed about whom we could say
        i.   We do not know with absolute certainty that during that person's life or within twenty-one years after that person's death the interest will vest;

        ii. We do not know with absolute certainty that during that person's life or within twenty-one years after that person's death the interest will fail; but

       iii. We can say with absolute certainty that it will either vest or fail during that person's life or within twenty-one years after that person's death

G. Things to keep in mind when applying the common law RAP

  1. Each interest subject to the RAP must be evaluated separately

  2. Each interest is evaluated at the time it is created

  3. Testamentary interests are created at the time the testator dies, not when the will is drafted or executed

  4. You cannot get married after you are dead

  5. You cannot have children after you are dead

  6. Additional children cannot become members of a class after the parents are deceased because no more children can be born after the parents are dead

  7. Any living person is presumed fertile for purposes of having children regardless of age or health concerns

  8. The RAP is not applied based on probabilities

  9. The RAP is based on knowing to an absolute certainty whether an interest will vest or fail during the perpetuities period

  10. A measuring life must be a natural person who is alive (or conceived) at the time of the original transfer

  11. Anyone who is born after the original transfer cannot be a measuring life unless they were conceived at the time of the original transfer

  12. Generally, any shifting executory interest which follows a fee simple defeasible estate is void under the RAP unless the executory interest is in a life estate

H. Class gifts and the common law RAP

  1. A class gift can be a vested remainder subject to open, an executory interest or a contingent remainder

  2. The "all or nothing rule" applies to all class gifts that are subject to the RAP

    a. Under the all or nothing rule the entire gift to all class members is void under the RAP unless it can be stated with absolute certainty at the time of the original transfer that every class member's interest will vest or fail during the perpetuities period

I. What happens when a future interest violates the common law RAP

  1. Under the "doctrine of separability" a transfer is rewritten without the void interest that violates the RAP

        a.   Exception—under the "doctrine of infectious invalidity" an entire transfer may be stricken by a court if the interest that is void under the RAP is essential to the transferor's intent such that elimination of the void interest totally frustrates the transferor's intent

   2.   The merger doctrine may apply after elimination of an interest that is void under the RAP

   3.   The doctrine of destructibility of contingent remainders, if in force, may save a contingent remainder from violating the RAP

   4.   The rule of convenience may save a class gift from violating the RAP

J.   Modern status of the RAP

   1.   The harshness of the common law RAP has been reduced by the following

        a.   The "cy pres doctrine," which allows a court to modify a transfer that violates the RAP so that it is valid but still consistent with the original transferor's intent

        b.   The "wait & see doctrine," which requires waiting and seeing what actually happens during the perpetuities period instead of trying to guess what might happen

            i.   If an interest subject to the RAP ends up actually vesting within the perpetuities period it is saved by the wait & see doctrine

           ii.   If an interest subject to the RAP ends up not vesting during the perpetuities period it is not saved by the wait & see doctrine

   2.   Uniform statutory rule against perpetuities (USRAP)

        a.   The USRAP is a combination of the common law RAP, the cy pres doctrine, and the wait and see doctrine

        b.   If an interest is valid under the common law RAP then it is valid under the USRAP

        c.   If an interest is void under the common law RAP then the parties must wait to see if the interest actually vests or terminates within the ninety year waiting period which starts to run when the original transferor created the interest subject to the RAP

        d.   If an interest is invalid under either the common law RAP or the ninety year wait and see period, it can be modified by a court, consistent with the transferor's intent, to make it valid

Application of the Common Law RAP in a "Nutshell"

(1) Identify the existence of any contingent remainders, executory interests and vested remainders subject to open

(2) Evaluate each future interest separately under the RAP

(3) Evaluation of each future interest under the RAP is made at the time it was created by the original transfer

(4) Identify measuring lives who must be natural persons alive at the time of the transfer (or conceived at the time of the transfer and subsequently born alive) that are mentioned in the original transfer or associated with the original transfer

(5) Try each measuring life with each future interest subject to the RAP

(6) If a future interest is valid based on at least one measuring life it is valid under the RAP

(7) If a future interest is invalid under all measuring lives it is void under the RAP

(8) Rewrite the original conveyance by striking out any future interests that are void under the RAP

Chapter Eighteen

Sample Exam Questions with Answers and Explanations

The following fifty questions should be answered in ninety minutes under test conditions. After answering all of the questions compare your answers to the answers and explanations at the end of the chapter. Assume the common law Rule Against Perpetuities (RAP) applies.

Sample Exam Questions

Please consider the following conveyance for Questions 1–2

Grantor conveys Blackacre to A and his heirs so long as A does not marry B, but if A does marry B, then to C forever.

(1) Which of the following *most* completely describes C's interest if all the parties are alive and A is unmarried?

    (a) C has a contingent remainder in fee simple absolute

    (b) C has a possibility of reverter

    (c) C has a springing executory interest

    (d) C has a shifting executory interest

(2) Which of the following statements is the *most* correct if all the parties are alive and A is unmarried?

    (a) C's interest violates the RAP

    (b) The marriage condition is an unenforceable direct restraint on alienation

    (c) A's heirs have a future interest in Blackacre

    (d) C has a future interest in a fee simple absolute

Please consider the following conveyance for Questions 3–6

Owner conveys Blackacre to Arnold and his heirs so long as Arnold does not go into the real estate business with Bill, but if Arnold does go into the real estate business with Bill, then to Carl for his lifetime.

(3) Which of the following is the *most* correct, assuming all the parties are alive and Arnold has not entered the real estate business with Bill?

    (a) Arnold has a contingent remainder in fee simple absolute

    (b) Carl has a springing executory interest

    (c) Arnold has a fee simple interest

    (d) Carl has a contingent remainder in fee simple absolute

(4) Which of the following statements is *true* if all the parties are alive and Arnold has not entered the real estate business with Bill?

    (a) Carl's interest violates the RAP

    (b) The condition on the conveyance to Arnold is unenforceable as a direct restraint on alienation

    (c) Carl's interest is a shifting executory interest

    (d) Carl's interest is an alternate contingent remainder

(5) Which of the following *most* correctly describes Owner's interest if all the parties are alive and Arnold has not entered the real estate business with Bill?

    (a) Contingent remainder in fee simple

    (b) Shifting executory interest

    (c) Right of entry

    (d) None of the above

(6) Which of the following statements is *true*, assuming all the parties are alive and Arnold has not entered the real estate business with Bill?

    (a) Carl has a contingent interest in Blackacre which will never become a present possessory estate

    (b) Owner or his heirs will eventually recover possession of Blackacre

    (c) Carl's interest in Blackacre may become a present interest

    (d) Carl's interest in Blackacre violates the RAP

Please consider the following conveyance for Questions 7–8

Sandra conveys Blackacre to Elmer and his heirs until such time as Blackacre ceases to be used as a farm, then to Robert. Assume all the parties are alive and Blackacre is being used as a farm.

(7) Which of the following is *incorrect*?

    (a) The conveyance creates a reversionary interest

    (b) The conveyance creates a defeasible fee

    (c) The conveyance creates an executory interest in Robert

    (d) The conveyance creates a future interest in Sandra

(8) Which of the following *most* accurately describes Elmer's interest in Blackacre?

    (a) A contingent present possessory estate

    (b) A vested remainder subject to divestment

(c) A present possessory estate

(d) A contingent remainder

Please consider the following conveyance for Questions 9–11

Grantor conveys Blackacre to Alfonso for life, remainder to Ben and his heirs provided that Ben becomes an attorney during Alfonso's lifetime, but if Ben does not become an attorney during Alfonso's lifetime, then to Kathy. Assume all the parties are alive and that Ben is a first year law student at Suffolk Law School.

(9) Which of the following *best* describes Ben's interest in Blackacre?

(a) A reversion

(b) A contingent remainder

(c) An indefeasibly vested remainder

(d) A vested remainder subject to complete defeasance

(10) Which of the following *best* describes Kathy's interest in Blackacre?

(a) A shifting executory interest

(b) A contingent future interest

(c) A fee simple subject to a condition subsequent

(d) A springing executory interest

(11) Which of the following is the *most* correct?

(a) Alfonso's estate violates the RAP

(b) Kathy has a contingent future interest

(c) Ben's estate violates the RAP

(d) Kathy's estate violates the RAP

(12) Oswald makes the following conveyance of his ranch known as The Ponderosa:

".... to Beatrice and her heirs, on the condition that if Beatrice or her heirs ever sells or attempts to sell The Ponderosa, all right, title and interest in The Ponderosa shall automatically vest in Andrew and his heirs."

What interest does Andrew have in The Ponderosa?

(a) A possibility of reverter

(b) A contingent future interest

(c) A right of entry

(d) None of the above

(13) Oscar, the husband of Amy, devises Blackacre in his will to Amy, his wife, for life, then to such of their children who graduate from Suffolk Law School. At Oscar's death Amy is alive and they have two surviving children currently attending high school. What interest, if any, do the children have in Blackacre?

(a) They have future interests

(b) They have no interest because their interest is void under the RAP

(c) They have vested remainders subject to open

(d) They have vested remainders subject to divestment

(14) Sheldon makes the following devise in his will:

"I, Sheldon, hereby bequeath and devise my summer home to my only child, Ruth, for her lifetime, and following her death to my beloved grandchildren then living."

At Sheldon's death Ruth has three children. At Sheldon's death, which of the following *best* describes the interest the grandchildren have in the summer home?

(a) A contingent remainder

(b) A vested remainder subject to open

(c) Alternative contingent remainders

(d) An executory interest

Please consider the following conveyance for Questions 15–17

Mindy conveys Blackacre to Larry for life, remainder to Larry's children.

(15) *Assume the following for this question only*: Larry had one child, Andrew, living at the time of Mindy's conveyance, which of the following is the *most* correct?

(a) Andrew has a partially vested remainder

(b) A contingent remainder exists in Larry's children since Larry could have additional children in the future

(c) Larry's children, both born and unborn, have a vested remainder in Blackacre

(d) Mindy has a possibility of reverter in Blackacre

(16) *Assume the following for this question only*: Larry had one child, Alvin, living at the time of Mindy's conveyance. Alvin predeceased Larry, and left a will that conveyed all his property to his wife, Sara. Larry subsequently had four additional children who were alive at Larry's death. At Larry's death which of the following is the *most* correct?

(a) The interest in Larry's children is void under the RAP

(b) Each child living at Larry's death owns a 1/4 share of Blackacre

(c) Each child living at Larry's death owns a 1/5 share of Blackacre

(d) Each child living at Larry's death owns a 1/6 share of Blackacre

(17) *Assume the following for this question only*: Larry had no children living at the time of Mindy's conveyance. Larry subsequently has four children but only two of these children survive Larry. At Larry's death which of the following is the *most* correct?

(a) The interest in Larry's children is void under the RAP

(b) Each child living at Larry's death owns a 1/5 share of Blackacre

(c) Each child living at Larry's death owns a 1/2 share of Blackacre

(d) Each child living at Larry's death owns a 1/4 share of Blackacre

(18) Elston conveys Blackacre to Roy for his life, remainder to the heirs of Kevin. Assuming Kevin and Roy are alive at the time of the conveyance, which of the following *best* describes the property interest of the "heirs of Kevin" at the time of the conveyance?

   (a) A vested remainder in fee simple

   (b) A contingent remainder in fee simple

   (c) A vested remainder subject to complete defeasance

   (d) Void under the RAP

Please consider the following conveyance for Questions 19–20

Molly conveys Blackacre to Andy and his heirs until such time as Blackacre ceases to be used as a farm, then to Bob for life if Bob is then alive. Assume all the parties are alive and Blackacre is being used as a farm.

(19) Which of the following is *not* correct?

   (a) The conveyance creates a reversionary interest in Bob

   (b) The conveyance creates an executory interest in Bob

   (c) The conveyance creates a defeasible fee

   (d) The conveyance creates a reversionary interest in Molly

(20) Which of the following is the *most* correct?

   (a) Bob's interest is void under the RAP

   (b) Andy's interest is a fee simple determinable

   (c) Andy's interest is a fee simple subject to an executory limitation

   (d) Andy's interest is a fee simple subject to a condition subsequent

(21) Shelly makes an inter vivos transfer of Blackacre which states:

"To Alice and her heirs on the condition that alcohol is never sold on Blackacre, remainder to Rachel and her heirs in the event alcohol is sold on Blackacre."

Which of the following is the *most* correct?

   (a) Alice has a reversionary interest in Blackacre

   (b) Rachel has a remainder interest in Blackacre

   (c) Rachel has an executory interest in Blackacre

   (d) Shelly has a right of entry

Please consider the following fact pattern for Questions 22–24

Cobalt Realty Corporation (CRC) leases the Empire State Building to Albert's Fine Clothing (AFC) for ten years. The lease begins on January 1, 1990. On December 1, 1994, AFC exclusively leases its interest in the Empire State Building to Steve's Fine Furniture (SFF) for four years, under a lease which provides for a lease term beginning on January 1, 1995.

(22) On June 15, 1996, which of the following is the *most* correct?

   (a) Only AFC has a reversionary interest

    (b) Only CRC has a reversionary interest

    (c) AFC has an executory interest

    (d) CRC and AFC have reversionary interests

  (23) On June 15, 1999, which of following is the *most* correct?

    (a) CRC and AFC have reversionary interests

    (b) Only AFC has a reversionary interest

    (c) AFC has an executory interest

    (d) Only CRC has a reversionary interest

  (24) On December 2, 1994, which of the following is the *least* correct?

    (a) SFF has a future interest

    (b) AFC has both a present and a future interest

    (c) SFF has both a present and a future interest

    (d) CRC and AFC have future interests

Please consider the following fact pattern for Questions 25–26

  Sharon makes a gift of Blackacre. The document evidencing the transfer states:
"Sharon conveys Blackacre to Alfred for his use and enjoyment during his life, and upon his death Blackacre shall automatically pass to Alfred's children, but if Alfred should die without any surviving children then Blackacre shall automatically pass to Stephen and his heirs."

Assume Alfred and Stephen are alive and Alfred has one child Renee at the time of the gift.

  (25) Renee's interest is *best* described as?

    (a) Vested remainder

    (b) Executory interest

    (c) Contingent remainder

    (d) Void

  (26) Which of the following is the *least* correct?

    (a) Alfred's children have a future interest in a class gift

    (b) Alfred's unborn children have a vested remainder

    (c) Stephen has an executory interest in fee simple absolute

    (d) The interest in Alfred's children is void under the RAP

  (27) Larry's will provides, in part:

"I, Larry, leave Blackacre to my beloved son, David, for his use, ownership and enjoyment during his lifetime, and upon his death my beloved grandson, Bernard, shall become the absolute owner of Blackacre."

Subsequent to Larry's death, David sells Blackacre to Realty Investment Company (RIC). Thereafter, Bernard buys Blackacre from RIC. If David and Bernard are still alive which of the following *best* describes Bernard's interest in Blackacre?

    (a) A vested remainder

(b) A life estate pur autre vie

(c) A fee simple absolute

(d) A contingent remainder

(28) Amy leases Blackacre to Lenny for ten years. Which of the following *best* describes the interest in Blackacre that Amy owns during the third year of the lease?

(a) A possibility of reverter

(b) A right of entry

(c) An executory interest

(d) A future interest

(29) Owner conveys Blackacre to A and his heirs until such time as Blackacre ceases to be used as a single family dwelling, then to C and his heirs if C is then alive. Assume all the parties are alive and Blackacre is being used as a single family dwelling. Which interest listed below was *not* created by the conveyance?

(a) An executory interest

(b) A reversionary interest

(c) A defeasible fee

(d) A contingent remainder

(30) Owner conveys Blackacre to A for life, remainder to B, but if B does not graduate from Suffolk Law School, then to C. Assume all the parties are alive and B has not graduated from Suffolk. Which of the following is *correct*?

(a) C's interest violates the RAP

(b) B's interest violates the RAP

(c) C has a contingent future interest

(d) C has a contingent remainder in fee simple

(31) A conveys Blackacre "… to B and his heirs, but if B or his heirs should ever attempt to sell Blackacre then A shall have the right to reenter and retake possession of Blackacre." What interest does A have in Blackacre?

(a) A right of entry

(b) A shifting executory interest

(c) A possibility of reverter

(d) None of the above

(32) Owner drafts a valid will which gives Blackacre to A for life, then to the children of A that are alive at Owner's death and have graduated from Suffolk Law School. A has no children when the will is executed. At Owner's death one year later, A is alive and A has only had two children, C1 and C2, who are currently attending high school. What interest, if any, do the children have in Blackacre?

(a) They have alternative contingent remainders

(b) They have vested remainders subject to open

(c) They have contingent remainders

(d) They have shifting executory interests

(33) Owner devises Blackacre to A for life, and then to C and her heirs. A sells his interest to B who in turn sells his interest to C. If A, B and C are alive which of the following describes C's interest in Blackacre?

(a) Life estate pur autre vie

(b) Contingent remainder

(c) Vested remainder

(d) Fee simple absolute

Please consider the following conveyance for Questions 34–35

O devises Blackacre "… to A for life, then to B and her heirs, but if A is survived at death by any children, then to such children and their heirs." At O's death A and B are both alive and A has two healthy children, C and D.

(34) Which of the following is *true*?

(a) C and D have alternative vested remainders subject to open

(b) C and D have alternative contingent remainders subject to open

(c) B has a contingent remainder in fee simple absolute

(d) D has an executory interest

(35) Which of the following is *true*?

(a) B has a vested remainder

(b) B has an indefeasibly vested remainder

(c) B has a contingent remainder

(d) B has an executory interest

(36) A conveys Blackacre to B for life, remainder to C for life. Thereafter, A conveys all of her right, title and interest in Blackacre to X. Subsequently, A, B and C die intestate. A is survived by only one heir, Y. B leaves Z as his sole heir. C leaves U as her sole heir. Which of the following is *true*?

(a) U owns Blackacre in fee simple absolute

(b) Y owns Blackacre in fee simple absolute

(c) X owns Blackacre in fee simple absolute

(d) Z owns Blackacre in fee simple absolute

(37) A conveys Blackacre to B for life, remainder to the children of B. A and B are alive. B has no children. Which of the following is the *most* correct?

(a) B has a fee simple absolute

(b) B has a life estate, the children of B have a contingent remainder and A has a reversion

(c) B has a life estate with a reversion in A

(d) B has a life estate, the children of B have a vested remainder subject to open and A has a reversion

Please consider the following conveyance for Questions 38–40

O conveys Blackacre "… to A, as his farm, for so long as he lives, but if A shall ever cease to farm Blackacre, then to B for the remainder of A's life, and upon A's death, to the children of A."

(38) B's interest in Blackacre is *best* described as?

    (a) A contingent remainder

    (b) An executory interest

    (c) A vested remainder subject to complete defeasance

    (d) An alternative life estate pur autre vie

(39) A's interest in Blackacre is *best* described as?

    (a) A defeasible fee

    (b) A life estate subject to being divested by a condition subsequent

    (c) A vested remainder

    (d) A determinable life estate pur autre vie

(40) The interest of A's children is *best* described as?

    (a) Void

    (b) A remainder

    (c) A shifting executory interest

    (d) A springing executory interest

(41) Acme Enterprises owns the Ada International Trade Center which is a ten story office building. Acme enters a lease on December 1, 1992, with Gilbert's Anonymous, Inc., an association organized to prevent obsessive use of Gilbert's law student study aids. The lease includes the following clauses:

> "The leasehold interest of Gilbert's Anonymous, Inc. in the Ada International Trade Center shall commence on January 1, 1993 and it shall last for a term of ten years for an annual rental of $12,000, with an equal portion of said rental being due and payable on or before the 15th of every month.
>
>   ∗ ∗ ∗
>
> Lessee shall not sublet said leased premises, but if said lessee sublets said premises the lessor shall have the right to re-enter and take immediate possession of said premises."

Which of the following *most* accurately describes the interest Gilbert's Anonymous, Inc. has in the Ada International Trade Center?

    (a) A property interest

    (b) A defeasible leasehold interest

    (c) An estate

    (d) A leasehold interest

(42) O makes the following conveyance:

"To A for life, and if B survives A, remainder to B"

Which of the following is *correct*?

    (a) B has a contingent remainder

    (b) B has an executory interest

    (c) B has a vested remainder

    (d) B has vested remainder subject to complete defeasance

(43) O makes the following conveyance:

"To A for life, remainder to B, but if B dies during A's lifetime, then to C"

Which of the following is *correct*?

    (a) B has a contingent remainder

    (b) B has an executory interest

    (c) B has a vested remainder

    (d) C has a remainder

(44) O makes the following conveyance:

"To A for life, and if B survives A, remainder to B, but if B fails to survive A, then to C"

Which of the following is *correct*?

    (a) B has a contingent remainder

    (b) B has an executory interest

    (c) B has a vested remainder

    (d) C has an executory interest

(45) Jacob executes a valid will that gives Blackacre to Miriam for life, then to Susan for life, then to John who shall never sell or transfer the property. Three weeks before Jacob's death he executes a valid deed which states "I hereby give Blackacre to Wally." Which of the following is *correct*?

    (a) Wally does not own any interest in Blackacre

    (b) Wally owns Blackacre subject to preexisting life estates in Miriam and Susan

    (c) Wally owns a life estate pur autre vie in Blackacre

    (d) Wally owns a fee simple absolute in Blackacre

(46) Ollie conveys Blackacre to Andy for life, then to Barry for life, then to Carl, but if alcohol is ever sold on Blackacre then to David. Which of the following is the *most* correct?

    (a) Ollie has a reversion in Blackacre

    (b) Carl has a fee simple defeasible in Blackacre

    (c) Carl has a fee simple absolute in Blackacre

    (d) David has a shifting executory interest in Blackacre

(47) Alan conveys Blackacre to Bonnie on condition that Blackacre is only used for residential purposes. Blackacre is currently being used for residential purposes. Which of the following is the *most* correct?

(a) Bonnie owns a fee simple absolute in Blackacre

(b) Alan owns a possibility of reverter in Blackacre

(c) Alan owns a right of entry in Blackacre

(d) Alan owns no interest in Blackacre

Please consider the following conveyance for Questions 48–49

Fred hereby conveys Blackacre to Linda for life provided that Linda does not use Blackacre for commercial purposes and if she does use Blackacre for commercial purposes it shall go to Lois for the remainder of Linda's life, then to Bernie for Marc's lifetime, and then to Marc.

(48) Which of the following is the *most* correct?

(a) Lois has a contingent remainder in a life estate

(b) Lois has an executory interest in a life estate pur autre vie

(c) Bernie has a defeasible future interest

(d) Bernie has an ordinary life estate

(49) Which of the following is the *most* correct?

(a) Marc has a contingent remainder

(b) Marc has a shifting executory interest

(c) March has a spring executory interest

(d) Marc has a vested remainder

(50) Barack conveys a life estate in Blackacre to John on the condition that Blackacre is only used for farming, but if it is not used for farming then to Hillary for as long as Bill is living. Assume Blackacre is being used for farming. Which of the following is the *most* correct?

(a) John has a determinable interest in Blackacre

(b) Bill has a future life estate in Blackacre

(c) The interest conveyed to Hillary is void under the RAP so Barack has retained a reversionary interest in Blackacre

(d) Barack has retained a reversion in Blackacre

Answers and Explanations

(1) (d) C has a nonreversionary future interest which can only be a remainder or an executory interest. C's future interest will only become a present possessory interest if the prior estate is prematurely terminated by violation of the marriage condition, so C's interest is an executory interest rather than a remainder. If C's interest becomes a present possessory interest in the future it will be transferred from A, a grantee, not from a grantor, so it is a shifting executory interest rather than a springing executory interest.

(2) (d) If A is used as a measuring life it can be stated with absolute certainty at the time of the original conveyance that at A's death she will either be married to B or not married to B. She cannot marry B after she is dead so C's interest is valid under the RAP. The marriage condition is not a direct restraint on alienation because it does not expressly restrict A's right to transfer Blackacre. The condition only indirectly interferes with A's ability to transfer Blackacre. A's heirs do not have any interest in Blackacre. The reference "to his heirs" in the conveyance are words of limitation which indicate that A received a fee simple interest from the grantor. The correct answer is (d) because the wording used ("forever") indicates C has a future interest in a fee simple absolute. Of course, because C has an executory interest, she may or may not ever get a present interest in Blackacre. However, if she does get a present interest it will be a fee simple absolute.

(3) (c) Arnold has a present possessory estate in Blackacre, not a future interest (remainder). Carl has a future interest that will only become a present possessory interest if the prior estate is prematurely terminated by violation of the condition so Carl has an executory interest rather than a remainder. However, if Carl gets a present interest in Blackacre he will acquire it from Arnold, not Owner, so he has a shifting executory interest rather than a springing executory interest. Arnold has fee simple defeasible interest (fee simple subject to an executory limitation) in Blackacre which is a type of fee simple interest.

(4) (c) Carl's interest does not violate the RAP because Carl can be used as a validating life. Carl has a future interest in a life estate so Carl's interest cannot vest once he is dead. Additionally, Arnold can be a validating life because he cannot enter the real estate business once he is dead. The condition is not a direct restraint on alienation because it does not expressly restrict Arnold's right to transfer Blackacre. Carl has a nonreversionary future interest which must be either a remainder or an executory interest. Carl's future interest will only become a present possessory interest if the prior estate is prematurely terminated by violation of the condition. Therefore, Carl's interest must be an

executory interest rather than a remainder. Additionally, if Carl's interest becomes a present possessory interest in the future it will be transferred from Arnold, a grantee, not from the grantor, so it is a shifting executory interest.

(5) (d) The original grantor (Owner) cannot retain a future interest that is a remainder or an executory interest. Any future interest retained by the grantor would have to be a possibility of reverter, a right of entry or a reversion. Owner gave Arnold a fee simple subject to an executory limitation. A right of entry would only be created if Owner gave Arnold a fee simple on condition subsequent.

(6) (c) It is unknown whether Carl's interest will become a present possessory estate in the future because it is unknown at the time of the original conveyance whether Arnold will or will not violate the condition, so (a) is incorrect. Likewise, Carl's interest does not violate the RAP. Carl has a life estate so he can be used as a validating life. Owner may or may not get possession of Blackacre in the future. If Arnold goes into the real estate business with Bill and one year later Carl dies, Blackacre will revert to Owner. However, if the condition is never violated it will be impossible for Owner to get possession of Blackacre once Arnold, Bill and Carl are dead, so (b) is incorrect. Carl may get present possession of Blackacre if the condition is violated during his lifetime.

(7) (c) Sandra gave Elmer a fee simple defeasible estate because it could last forever unless it was terminated by the violation of the condition, so (b) is not the answer. Robert's interest appears to be a shifting executory interest because it will only become a present possessory estate if the prior estate is prematurely terminated by violation of the condition. However, Sandra attempted to create a shifting executory interest in Robert in fee simple absolute. It is unknown when, if ever, Robert's interest will vest. All measuring lives could die and one-hundred years later the condition could be violated. Or, it could be violated two days after the original conveyance. Hence, Robert's interest is void under the RAP. The grant is then rewritten leaving only the condition. As a result it is no longer a fee simple subject to an executory interest. It becomes a fee simple determinable or a fee simple on condition subsequent. Either estate would result in the original grantor, Sandra, retaining a future interest that is a right of entry or a possibility of reverter. Such future interests are referred to as reversionary interests. (c) is incorrect (and, therefore the answer) because by operation of law the RAP eliminates the executory interest that Sandra attempted to create in Robert.

(8) (c) Choice (a) is incorrect since no such interest exists. Elmer has a present estate, so choices (b) and (d) are incorrect because both choices are non-reversionary future interests.

(9) (b) Ben has a nonreversionary future interest in Blackacre which can only be a remainder or an executory interest. It is a remainder because it will

only become a present possessory interest at the natural end of the prior estate rather than by prematurely terminating the prior possessory estate. It is a contingent remainder because it is subject to a condition precedent (Ben must become an attorney). A reversion is a future interest retained by the original transferor.

(10) (b) Ben and Kathy have alternative contingent remainders, so (a) and (d) are incorrect. Additionally, (c) is incorrect because Kathy's interest is not subject to a subsequent divesting condition. She is subject to a condition precedent (Ben does not become an attorney).

(11) (b) Alfonso has a present life estate. Present estates are not subject to the RAP. Ben's interest is valid under the RAP. If Ben is used as a validating life it will be known with absolute certainty at Ben's death whether he is or is not an attorney. Likewise, Kathy's interest is valid under the RAP. Again, if Ben is used as a validating life it will be known with absolute certainty at his death whether Kathy's interest will vest or fail. (b) is correct because Kathy has a contingent future interest.

(12) (d) The condition attached to Beatrice's estate is an invalid direct restraint on alienation which is void as a matter of law. Therefore, the clause containing the void restriction is eliminated which leaves Beatrice with a present fee simple absolute in Blackacre.

(13) (a) The interest in the children is not a class gift because Oscar cannot have more children after his death. The children are subject to a condition precedent (graduating from Suffolk Law School) so they have contingent remainders which are subject to the RAP. The children can be used as validating lives. It will be known with absolute certainty at their deaths whether each of them did or did not graduate from Suffolk Law School, so the interest in the children is valid under the RAP. A contingent remainder is a future interest so (a) is the only correct answer.

(14) (a) Ruth's children are Sheldon's grandchildren, and Ruth's grandchildren would be Sheldon's great grandchildren. The children have a remainder because their interest will vest at the natural end of the prior estate. All of the children are subject to a condition precedent (they must be alive at Ruth's death) so they have a contingent remainder. The RAP does not invalidate the contingent remainder. Ruth can be used as a validating life because it will be known with absolute certainty at her death what children, if any, are alive at that time.

(15) (c) (a) is incorrect because no such future interest exists. Mindy does not have a possibility of reverter. Such a future interest is only created in association with a determinable estate which is not created by the conveyance. At the time of the conveyance one child of Larry (Andrew) was alive. This

child was not subject to any condition precedent. Larry could have additional children subsequent to the conveyance, so Larry's children have a vested remainder subject to open. A vested remainder subject to open is a type of vested remainder.

(16) (c) The vested remainder subject to open in the children (a class gift) is subject to the RAP. If Larry is used as the measuring life it can be stated with absolute certainty that the class will close at his death because you cannot have children after you are dead. Therefore, the remainder is valid under the RAP. Alvin was alive at the time of Mindy's original conveyance so his interest is vested. Consequently, Alvin's death does not destroy his interest. His interest passes to his wife Sara via his will. Prior to his death Larry had four more children. At his death the class closes and the vested remainder subject to open becomes a present possessory estate. Each of the five children is entitled to an equal share of the estate. However, Alvin's share goes to his wife Sara. Each of them is entitled to 1/5 of the estate.

(17) (d) At the time of the initial conveyance Larry's children had a contingent remainder because no children existed. Subsequently, the interest of each child vested upon birth. Once each child's interest vested it is not destroyed by a child's subsequent death. At a child's death the interest passes via will, or intestate succession in the absence of a will. Therefore, since four children were born, each is entitled to a 1/4 share of the estate.

(18) (b) The interest in the heirs is a remainder because it will only become a present possessory estate, if at all, at the natural end of the prior estate. No condition precedent exists which must be satisfied before the heirs can take possession. However, you cannot have heirs until you are dead. Therefore, at the time of the conveyance Kevin's heirs are unknown so the remainder in the heirs must be a contingent remainder rather than a vested remainder. The heir's interest is valid under the RAP. Kevin can be used as a validating life because it can be stated with absolute certainty that it will be determined who Kevin's heirs are at his death.

(19) (a) Andy has a fee simple subject to an executory limitation which is a type of defeasible fee. Bob has a shifting executory interest. Additionally, Bob's interest is only a life estate so Molly retained a reversion in Blackacre. Choice (a) is incorrect because a reversionary interest cannot be created in someone other than the grantor.

(20) (c) Bob's interest is valid under the RAP. Bob's future interest is in a life estate. If Bob is used as a measuring life it can be stated with absolute certainty that his interest will have vested or failed at his death. Andy has a present fee simple defeasible interest. The divesting condition provides for the estate to go to a third party if the condition is violated. Therefore, it cannot be a fee

simple on condition subsequent or a fee simple determinable. It can only be a fee simple subject to an executory limitation.

(21) (d) Alice has a present possessory fee simple defeasible interest in Blackacre. Alice cannot have a reversionary interest because such an interest can only be retained by the grantor (Shelly). The conveyance attempts to create a shifting executory interest in Rachel which vests upon violation of the condition. It is incorrectly called a "remainder" by the grantor. However, the executory interest is in a fee simple absolute in Blackacre. The problem is that it is unknown when or if Rachel's interest will vest. No measuring life will work under the RAP, so Rachel's interest is void under the RAP. Once Rachel's interest is eliminated Alice has either a fee simple determinable or a fee simple on condition subsequent. The language in the conveyance ("on the condition that") is typically indicative of a fee simple on condition subsequent estate. A right of entry is impliedly created by a fee simple on condition subsequent.

(22) (d) As lessor, CRC, has a reversion which becomes a present possessory interest at the end of the ten year lease to AFC. Additionally, AFC has a reversion which becomes a present possessory interest at the end of the SFF lease because the SFF lease ends before the AFC lease ends. AFC has subleased an interest to SFF.

(23) (d) The lease to SFF expires on June 15, 1999 so AFC will be in possession of Blackacre on that date. The only future interest in Blackacre on that date is CRC's reversion.

(24) (c) On December 2, 1994, SSF has a future interest in the building because the lease gives SSF the right to present possession at a future date (January 1, 1995). On December 2, 1994, AFC still has possession of the building so they have a present interest. AFC also has a future interest because they have a reversion at the end of the SFF lease. Additionally, CRC has a future interest because they have a reversion at the end of the AFC lease. (c) is incorrect (and, therefore the correct answer) because SFF has a future interest but not a present interest on December 2, 1994.

(25) (a) Alfred has a present life estate that is followed by a remainder in Alfred's children. It is a remainder because the interest will only vest, if at all, at the natural end of the prior possessory estate (At Alfred's death). At the time of the conveyance Alfred has one child, Renee. No condition precedent exists before Renee's interest can vest. Therefore, Renee has a vested remainder. However, other future born children of Alfred could enter the class so the children have a vested remainder subject to open. The survival condition (Alfred's children must survive Alfred) is a condition subsequent so it does not make the future interest in the children a contingent remainder. Stephen has a shifting executory interest because his interest will only become a present possessory

interest by cutting off the children's interest if the children fail to satisfy the survival condition.

(26) (d) The interest in Alfred's children is valid under the RAP. Alfred can be a validating life because it can be stated with absolute certainty that it will be known at Alfred's death if his children's interests have vested or failed. Alfred's children have a class gift which is a vested remainder subject to open because one child, Renee, already exists and she is not subject to a condition precedent. Stephen has a shifting executory interest because his interest will only become a present possessory interest by cutting off the children's interest if the children fail to satisfy the condition subsequent (survival condition).

(27) (c) Larry's will gave David a present life estate in Blackacre followed by an indefeasibly vested remainder in fee simple absolute in Blackacre in Bernard. When David sold Blackacre to RIC they purchased a life estate based on David's life (a life estate pur autre vie). When Bernard purchased Blackacre from RIC he owned a life estate in Blackacre based on David's life plus a vested remainder in Blackacre in fee simple absolute. Consequently, Bernard owned all of the existing interests in Blackacre so a merger occurs which gives him a present fee simple absolute in Blackacre.

(28) (d) Amy created an estate for years leasehold. The lease is not subject to any divesting condition. Amy retains a reversion in the lease which is a type of reversionary future interest. Amy's reversion will become a present possessory interest in Blackacre when the ten year lease ends. A possibility of reverter would only exist if a determinable estate was created. A right of entry would only exist if an estate on condition subsequent was created. An executory interest is a nonreversionary future interest which would be owned by a third party, not the lessor (Amy).

(29) (d) A has a fee simple subject to an executory limitation. C has a shifting executory interest in Blackacre. Owner retained a reversion because C's interest is a contingent future interest. C's interest is valid under the RAP because C can be used as a validating life. At C's death his executory interest will have either vested or it will be destroyed if it has not vested prior to his death.

(30) (c) A has a present life estate. B has a vested remainder subject to complete defeasance. C has a contingent future interest which is a shifting executory interest. It is not a remainder because it will not become a present possessory estate at the natural end of the prior estate. It will only become a present possessory estate if the prior estate is prematurely terminated due to B's failure to graduate from Suffolk. B's interest is not subject to the RAP. C's interest is valid under the RAP. B is a validating life because it is known with absolute certainty that at his death he will or will not have graduated from Suffolk. He cannot graduate after he is dead.

(31) (d) A attempted to create a fee simple on condition subsequent which would give A a right of entry if the condition is breached. However, the condition is an invalid direct restraint on alienation which is void by operation of law. Once the invalid restraint is stricken from the grant B has a fee simple absolute.

(32) (c) A has a present life estate. Owner appears to have created a class gift in A's children at the time the will was executed. However, a will only has legal effect at the decedent's death. At Owner's death, A has only two living children (C1 and C2). The will requires that any children of A must be alive at Owner's death so the future interest in A's children can only go to C1 and C2. No additional children of A can gain an interest in Blackacre. C1 and C2 will get Blackacre, if at all, at the natural end of the prior possessory estate (at A's death), so Owner's will created remainders in C1 and C2. C1 and C2 are each subject to a condition precedent (must graduate from Suffolk Law School), so the remainders are contingent remainders. The contingent remainders are valid under the RAP if C1 and C2 are used as validating lives. It will be known with absolute certainty if C1 and C2 have or have not graduated from Suffolk Law School at their deaths.

(33) (d) The original devise creates a life estate in A followed by an indefeasibly vested remainder in C in fee simple absolute. When C purchases the life estate from B a merger occurs resulting in C owning a present estate in Blackacre in fee simple absolute.

(34) (d) A has a present life estate. B is known and ascertained and no condition precedent exists so B has a vested remainder. However, B's interest is subject to a condition subsequent (if A is survived by any children) which can divest it. Therefore, the specific type of vested remainder given to B is a vested remainder subject to complete defeasance. A's children will only get Blackacre if they survive A which cuts off B's estate. Therefore, A's children have a shifting executory interest.

(35) (a) See answer for question 34.

(36) (c) A's original conveyance creates a present life estate in B followed by a vested remainder in C. A retained a reversion in Blackacre in fee simple absolute. B and C had life estates so no interest can pass to their heirs upon their deaths. A transferred her reversion to X during her lifetime, so upon her death no interest in Blackacre passed to her heir, Y. Because both B and C are dead, X has a present possessory estate in Blackacre in fee simple absolute.

(37) (b) B has a present life estate. B has no children so the remainder in the children of B is a contingent remainder. The contingent remainder is valid under the RAP. If B is used as the measuring life it can be stated with absolute certainty that it will be known at B's death whether B has children because B

cannot have any children after her death. A retains a reversion in Blackacre because she conveyed a life estate followed by a contingent remainder. The contingent remainder might never vest because B could die without ever having children.

(38) (b) B has a future interest which will only become a present possessory estate if A violates the condition (ceases to farm Blackacre). B's interest will not become a present possessory estate at the natural end of the prior estate. Therefore, B has a shifting executory interest.

(39) (b) A has a present possessory life estate in Blackacre which is subject to a condition that can divest A's estate and transfer it to B. Therefore, A has a defeasible life estate. Upon violation of the condition the estate does not go back to the original grantor so A does not have a determinable life estate or a life estate subject to a condition subsequent. She has a life estate subject to an executory limitation. Choice (a) is incorrect because she has a defeasible life estate not a defeasible fee estate. Choice (c) is incorrect because she has a present estate rather than a future interest. Choice (d) is also incorrect because her estate is neither determinable nor based on someone else's life. Choice (b) is correct because A has a life estate which is defeasible based on the condition to continue farming. This divesting condition is a condition subsequent not a condition precedent.

(40) (b) The interest in A's children can only become a possessory interest, if at all, at the end of the prior possessory estate, so the children have a remainder. The interest in A's children is not an executory interest because it will not become a possessory estate by prematurely cutting off the prior estate. The interest in A's children is valid under the RAP. A can be a validating life because it can be stated with absolute certainty that the interest in A's children will either vest or fail at A's death.

(41) (b) Gilbert's Anonymous, Inc. has a ten year estate for years lease which is subject to a divesting condition (cannot sublet). If Gilbert's sublets the lease, the lessor has the right to immediately retake possession of the leased property. Therefore, Gilbert's has a defeasible leasehold. More specifically, it would be a leasehold on condition subsequent which means the lessor retained a right of entry. (a), (c) and (d) are all correct statements. However, the question asks for the answer which "most accurately describes" Gilbert's interest which is (b).

(42) (a) A has a present life estate. B has a remainder because it will only become a present possessory estate, if at all, at the natural end of the prior estate (at A's death) rather than by prematurely cutting off or terminating the prior possessory estate. However, it is a contingent remainder because it is subject to a condition precedent (B must survive A).

(43) (c) A has a present life estate. B has a remainder. B's interest is not subject to a condition precedent that must be satisfied before B's interest can vest.

B's interest is subject to a condition subsequent that can divest B's interest. Therefore, B has a vested remainder. More specifically it is a vested remainder subject to complete defeasance. C, therefore, has an executory interest because C's interest will only become a present possessory interest if B's interest is prematurely cut off because B predeceases A.

(44) (a) A has a present life estate. B has a contingent remainder because it is subject to a condition precedent (B must survive A). C also has a contingent remainder because it is also subject to a condition precedent (B must fail to survive A). B and C have alternative contingent remainders.

(45) (d) Jacob's will has no effect until he is dead. Upon his death his will only transfers property mentioned in the will if he still owns it. Prior to his death Jacob gave Blackacre to Wally, so at his death Jacob no longer owned Blackacre. The wording of the will "to Wally" transfers a fee simple absolute interest in Blackacre to Wally.

(46) (c) Ollie's conveyance gives Andy a present life estate in Blackacre. It gives Barry a vested remainder in a life estate followed by a vested remainder in a fee simple in Carl. All three interests are subject to a condition subsequent (sale of alcohol). The condition provides that Blackacre goes to David only if the condition is broken. Hence, David appears to have a shifting executory interest in a fee simple. David's interest is void under the RAP. It cannot be stated with absolute certainty when or if the condition will be violated. The condition could be violated the day after Ollie's conveyance. Likewise, fifty years after Andy, Barry, Carl and any other potential measuring life dies, the condition could be violated. The clause in the grant that gives the interest to David is eliminated which converts the conveyance to a present life estate in Andy, followed by a vested remainder in a life estate in Barry and then a vested remainder in a fee simple absolute in Carl. Ollie has not retained any interest in Blackacre.

(47) (c) Alan conveyed a fee simple defeasible estate to Bonnie because it is subject to a condition (residential activities). The conveyance does not provide for the estate to go to a third party upon breach of the condition, so by default it goes back to the original grantor (Alan). Therefore, Bonnie does not own a fee simple absolute or a fee simple subject to an executory limitation. Bonnie must therefore own either a fee simple determinable or a fee simple subject to a condition subsequent. The language "on condition that Blackacre is only used for ..." is typically associated with a condition subsequent. A right of entry is automatically retained by the grantor if a fee simple subject to a condition subsequent is created.

(48) (b) Linda has a present life estate subject to an executory limitation. If Blackacre is used for commercial purposes Linda's life estate is cut short and

it goes to Lois for the remainder of Linda's life. If Blackacre is not used for commercial purposes Linda's estate naturally ends at her death. Lois will only get Blackacre, if at all, if Linda's life estate is prematurely terminated because Linda violates the condition. Lois has a shifting executory interest in a life estate pur autre vie based on Linda's life. Bernie has a remainder because he will only get Blackacre, if at all, at the natural end of either Linda's ordinary life estate or at the natural end of Lois' life estate pur autre vie. Bernie's remainder is in a life estate pur autre vie based on Marc's life. Marc has an indefeasibly vested remainder in a fee simple absolute in Blackacre. Marc's heirs or will beneficiaries will get Blackacre at the end of the prior possessory estate which occurs at Marc's death.

(49) (d) See discussion for question (48).

(50) (d) John has a defeasible present life estate which is subject to an executory limitation. It is not a determinable life estate because Blackacre does not go to Barack upon violation of the farming condition. Hillary has a shifting executory interest because her interest will only become a present possessory estate by cutting off John's estate due to violation of the farming restriction. Hillary's future interest is in a life estate pur autre vie which is based on Bill's life. Bill has no interest in Blackacre. Hillary's interest is valid under the RAP. If Bill is used as a validating life it can be stated with absolute certainty that Hillary's interest will have either vested or failed at Bill's death. Barack did not convey all interests in Blackacre so he automatically retained a reversion. If John farms Blackacre until his death it will go back to Barack. If the farming restriction is violated Blackacre will go to Hillary, but upon Bill's death it will go back to Barack.

Index